The Reign of Elizabeth I

The Reign of Elizabeth I

EDITED BY
CHRISTOPHER HAIGH

THE UNIVERSITY OF GEORGIA PRESS
Athens

Published in 1985 in
the United States of America
by the University of Georgia Press,
Athens, Georgia 30602.

Phototypeset by
Wessex Typesetters Ltd
Frome, Somerset

Printed in Great Britain

ISBN 0–8203–0757–2

Contents

Preface

ONE of the traditional functions of a preface is to explain what is and excuse what is not in a book, in the hope of defusing some of the ire of critics. This collection of essays was planned as a coherent whole: whether it became one is for the reader to judge. The volume aims to survey the composition and workings of the Elizabethan political system, and to examine how its institutions responded to the issues which most worried politicians and churchmen. Given these intentions, the most obvious gaps are the regulation of economic activity and the promotion of naval and colonial enterprise. The real reasons for the omissions are the necessary constraints of the 'Problems in Focus' series; the public justifications are the appearance of a splendid study of the Elizabethan economy (David Palliser's *The Age of Elizabeth*), and my conviction that, as Drake and Ralegh have long had more attention than they deserved, a little neglect would be salutary.

A second, and essential, role of a preface to a collective volume is to thank all those who made the editor's task easier (while remaining silent about any who made it more difficult!). The contributors to this book do not form a party (still less a faction): they share no common ideology, and are deliberately representative of a wide range of approaches and generations. I was lucky to recruit a team of authors willing to play in the positions I earmarked for them, and luckier still that my team-mates turned up for the match. I am grateful to them, and especially to Jim Alsop, who joined as a late substitute and still managed to score before the final whistle. The team management (Sarah Mahaffy, Vanessa Peerless and Valery Rose) proved encouraging and helpful, and their patience was exceeded only by that of the editor's wife and daughters.

C.A.H.

Introduction

CHRISTOPHER HAIGH

> The all-glorious, all-virtuous, incomparable, invict and matchless pattern of princes, the glory, honour and mirror of womankind, the admiration of our age, ELIZABETH, Queen of England, was by the father's side truly royal, being daughter to Henry VIII, grandchild to Henry VII, and great-grandchild to Edward IV.

THE first full account of the life and times of Elizabeth I began with this fulsome praise of its heroine, and ended with little more restraint: 'No oblivion shall ever bury the glory of her name, for her happy and renowned memory still liveth and shall for ever live in the minds of men to all posterity, as of one who (to use no other than her successor's expression) in wisdom and felicity of government surpassed (without envy be it spoken) all the princes since the days of Augustus.' William Camden and his translators, in the 1620s,[1] had no doubt of the greatness of Elizabeth's contemporary and future reputations, and their confidence has been justified. Despite occasional sniping, especially from Clarendon, Lingard and Froude, Elizabeth's stock among historians has remained high, and never more so than in the past century. J. R. Green, in 1874, sketched what became the standard picture of Elizabeth, as a cool and skilful politician who, by cautious and moderate policies, restored national unity and pride and channelled the 'sudden burst of national vigour' which set England on the path to supremacy. The interaction between the ability of the Queen and the enthusiasm of her people became a dominating theme in later accounts. In Creighton's biography (1896) 'Elizabeth's imperishable claim to greatness lies in her instinctive sympathy with her people', and in Pollard's *History of England from the Accession of Edward VI to the Death of Elizabeth* (1910) the Queen is an expression of the will of the people who, by restraining religious conflict and extending public order, paves the way for liberty at home and empire overseas.[2] Elizabeth was a great queen, and she presided over a great age of national achievement.

Interest in Elizabeth and admiration for her seem boundless. More than seventy new biographies have been published since 1890, and between 1927 and 1957 they appeared at an average rate of one each year. Some biographers and students of the period have been critical (recently, Carolly Erickson and Charles Wilson), but by a large majority the verdict remains favourable – even laudatory. The most widely read of the professional historians have been among the most praising, and have endorsed the interpretation formulated by the generation from Green to Pollard. A. L. Rowse dedicated *The England of Elizabeth* (1950) 'to the glorious memory of Elizabeth Queen of England', and quoted Creighton in ascribing her greatness to 'her instinctive perception of what England wanted'; under her leadership, the deeds of the nation 'made the age the most remarkable in our history'. Sir John Neale's portrait of 'this amazing Queen', drawn in his best-selling 1934 biography and filled out in books and essays in the 1950s, was so flattering that a schoolgirl asked him if it was really true that he had fallen in love with his subject. One reviewer complained that in Neale's presentation 'Elizabeth comes too close to a new apotheosis', but the Neale account has become standard and few substantial challenges have been mounted.[3] By 1960, indeed, the essential political history of Elizabeth's reign seemed fixed, crushed into shape by the weight (physical and authoritative) of five detailed and dull tomes from Conyers Read and four livelier, but apparently incontrovertible, volumes by Neale. This introductory essay will examine some of the reasons for this adulation of Elizabeth and her era, and indicate how the complimentary certainties of the 1950s and after have been dissolving more recently.

I

The selling of Elizabeth began as soon as she ascended the

throne. Her image-making was seized by Protestant enthusiasts, she was packaged as a Protestant saviour and marketed as God's chosen bulwark against Antichrist. Broadside ballads identified her accession with the triumph of Protestantism, and in his 1563 *Acts and Monuments* John Foxe told how Elizabeth had been protected by God through the bloody reign of her sister so that she could restore true religion. Elizabeth was the Protestants' hope because she was the only hope the Protestants had, and in projecting her as *their* queen they sought to bind her to their cause. Each crisis of the reign brought forth further batches of ballads and prayers for her safety; in 1570 'A godly ditty or prayer to be sung unto God for the preservation of his Church, our Queen and realm, against all traitors, rebels and papistical enemies', and in 1586 'A godly ditty to be sung for the preservation of the Queen's most excellent majesty's reign':

> All English hearts rejoice and sing,
> That fears the Lord and loves our Queen;
> Yield thank to God, our heavenly king,
> Who hitherto her guide hath been.

If Protestants tried to catch Elizabeth's support by loyalty and praise, so too did needy towns: the grandiloquent addresses received from towns entered on progresses usually contained some petition or other. Historians have often quoted the recorder of Warwick's list in 1572 of

> the great benefits received from God by the happy and long-desired entrance of your Majesty into the imperial throne of this realm, after the pitiful slaughter and exile of many of your Highness' godly subjects, the restoration of true religion, the speedy change of wars into peace, of dearth and famine into plenty, of an huge mass of dross and counterfeit money into fine gold and silver, to your Highness' great honour.

No doubt the paean was heartfelt, but the spokesman was producing what was expected by the town's patrons, the Earls of Warwick and Leicester, and he was careful to stress its poverty and dependence on their favour. Economic self-interest was even more to the fore at Worcester in 1575, when the orator bewailed the collapse of the local cloth industry, pleaded for stricter control of trade, and claimed that only the Queen's visit had raised the citizens from their gloom.[4]

For the first two decades of the reign adulation of the Queen was, if not exactly spontaneous, at least popular rather than official. 17 November, the date of Elizabeth's accession, was from about 1570 celebrated in more and more parishes with bell-ringing, bonfires and joviality. But by 1576 'the Queen's day' was under official control, as an elaborate state festival with authorised prayers, municipal processions and propagandist sermons: 17 November 1558 was presented as a turning-point in the history of the nation, after which Elizabeth had delivered her people from darkness. As it became almost certain that Elizabeth would not marry and likely that she would not clarify the succession, political stability and confidence required some definition of the attributes of female monarchy and representation of focal issues of loyalty. By the late 1570s the Elizabethan 'cult of personality', which had begun in the fervent hopes of Protestants and the calculated panegyrics of supplicants, was under official management. Sir Henry Lee, the Queen's Champion, turned the Accession Day tilts from Court sports into ritualised public spectacles (admission a shilling), where chivalrous knights jousted for the favour of the Virgin Queen. Portraits no longer represented her in the real surroundings of the Court, but at the centre of complex allegories in which she was a Vestal Virgin or an omniscient philosopher or a ruler of the oceans. Approved pictures of Elizabeth (always young!) were replicated in miniatures and medallions and, for wider audiences, in woodcuts and engravings. In pageants and poems, especially after the Armada, Elizabeth was Astraea, the just virgin of Virgil's Fourth Eclogue, who had inaugurated a golden age of peace and eternal spring: in the Lord Mayor of London's pageant of 1591, Astraea overcame Superstition and Ignorance, and tended her flock as a virgin shepherdess.[5]

It is difficult to know how far, and how fast, such propaganda was effective, for our evidence is mainly the endless official repetitions of favoured themes or dissent so extreme as to bring the guilty before the courts. It took some time for the virgin-queen image to establish itself in the popular mind: there were stories in the Home Counties in 1560 that Elizabeth was pregnant by Robert Dudley, and claims in East Anglia and Kent in 1570–2 that Leicester and Hatton were the Queen's lovers, but there were few such scandals later. Much more serious than early attacks on Elizabeth's morals were the later denials of her competence as a ruler and her care for her subjects. Under the pressure of war taxation and economic distress in the 1590s, there was a good deal of hostile muttering in some counties. An Essex labourer was saying in 1591 that the people should pray for a king because 'the Queen is but a woman and ruled by noblemen, and the noblemen and gentlemen are all one, and the gentlemen and farmers will hold together so that the poor can get nothing'; 'we shall never have a merry world while the Queen liveth'. In the following year another labourer thought 'this is no good government which we now live under, and it was merry England when there was better government', while it was argued in both Essex and Kent that Philip of Spain would be a more solicitous ruler than Elizabeth.[6]

In the 1590s, as the war dragged on and prices soared, propagandists ignored the facts and resorted to the 'big lie' technique. From the presses came 'A joyful new ballad of our Queen's going to the Parliament, showing her most happy and prosperous reign and the great care she hath for the government of her people, made this year 1593', and 'A triumphant new ballad in honour of the Queen's Majesty and her most happy government, who hath reigned in great prosperity thirty-seven years' (1595). 'A pleasant new ballad of the most blessed and prosperous reign of her Majesty for the space of two and forty years, and now entering into the three and fortieth, to the great joy and comfort of all her Majesty's faithful subjects' was published in 1600, and it seems to have been reissued in the next two years with altered dates. By this point, the idealised queen and kingdom were far from the realities: the public Elizabeth was not a real person, but a cluster of images. In Dekker's play *Old Fortunatus* (1599), an old man is asked 'Are you then travelling to the temple of Eliza?' and replies:

Even to her temple are my feeble limbs travelling. Some call her Pandora, some Gloriana, some Cynthia, some Bel-phoebe, some Astraea, all by several names to express several loves. Yet all those names make but one celestial body, as all those loves meet to create but one soul. . . . Blessed name, happy country; your Eliza makes your land Elysium.

The Elizabeth who died in 1603 was not a woman, she was all-but a goddess: an engraving published early in the next reign was inscribed

This Maiden-Queen Elizabeth came into this world, the Eve of the Nativity of the blessed virgin Mary; and died on the Eve of the Annunciation of the virgin Mary, 160[3].

She was, she is (what can there more be said?)
In earth the first, in heaven the second Maid.[7]

II

It would, perhaps, be unfair to suggest that Elizabeth's admirers among modern historians have been directly influ-enced by such rhetorical excesses (though suspicions remain in the most fervent cases!). But the praise and propaganda contributed to the emotional climate within which the con-temporary observers upon whom we must rely lived. Behind the measured, scholarly tones of William Camden's *Britannia* and *Annales* lies a considerable pride in his country and its Queen, which probably owes as much to the atmosphere of his times as to real events. The *Annales* (subtitled, in the first English edition, *The True and Royall History of the famous Empresse Elizabeth, Queene of England, France and Ireland, etc. True Faith's Defendresse, of Divine Renowne and Happy Memory*) was subject to three formative influences. The first was, as Camden admits in his preface, a determination by himself and his patron Lord Burghley that Elizabeth's achievements should be accurately recorded for posterity. Camden, who had been born in 1551, lived through her reign and, with Burghley's encouragement, began to study its official records in about 1596: he intended that the Queen's greatness should be displayed by quotation of evidence and not depend upon his own claims. But the task of research proved daunting and Camden gave up after 1598 – though he began to work again in 1608, perhaps under pressure from King James to provide a favourable version of the life of his mother, Mary, Queen of Scots. Camden certainly did not write a whitewash of Mary at her son's dictation, but it seems that James's sensitivities formed a second influence on the content of Annales. The affairs of Scotland and its Queen took up much of the volume, and Camden treated Mary with sympathy: her Scots enemies were blamed for many of her troubles, her defence in 1587 was carefully set out, balanced judgements for and against her were given, the pressures upon Elizabeth for execution were stressed, and the case of Secretary Davison was reported in great detail. Most strikingly, Camden answers by implication the criticism which had been made of the conduct of James himself. James had 'laboured all that possibly he could . . . to save her life, and omitted nothing that became a most dutiful and pious son'; after Mary's execution 'the King of Scots, her only son, who respected his mother with the greatest piety that could be imagined or found in a son, took exceeding great and hearty grief mixed with deep displeasure at the same, and very much lamented and mourned for her'. On this issue Camden, usually moderate and restrained, wrote what was expected not what was true.[8]

The third influence upon Annales also relates to King James, but this time shows Camden's independence. At the death of Elizabeth in 1603, there was a good deal of relief at the passing of 'petticoat government' and enthusiasm for the accession of an experienced, but still only middle-aged, king: the 17 November celebrations were transferred to 24 March, the Accession Day of James. But, reports Bishop Goodman,

after a few years, when we had experience of the Scottish government, then – in disparagement of the Scots and in hate and detestation of them – the Queen did seem to revive. Then was her memory much magnified – such ringing of bells, such public joy and sermons in commemoration of her, the picture of her tomb painted in many churches; and, in effect, more solemnity and joy in memory of her coronation than was for the coming in of King James.

This response was partly a matter of nostalgia and a feeling that the world (not to mention the government of England) was subject to corruption and decline: as James's public stock went down, Elizabeth's went up. What is significant for us, however, is that perceptions of the Elizabethan period now altered and history was rewritten for political purposes.[9]

Camden's history of Elizabeth's reign was written between 1608 and 1617, as Stuart government, for some at least, turned sour. The first three parts (up to 1588) were published in Latin in 1615 and in English translation in 1625: they formed an implied condemnation of Jacobean domestic policy and profligacy. Book IV (covering the rest of the period up to 1603) appeared in Latin in 1625 and in English in 1629: by its attention to Elizabethan military and naval successes, it implied criticism of the Stuarts' supine foreign policy. Camden presented Elizabethan England as a golden age of wise rule and national achievement. The Queen's priorities were to secure purity in religion, safe defence for her realm and the devotion of her people: she fulfilled these aims without incurring heavy debts and without lavish gifts to her servants – 'In which regard both her kingdom and successors ought to have her provident care in grateful remembrance.' Elizabeth ruled well, and her people responded: coastal towns built ships for the navy, the nobility provided stocks of arms, and the common people cheerfully paid the taxes they knew would be well spent. In this best of all possible worlds, financial incentives were restored and the country people actually worked harder; they 'began to ply their husbandry more diligently than before, yea and above that which the laws afterwards made required, by breaking up grounds which had lain untilled beyond all memory of man'. In 1561, 'In the midst of these best cares of Queen and people, whilst the commonwealth seemed to revive, to the general rejoicing of all men, this said accident befell . . .' – the steeple of St Paul's fell down, but it was a minor blot on the glory of the new age. The contrast with the reign of James was clear enough, but for inattentive readers Camden pointed the lessons in asides and qualifications: Elizabeth 'always made peace the prime thing in her counsels and undertakings, yet never neglected or threw off all care of arms'; she avoided debt, 'But the truth is, she was providently frugal, and scarcely spent anything but for the maintenance of her royal state, the defence of her kingdom or the relieving of her neighbours.' And for those who needed pictures to point the differences in foreign policy, the 1625 English edition appeared with an illustrated title-page depicting Drake's attack on Cadiz in 1587, the Armada victory in 1588, the burning of San Juan de Puerto Rico in 1591, and the expedition to Cadiz in 1596.[10]

The emphases of the *Annales* were conditioned by the atmosphere in which it was written and published. In the first years of James I, Elizabeth was praised for the peace and prosperity of her reign; but by the 1610s and after it was usual to stress the glories of her rule and her patronage of international Protestantism and English sea power. The virtues and successes of Elizabeth were therefore defined by the flaws and omissions of James, and Camden wrote a commentary on the rule of James in the guise of a history of the rule of Elizabeth. Now it is no new perception that 'all history is contemporary history', or that all historical evidence must be used critically: these are well-recognised characteristics of our discipline. But Camden was not just any old historian, and the *Annales* is not simply one historical source. Camden was the first, and the formative, historian of the age of Elizabeth: he established the historiographical agenda, and fixed the relationship between the Queen and the events of her reign. He stressed the chaos produced by her predecessors, listed the problems she faced at her accession, and credited her with coherent and moderate policies to heal the ills of the realm. Camden rationalised Elizabethan political history, and made Elizabeth a rational politician – and William Camden's Elizabeth became John Neale's Elizabeth.[11]

Camden's main and lasting achievement was the definition of the structure and ingredients of the political history of Elizabeth's reign: since the *Annales*, it has consisted of the early solution of inherited problems and the ensuing defence of her solutions against challenges from Puritans, papists, self-seeking politicians and Philip of Spain.[12] His influence has not, however, been confined to continuing use of his organising scheme: many of his attitudes and specific judgements have been repeated through the years. Camden's version of the history of Elizabethan Protestantism was that the Queen and Parliament established an authentic and acceptable Protestant position in 1559, but that this was threatened thereafter by Puritans, a schismatic presbyterian sect supported by greedy nobles who coveted Church lands; the Puritan menace to the integrity of the Church and the security of the state was beaten off by Archbishop Whitgift, who restored order and unity by fair but firm discipline. There was no substantial revision of this story until very recently, when historians such as Patrick Collinson and Peter Lake pointed out the dynamic character of Protestantism and suggested that, by seeking to restrain the evangelistic impetus of preachers, it was Elizabeth and Whitgift, not Puritans, who were the disruptive forces.[13] Camden's presentation of central politics in terms of factional rivalry between leading courtiers with followings has also been influential: Leicester against Sussex in 1565, Leicester and Norfolk against Cecil in 1569, Leicester against Essex in 1576, and Robert Cecil and Raleigh against Robert, Earl of Essex, in 1597 and after, have become classic matches in the Elizabethan fixture-list – questioned only recently by Wallace MacCaffrey and Simon Adams.[14]

Camden's account of factional politics has carried authority partly because of the support it received from another jaundiced Jacobean, Sir Robert Naunton – who was a critical Caroline by the 1630s. Naunton, born in 1563, was on the fringes of government service from 1596; he held high office from 1618 (until he was suspended in 1621 during foreign policy disputes) and again from 1624 – though his alienation led to virtual exclusion from the Council in 1630 and dismissal in 1635. Naunton's views were much the same as Camden's; he was anti-Catholic and anti-Spanish, and also came to see Elizabeth's reign as a golden age in which Protestant truth was restored and defended against all comers. Naunton's notes on Elizabeth and her courtiers, written in the early 1630s, were published (by others) as *Fragmenta Regalia* in two separate editions in 1641 – presumably as criticisms of Charles I. He saw as a principal reason for the Queen's success the fact that 'she ruled much by faction and parties, which herself both made, upheld and weakened, as her own great judgement advised, for I disassent from the common received opinion that my lord of Leicester was absolute and above all in her grace'. By encouragement of factions, Elizabeth remained open to many influences and ran a broad-based regime: the contrast with the dominance of Buckingham and the exclusiveness of the Court of Charles I was clear. Naunton's perception of Elizabethan politics (of which he had known little at first hand) was much influenced by his experience of her successors, and he wrote to influence events. But his characterisations have been widely used by modern historians, and the factional conception of politics became dominant through the work of Conyers Read and J. E. Neale.[15] Another important element in the Camden story, ably reinforced by Robert Naunton, has survived to play a crucial role in the modern historiography of Elizabethan England.

III

The laudatory line of succession seems clear. Protestant enthusiasts presented Elizabeth as saviour of their religion in the hope that she would grow into the role (which she refused to do). Townsmen and courtiers praised her as a caring benefactress in the hope of reward (but her prudence hardened into parsimony). Official propaganda paraded her as ever-young and omnicompetent to sustain confidence in the regime through difficult times (while she grew old and irritable, and lost control of her military commanders). In the second half of the reign of James her image was refurbished as a model for the King (but it was a mirror-image of him, in which his defects were reversed into her virtues). And under Charles she was cast (by Sir John Eliot as well as Naunton) as the friend of Parliaments and leader of a Protestant crusade[16] – how Peter Wentworth and Francis Walsingham would have laughed! Each fragment of the picture – every piece more than a little absurd in itself – has locked together into a composite portrait which has held a compelling attraction for some English historians. The magnetism of the 'Camden version' has not been uniformly effective, however, and (at the risk of straying somewhat beyond the competence of the present writer) it may be worth asking when and why it has exercised its power.

After she had been roundly criticised by Macaulay, Lingard and, above all, Froude, and ignored on 17 November 1858 (the *Times* leader, Neale says, was on the subject of manure), Elizabeth's reputation soared in the late nineteenth century. There had been only one new biography of her in each decade until the 1890s, when there were six – and one of them, Creighton's, balanced its mild deflation of the Queen with enthusiasm for the expansionary efforts of her people. It seems that, at the high point of English imperialism, romantic nationalists saw the reign of Elizabeth as the origin of an inexorable movement which had triumphed in their own day. In 1893–4 Froude lectured at Oxford on the Elizabethan sailors who fought off Spain and began the push towards empire, and in 1895 J. R. Seeley's *The Growth of British Policy* traced from Elizabeth's period a 'national' (rather than dynastic) foreign policy based on sea power and overseas expansion.[17] The next wave of Elizabethan enthusiasm came in the rather different circumstances of economic depression and appeasement: thirteen biographies were published in England between 1927 and 1936, and three others abroad in 1937. The 1930s crop included Neale's biography, probably the best (and one of the most adulatory) of all: it was republished in 1952 to mark the dawn of what was then represented as a new Elizabethan age. The coronation of Elizabeth II in 1953 was celebrated by a batch of articles on Elizabeth I's crowning, and it presumably pointed to the commercial possibilities of 1958: Sir John Neale marked 17 November 1958 with a volume of essays, and there were four biographies in 1957–9 (thirteen in 1954–63). Elizabethan historians were served well by 1953 and 1958: there was money to be made. But the coincidence of dates does not entirely explain the rapturous tones. Perhaps eulogy of the colourful Elizabethan Court and the muscular vigour of Elizabethans was, for Neale and A. L. Rowse, a protest against the drab uniformity of the post-war world; certainly they drew parallels between England's resistance to Spanish Catholicism under Elizabeth I and resistance to German Nazism under Churchill.[18]

The dominating interpretative concept in Neale's writings of

the 1950s was, however, not Churchillian leadership but the
Cold War. He prefaced the 1952 edition of his biography with a
note that he had changed the 1934 version only by minor
corrections, and that although the book had been written
'before such words as "ideological", "fifth column", and "cold
war" became current' nevertheless 'the ideas are present'. In
some respects Neale's work in the 1950s was a reversion to a
1934 stance from directions he had been taking in the 1940s. In
a formative essay on 'The Elizabethan Political Scene' (1948)
and in *The Elizabethan House of Commons* (1949), Neale sketched
a new framework for an understanding of early-modern
English politics – which was to become especially influential in
the late 1970s. The conventional picture of authoritative
monarchical rule checked intermittently by representative
institutions was replaced by a conception of interacting
clientages, kept in uncertain balance by royal manipulation of
patronage. But in the 1950s it was as if Neale had forgotten
what he had written. He was dominated by the idea of Cold
War, and drew specific parallels between the ideological
conflicts of his own day and the religious conflicts of the
sixteenth century. He argued that the Reformation brought a
clash between two revolutionary ideologies, represented in
England by fanatical Puritans and by the Jesuits and their
followers. But Elizabeth was liberal-minded and tolerant, with
a comprehensive vision of her duty towards the whole people,
so she restrained the persecuting intentions of the Puritan-filled
House of Commons. This brought about the running constitutional conflict which forms the theme of Neale's *Elizabeth I and
her Parliaments*, but which is vigorously rebutted by Professor
Elton in Chapter 3 of this collection. Neale's use of contemporary analogies and comparisons led him into a misunder-
standing of Elizabethan political history.[19]

IV

Neale's view that Elizabeth checked the aggression of the
Puritan militants provided further support for his conviction
that she was a great queen: 'Had it not been for her, the broad
way of English life would have been narrowed and an

experiment made with what we today term the ideological state.' Because of Elizabeth's humanity and determination, England remained England. In moderating ideological conflict, the Queen made possible that 'greatness of the Elizabethan age' which Neale, and so many other historians, thought accompanied her rule. Now, it has been suggested in this survey that the glowing accounts given by modern historians of Elizabeth and her reign have been influenced by the propaganda of her contemporaries, by the misrepresentations of critics of Stuart government, and by modern political and social pressures. But historical judgements may be conditioned by such forces and still be *right*, if they are supported by the evidence. For Neale, the evidence was clear: Elizabeth was a great queen, and under her England experienced a great age – indeed, the case was so obvious that he scorned any suspicion that he had to prove it![20] It is not proposed to debate the question of 'greatness' here (it is a semantic issue which seems less important to hard-nosed historians in the present intellectual climate than it was to romantic nationalists a generation ago), but to examine the alleged national harmony and confidence which are said to have contributed to great deeds.

Camden was one of the first historians to write of an Elizabethan golden age of English unity and achievement and, like those who came after, he established this by contrasts with divisions and disasters under her predecessors. Henry VIII had ruined the economy by war and currency debasement; under Edward VI the nobility were riven by unrestrained faction and the people were in tumult; and under Mary the reimposition of papal authority brought religious conflict at home and contributed to military humiliation abroad. But Camden's Elizabeth soon solved these difficulties, as did Neale's Elizabeth and Joel Hurstfield's Elizabeth: the theme of Hurstfield's *Elizabeth I and the Unity of England* (1960) was that she 'brought unity and strength to a divided England' and led the country to 'within striking distance of the time of her imperial greatness'. More soberly, Wallace MacCaffrey has argued (in 1968 and 1981) that the first phase of the reign saw the resolution of a national political crisis which had begun in 1529: between 1558 and 1572, Elizabeth, Cecil and Leicester learned to cooperate and to neutralise some of the forces of disruption; and thereafter they established a political stability which lasted at least until the aftermath of the Armada. In Chapter 2 of this present volume, Simon Adams supports part of the MacCaffrey analysis by stressing the essential cohesion of Council and Court in the 1570s and 1580s, which brought a political homeostatis.[21]

Elizabeth has always seemed the luckiest of the Tudors: she inherited chaos, lived long enough for it to go away, and died before it returned. But her historical context has been subject to a good deal of revisionary argument in recent years, and in so far as her reputation has depended upon disasters before and after her reign it must now be at risk. Early modern English history has been enduring two forms of revision. The first reflects little more than the aggressive perversity of historians of all periods: rather than repeat what we were taught, we turn inherited views upside down to demonstrate our own inventiveness. So Michael Bush makes Pollard's naive and idealistic Somerset into a hard-headed (and hard-hearted) politician who ruled with a firm hand; Dale Hoak makes W. K. Jordan's grasping and short-sighted Northumberland into 'one of the most remarkably able governors' in Europe; and Jennifer Loach and Ann Weikel make everyone's weak and unpopular Marian regime into a purposive and effective government. As 'the mid-Tudor crisis' is argued out of existence, Elizabeth's early problems seem less severe and her own reign less notable – and if Jenny Wormald's attempt to turn 'the wisest fool in Christendom' into a competent king is successful, Elizabeth's reputation will not be able to rely on contrasts with James I.[22]

The second form of revision, more specific to the early modern period and often called 'revision*ism*', is a revolt against Whig-Protestant interpretations which stress the speed of historical change and the triumph of progressive forces. The history of the two centuries from, say, 1450 to 1649 has generally been written in terms of two sequences. In the first, historians have traced a political emancipation of the Crown from the nobility, a construction of a centralised state in partnership with the gentry, and a breakdown in that relationship which culminated in the Civil Wars of the 1640s. The second theme interprets the Reformation and its consequences:

it is argued that a movement of popular discontent with the medieval Church was endorsed by official alteration of the state religion from Catholicism to moderate Protestantism, but more radical forms of Protestantism (called 'Puritanism') emerged to challenge the Church of England and (because the Crown tried to maintain Anglican uniformity) the monarchy. But 'revisionists' have argued that to divide the past into progressive movements is to elongate causal sequences, exaggerate change and make the past more crisis-ridden than it really was; instead, they have emphasised continuities and played down the importance of progressive movements.[23] Now not all early-modern historians (and not all contributors to this volume) are 'revisionists', but the revisionist attitude has important implications for our understanding of the reign of Elizabeth I.

A significant feature in Neale's argument that Elizabeth's was 'an age of greatness' was his view that her reign was, to purloin a phrase used of a later era, an 'age of equipoise', a period of balance in which 'conservative elements' and 'new forces' cancelled each other out. Within the political and social harmony which resulted, individual freedom and national achievement became possible.[24] But since recent historians have often emphasised the continuing power of 'conservative elements' and doubted the vigour of 'new forces', the balance may not have existed at all. Although a 'revisionist' view of the English Reformation does not, and probably will not, command general acceptance, a growing company of historians has suggested that Catholic belief and practice retained their hold among the people of Tudor England must more successfully than had been supposed: in 1982 this approach gained the ultimate accolade of the fashionable novelty as the theme of a set of Ford Lectures at Oxford.[25] If the Reformation was a slow and difficult process, and if Protestantism made only tardy progress at the popular level, then our perspective on the reign of Elizabeth must shift decisively. Catholic survival, not Protestant militance, was the major ecclesiastical problem, and Puritan enthusiasts were not dangerous deviants but the government's allies against a common foe. Hemmed in by popery and ignorance, the Protestant ethos was not a crusading confidence sustained by a Foxeian version of history which would culminate in a final victory over the powers of darkness; rather, as Carol Wiener has argued, it was a frenetic, almost despairing, anxiety which saw a Jesuit under every bed, Catholic plotters in every closet, and a Spanish armada around every headland.[26]

The buoyant confidence which is said to have sustained Elizabethans was hardly evident in the autumn of 1584, when the rulers of the realm were close to panic. The successes of Spanish forces against the Netherlands rebels and the murder of William the Silent, the Dutch Protestant leader, seemed likely to lead to the defeat of England's continental allies and to a Spanish invasion of England itself. At home, the interrogation of Catholic plotters had drawn attention to the risk that Elizabeth too might fall victim to assassins, and to the presence, in Mary, Queen of Scots, of a claimant to the throne whose very life was an invitation to Spanish conquest and Catholic conspiracy. In the Privy Council, desperate men turned to desperate measures: they accepted a plan for the creation of an 'Association' of men bound by oath to protect Elizabeth and, if their protection should fail, to hunt down her murderers and resist the succession of any candidate on whose behalf the killing had been carried out. The Association was to be a political vigilante group, pledged to use lynch law to safeguard the throne. Its conception and organisation show an astonishing lack of confidence in the formal mechanisms of government and in the breadth of support which the regime enjoyed. In 1569 a similar association had been proposed in the fearful weeks before the Revolt of the Earls, and there were renewed suggestions at the end of the reign to safeguard the Protestant succession. It is true that the alarm of the autumn of 1584 soon subsided, and that in 1585 resistance to traitors was brought under the statutory control of the Council and the judges, disguising vendetta in the respectable clothes of legal process. But in a period of apparent crisis the councillors had not mobilised the resources of the Tudor state, they had appealed to the force of their own supporters. The realities of the Elizabethan polity had been laid bare.[27]

The Association of 1584 demonstrated the nervousness of England's Protestant rulers: it also showed the distribution of political power, and the continuing influence of 'conservative elements'. The Privy Council did not recruit members for the Association through the official structures of shrievalty, county sessions or militia, or even through the all-embracing hierarchy of the Church. Instead, they enlisted the co-operation of nobles and magnates, who were expected to lead the senior gentry into an Association which would harness their private power. Some of the nobles who were active in organising county branches of the Association on behalf of the Council were lords-lieutenant. But others were not, and its seems to have been the informal influence of social leaders, rather than the formal authority of office-holders, that was pressed into service. If the political power of the nobility was being sapped by a 'crisis of the aristocracy', and if a new class had become dominant as a result of 'the rise of the gentry', then Elizabeth's councillors did not know much about these movements. When danger threatened, as in 1584, Elizabeth and her advisers turned to the magnates of the kingdom. In 1588, as the Armada approached, the Queen was protected by a huge bodyguard drawn mainly from the private followings of nobles and courtiers, and in 1599, during another invasion scare, nobles were summoned to Court with their horsemen to safeguard the monarch. In some respects, of course, the power of the aristocracy *was* undermined. The crisis of 1569–70 broke the influence of the Dacres, Nevilles and Percies in the north, and the Howard dominance of Norfolk ended in 1572. Financial problems eroded the regional influence of some families, such as the Cliffords, and the division of estates among heirs-general weakened the position of others, such as the Stanleys. But there is a growing recognition among historians of the significance of the nobility as Court patrons, as members of the House of Lords, as county governors, as local power-brokers, and as the men to whom the Crown naturally entrusted its most delicate tasks – such as dealing with Mary, Queen of Scots.[28] The surviving importance of the nobility – like the surviving importance of Catholicism – will be an important theme in the revision of Elizabethan history.

V

If historians of a (more or less) 'revisionist' cast of mind have challenged Neale's Elizabethan balance by stressing the continuity of 'conservative elements', their doubts on the strength of 'new forces' have been even more pronounced and disruptive. One of the foundations of Elizabeth's reputation among modern historians has been her apparent success in holding in check those movements which were to bring civil war forty years after her death. But one of the most obvious (if controversial) developments in the recent historiography of early-modern England has been the attempt to shorten the causal sequence leading to the Civil War. Conrad Russell has reinterpreted the parliamentary difficulties of the years 1604 – 29 and denied that there was any emerging constitutional crisis resulting from parliamentary pretensions. Patrick Collinson and Nicholas Tyacke have suggested that there was a Calvinist consensus in religion in the reign of James I, which was to be disrupted only by the influence of Laud and the Arminians from 1625. John Morrill and Kevin Sharpe have argued that royal government in the 1630s was stable and effective, and Anthony Fletcher has sought the origins of the war in the political misunderstandings and suspicions of 1640–2.[29] If historians of early-Stuart England have abolished the long-term causes of the Civil War, wherein lies the greatness of Elizabeth I?

It has to be admitted that the 'revisionist' advance has been bitterly resisted, both by specific study of parliamentary problems and by general attacks on 'revisionist' assumptions and methodology.[30] But the Elizabethan consequences of early-Stuart revisions can be seen in this volume, and several contributors seek to emancipate the reign of Elizabeth from slavery to the origins of the Civil War. The redefinition of 'Puritanism' has been in train for some years, and in Chapter 7 Patrick Collinson incorporates some of its perceptions into a wide-ranging account of Elizabethan Protestantism. Many of the difficulties which have arisen in our understanding of Puritanism resulted from failures to distinguish the various usages of the term: as Professor Collinson has remarked, since 'puritan' was a term of abuse 'the Puritanism was in the eye of the beholder'. In his own early work, Collinson showed that Puritanism narrowly defined (that is, the demand for a thorough reconstruction of the Church of England along presbyterian lines) was a small-scale, though well-organised, movement of ministers, able to seize the leadership of their colleagues only in times of crisis and in disarray after 1590. Puritanism more loosely defined (as 'the hotter sort of Protestants') has been reinterpreted as 'mere Protestantism', as the mainstream of English evangelical reformed religion, and its structures (exercises, lectureships, conferences) as practical solutions to pastoral problems rather than cells of subversion. Although it is argued in Chapter 8 that godly preaching and moral regulation could be disruptive in the parishes, it is now difficult to see in any 'rise of Puritanism' a challenge to the Church of England or to the Crown. If we define Puritanism tightly, it was too small a force to be dangerous; if we define it more generously, it was too amorphous and too establishment-minded to be seriously troublesome.[31] In either case, it was not a powerful revolutionary movement ably checked by Elizabeth I.

Thus some ecclesiastical historians have denied that the Elizabethan disputes over religion were part of an inexorable polarisation of opinion which was to culminate in civil war. The same strategy can be observed in recent studies of Elizabethan Parliaments, most notably by Michael Graves and Geoffrey Elton – indeed, 'revisionism' was virtually invented by Professor Elton in an influential essay of 1965. In Chapter 1 of this volume, Norman Jones attacks the view that Elizabeth and her Council put moderate religious proposals to the Parliament of 1559, but were forced by Puritan militants in the Commons to concede a radical settlement. In the Jones version, one finds the classic ingredients of parliamentary revisionism: an emphasis on royal management, a denial of Commons initiative, a diminution of Puritan influence and a recognition of the significance of the House of Lords. In Chapter 3, Professor Elton gives an elegant demonstration of the application of 'revisionist' techniques: he stresses the importance of routine parliamentary business rather than constitutional issues; he shows that co-operation rather than conflict was the normal relationship between Crown and Commons; he suggests that any disputes which arose took place *within* the Council and the two houses of Parliament, not *between* those institutions; and argues that when harmony was disrupted it was often as a consequence of the politics of the Court. There is little evidence of the constitutional pretensions often ascribed to the Elizabethan Commons, and no sign that MPs had set out on 'the high road to civil war'.[32]

Two further (and connected) sources of conflict are thought to have tested Elizabeth's political skills and, as she lost control in the 1590s, to have contributed towards the slide to disaster – the relations between factions and the relations between Court and counties. Under the influence of Camden, Naunton and, more recently, Neale, historians have seen the politics of the Elizabethan Court in terms of bitter struggles between antagonistic factions competing for the control of patronage and policy. Although factionalism has been a much-used weapon in the revisionist armoury (employed to explain the development of the political Reformation and to explain away troubles in early-Stuart Parliaments), its importance in the reign of Elizabeth is questioned by Simon Adams in Chapter 2. Dr Adams doubts whether the conflicts between William Cecil and Leicester, which play so large a part in Conyers Read's two-volume biography of the former, really existed – at least after 1569. He does not think that Court politics was organised in factions, and (like some ecclesiastical historians) he detects a Calvinist consensus in Court and Council in most issues. The Essex phenomenon of the 1590s may thus be a unique and personal one, and even his divisiveness may have been exaggerated: Professor Wernham has recently stressed the cohesion of the Council during the years of military strain from 1588 to 1595.[33] The newly promoted 'crisis of the 1590s' may also have been overdone. The Crown's demands for men and money to fight its wars, its failure to secure the continuing favour of county leaders by patronage, and its use of new administrative methods are said to have produced a break-down of trust and co-operation between centre and localities. But, in Chapter 5, Penry Williams suggests that, despite some resistance to taxation and some troubles caused by the ambitions of Essex, government was effective in difficult circumstances and its ends were achieved.[34]

The assumption that there were divisions and dissensions in Elizabethan society which led to civil war and revolution in the mid seventeenth century has also been challenged by economic and social historians. The attack has been directed against the views and influence of R. H. Tawney, especially on the social consequences of the growth of capitalist agriculture. The once-famous 'rise of the gentry' by efficient farming, at the expense of a feudal aristocracy who declined through out-moded estate-management, is now thought to have been a crude simplification. Instead, the expansion of the gentry class is stressed, as yeoman-farmers profited from rising food prices to raise their own social status – and as more gentlemen meant better supervision of the lower orders, the stability of the nation may have been enhanced. Tawney's view that enclosure and exploitation by capitalist gentleman-farmers broke the English peasantry and drove copyholders into wage-labour has also been assailed: the legal rights of tenants have been emphasised, and the disintegration of the peasantry seen as a long-term and gradual movement rather than a sudden social crisis. Cata-clysmic interpretations of economic history have been denounced: all was for the best in the England of Elizabeth. Population pressures stimulated economic growth, poverty was contained by economic expansion and charitable pro-vision, agricultural improvements increased the food supply, industry and trade advanced with new techniques and new markets, trade was in balance or even surplus, a benign regime preserved social order and enlightened councillors pursued helpful policies of industrial diversification and import sub-stitution – or so it has been forcefully and skilfully argued.[35]

VI

At this point, perhaps, we should take stock, for the historio-graphical wheel has come almost full circle. A 'revisionist' argument which diminished Elizabeth's achievement by weakening the forces she is said to have controlled has apparently rehabilitated her reign as an era of concord. We are back – give or take a bread riot or two – with an Elizabethan golden age! Harmony at Court, harmony in Parliament, harmony (or, at least, no *serious* disputes) in the localities, harmony in religion, harmony between social classes – perhaps Neale's idyllic picture was right after all! There is a risk that, in their determination to escape from a polarising and crisis-laden Civil War perspective, historians will fall into a false 'Merrie England romanticism which explains away every problem and sees near-success in each disaster. It is therefore reassuring (to the editor) that this collection includes Chapter 9, from Paul Slack — who asserts the reality of social difficulties in Elizabeth's reign, and counters recent emphasis on economic progress. Dr Slack argues that the growth of population produced increases in prices and falls in real wages which caused hardship to the poor, and brought a mobility by the destitute and fear of disorder by the propertied which do not suggest a stable and confident society. Paul Slack is not alone in his more pessimistic tone. In Chapter 4, James Alsop highlights the deficiencies of Elizabethan administration by the example of the Exchequer which (like all bureaucracies?) was operated in the interests of office-holders rather than of Crown or public — and where the Queen found it as difficult to enforce her will as she did in the most distant of her counties. It has, indeed, been claimed that the main task of the machinery of the Elizabethan state was not to provide government, but to generate the privileges and profits which bought the co-operation of those who *did* govern — the men of independent power in the counties.[36] There is pessimism, too, in George Ramsay's discussion (in Chapter 6) of Elizabeth's foreign policy — hardly a policy at all, but a series of opportunistic expedients and nervous delays which tried to reconcile conflicting commercial, religious and strategic interests on a shoestring budget. And in Chapter 8 there is an account (with a gloom that Elizabeth's Protestant councillors and her bishops came increasingly to share) of the Church of England's evangelistic failure, and of the ways in which unprotestantised parishioners attempted to dictate the liturgical and pastoral practices of established religion.

Nor should it be supposed that the other contributors to this volume could be convicted of naive optimism. Professor Elton notes that the Queen's rigid definition of her own prerogative competence caused difficulties with counsellors of all kinds, and even Professor Collinson (whose brief was to chart the progress of Protestantism among those with whom it succeeded) points out the appalling condition of church fabric!

There is a possibility that in any collection of thematically organised essays the ups and downs of political and social stability may be obscured and a misleading impression of calm given. Perhaps we do not adequately reflect the problems of the years 1568–72 – or perhaps it is only the editor who feels that this really was a period of danger, when the tensions within the regime were barely contained and when the widespread disaffection among nobles and people was demonstrated by plots and rebellion.[37] But the major difficulties of 1594–8 *are* clearly shown. Dr Adams establishes that the Council of the 1590s was a narrow, self-perpetuated oligarchy, whose few members took pluralistic shares of the great offices of kingdom and Household and passed them on to their sons. No wonder that Essex and his allies thought themselves excluded from a charmed circle, and finally tried to break in by violence. Dr Williams demonstrates that there was real resentment of the burdens of the war and of the means the Crown used to reward its favoured followers, and Professor Elton concedes that constituency opposition to monopolies pushed MPs into rare criticism of royal policy. These military and financial demands should be seen within the social context sketched by Dr Slack, in which harvest failure, epidemic, crime and rioting combined to produce a multiple dislocation. The years 1594–8 saw a political and social disequilibrium which seems to have been worse than the crisis of 1555–8 and as bad as that of 1626–30.[38] We may argue that Elizabeth's reign did not see problems which led to the Civil War, but we should not suppose that her reign had no problems.

The last paragraph of an introduction is no place to attempt a balanced conclusion. Instead, this survey might end as it began, with a glance at attitudes towards Elizabeth. The crisis of 1594–8 passed (as did those of 1555–8 and 1626–30), without apparent damage to the fabric of society or state. But the myth of Gloriana had been severely dented, and to some even Spanish rule (not to mention Scottish) seemed preferable. Although official iconography still depicted her as a young beauty and the balladeers still celebrated her peaceful reign, there was a widespread wish in her last years that the old woman would be gone: the French ambassador recorded in 1597 that Elizabeth's government 'was little pleasing to the great men and the nobles, and if by chance she should die it is certain that the English would never again submit to the rule of a woman'. His certainty, it is true, proved unfounded, but men now looked to a king: in 1603 an ambassador bewailed the 'strangely barbarous and ungrateful' conduct of Londoners in lighting bonfires to James on the day of Elizabeth's death, as she finally lost the loyalty which had been ebbing for years. The prospects were now in Scotland: 'There is much posting that way,' reported John Chamberlain, 'and many run thither of their own errand, as if it were nothing else but first come first served, or that preferment were a goal to be got by footmanship.' But Elizabeth had secured her own future, and bequeathed to James problems which could not be solved: as his failure became clear, her reputation recovered.[39]

1. Elizabeth's First Year: The Conception and Birth of the Elizabethan Political World

NORMAN L. JONES

I

ELIZABETH Tudor was a very conservative woman with well-developed ideas about her place in the world. At twenty-five she had already learned hard political and personal lessons, and they had shaped her vision of herself as monarch, blending naturally with political ideas derived from her humanistic education and the traditions of English kingship. With a temper as fiery as her red hair, her personality led her to be cautious and stubborn, sure of her authority and petulant in the face of change. In a land and time when the personal rule of the monarch was very real, these traits had a profound impact on the course of English history from 17 November 1558, when she acceded to the throne.

To understand what happened when she took the nation's helm, it is important to realise that Elizabeth believed Bracton's famous dictum that the king is under God and the law. God, of course, put the king in charge of England, as Henry VIII had told the Pope, and so the monarch ruled the Church as well as the state. The monarch made the law in her courts, in her Parliament and by her proclamations, but the law constrained the monarch's behaviour, requiring that its forms be honoured. After all, as Elizabeth knew well, God and the law were the supports that kept a monarchy intact. This same belief, however, imposed great responsibilities on a ruler.

Responsible before God for her people, she was careful never to let them challenge her right to that responsibility. Politics and theology taught her that, when the people overreached themselves in religion or government, revolt and bloodshed were likely to follow. Stability, she believed, was what God wanted and what would be the best for her beloved people, as well as what best pleased her cautious, conservative personality, so she devoted herself to maintaining the *status quo*, showing great reluctance to innovate.

However, in November 1558 innovation was required by circumstances. The events of her life had made it impossible for her to accept Queen Mary's religion and, since religion was also ideology in the sixteenth century, to change the nature of the Marian settlement of religion was to change England's place on the political map. Thus for Elizabeth the choice was clear, if uncomfortable; she had to return to the Protestant *status quo ante* of her late brother, as it had been recognised in law. Personally, although she had conformed under Mary, there was little chance that she would keep England attached to the papacy. The living symbol of her father's break with Rome, she had never been recognised as legitimate by the Catholic Church. Moreover, she believed firmly that she was the rightful ruler of all England, including its Church, and no pope could agree with that. During Mary's reign Catholicism had been tainted by heresy persecutions, Spanish hegemony and a disastrous war, so that many English patriots, and Protestants, looked to Elizabeth as their champion. Her surest supporters, Elizabeth could not abandon them. Last, but not least, Elizabeth was a convinced Protestant. Though impatient with theological quibbling, there is no doubt that she accepted the basic tenets of the reforming movement and did not believe in transubstantiation or the papal supremacy. However, though we know she was more than a Henrician Catholic, it is impossible to pin her to one of the specific 'isms' of the Reformation. With some logic on her side she seems to have thought that beyond the basic issues of faith and grace there were only 'adiaphora' – things which she could regulate in accord with the needs of the nation.

Tightly bound to the question of the religion Elizabeth would impose on the nation was the question of what man she would impose on herself. In 1558 no one, perhaps not even Elizabeth, could imagine a forever-virgin queen. It was assumed that she would marry and provide an heir to the throne; and it was assumed that the man whom she married would in some sense rule her. Thus the world waited for Elizabeth to play what one of her diplomats described as 'the card of our negotiations' by bestowing herself on someone. Suitors quickly appeared, led by her dead sister's husband, Philip II, and everyone assumed that Elizabeth's choice of a mate would indicate the nation's religious future. Elizabeth found herself in a difficult position. The nation would not willingly accept a foreigner for king, as Mary's reign had proved, but there were no suitable candidates at home. Besides, she did not like the idea of marriage – perhaps because of her childhood experience with so many unfortunate stepmothers. Together these problems would prevent her from choosing a husband and teach her the political value of remaining marriageable.

The issues of religion and marriage were closely related to a third pressing trouble. England, at the behest of Philip II, had allied itself with Spain against France and Scotland in a war that had lost her Calais and more treasure than she had. Now, humiliated and nearly bankrupt, England was engaged in negotiations to end the fighting. The talks, however, were suspended at Mary's death and the English representatives returned home for instructions. Elizabeth had to decide what those instructions would be, defining in the process her relations with her Spanish ally and her bellicose neighbours. In the meantime she had to ensure that the realm was ready for war if the talks failed and a Franco-Scottish army crossed the northern border. Whether or not the war ended, Elizabeth faced a financial crisis. The fighting had further stimulated the inflation that was plaguing the economy, new taxes were needed to replenish the treasury, and the coinage was badly inflated after years of debasement.

Before she could face any of these issues, however, Elizabeth had to create a government which would work for her. To achieve this she needed to choose a new Privy Council, replacing those on Mary's Council who would not serve her interests. The Spanish ambassador, the Count of Feria, reported that by 14 November, three days before Mary's death, a new Council was coalescing, and that the members of Mary's

Council were 'extremely frightened of what Madam Elizabeth will do to them. They have received me well, but somewhat as they would a man who came with bulls from a dead pope.'[1] Mary's Chancellor, Archbishop Heath, arranged a meeting with Sir William Cecil, who was obviously to be the linchpin of the new regime, to discuss the state of the realm and affairs of religion, as well as to prepare for a transition of power.

Around Cecil Elizabeth gathered nineteen other privy councillors, divisible roughly into three groups. At the periphery of the Council were great lords with strength in their localities. Seldom attending meetings of the Council, they were named primarily because they were too important to be ignored. On the semi-periphery were civil servants whose experience made them invaluable, such as William Paulet, Marquis of Winchester and Lord Treasurer, who, as a financial expert, had held his office under both Edward and Mary.[2] At the centre of the new Privy Council lay a small group who shaped the policy followed by the government. Dependent upon their close connection, through friendship and blood, to the Queen, they were remarkably stable. William Cecil would lead the Council until the 1590s, while Sir Francis Knollys, Vice-Chamberlain, would live until 1596. Nicholas Bacon, Lord Keeper, who was Cecil's brother-in-law, remained at his post until 1579; Lord Admiral Clinton served until 1584, and Lord William Howard, Lord Chamberlain, lived until 1573. It was this group, in union if not always in harmony with the Queen, that helped Elizabeth deal with the problems of religion, war, foreign policy, economic distress and domestic unrest in her first year, and that set the nation on the course it would follow through the reign.

II

What happened when the Queen and her new councillors began to impose their desires on the nation has been the subject of historical debate, for Elizabeth was careful to hide her true intentions toward religion. Subscribing to Nicholas Throckmorton's advice that 'neither the old or new should wholly understand what you mean [to do]',[3] she succeeded in confusing contemporaries and historians alike. The oldest historiographic tradition, represented by John Foxe, William Camden and John Strype, held that Elizabeth set out to create the Anglican Church and, despite stiff Catholic resistance, succeeded. Refined by later historians, the story of 1559 was told in this way until the early 1950s, when J. E. Neale startled his colleagues with a new interpretation of the Queen's intentions toward religion. Elizabeth, he asserted, did not wish to establish a thoroughly Protestant Church, desiring instead to return to her father's Catholicism without the Pope. Her plans were thwarted, Neale believed, by a Puritan party in the House of Commons. Led by returned religious exiles, this group forced Elizabeth to compromise between her ideal of a conservative religious settlement and their ideal of a settlement modelled on the Swiss Reformation. It was this conflict, he thought, that made the Parliament of 1559 so stormy, not Catholic opposition to the change in religion. Forcefully argued, Professor Neale's vision of a conservative Queen opposed by a Puritan opposition became the stuff of textbooks. Recently, however, his interpretation has been challenged and rejected by several historians, who have shown that John Foxe's account was generally accurate.

Historians are left to guess the course of events after the fact; Elizabeth had to prepare for them before they occurred. To help her do this she received advice, solicited and otherwise. The most important and detailed counsel was contained in Richard Goodrich's 'Divers Points of Religious Contrary to the Church of Rome', and the anonymous 'Device for Alteration to Religion'. Their forms suggest that they were written in response to an official request, and they imply that from the very beginning Elizabeth intended to revive the royal supremacy over the Church and reintroduce the *Book of Common Prayer* of 1552 as soon as it was politically feasible. Goodrich's document contained sound legal and political information, showing Elizabeth how far she might take religion without breaking the law, and warning of the dangerous effects too quick a transition from Catholicism to Protestantism might have. He was especially concerned about the threat presented by the leaders of the Marian regime, urging that they be imprisoned before a religious alteration was undertaken. While preparations were under way for the legislation of reform by Parliament, he insisted that the realm could use the English litany and suffrages used in Henry VIII's time, and that the Queen could have a mass in which the host was not lifted up for adoration.[4] Although some of Goodrich's caution was ignored, much of his outline was echoed by later events. In particular, Elizabeth followed it in reforming the service in her chapel on Christmas Day 1558. In a dramatic episode she ordered Bishop Oglethorpe not to elevate the host; he refused, and when he reached that point in the mass Elizabeth rose and stalked from the chapel, making clear to all that she did not accept transubstantiation. Two days later she proclaimed that the realm could use her chapel service, which included the English litany printed for Henry VIII in 1545.

The 'Device for Alteration of Religion' is even more interesting, for it is broader in scope, seeing the return to Protestantism as part of a complicated web of problems. It is arranged in a series of questions and answers. When should the alteration occur? It ought to be done soon if proper precautions have been taken. What dangers will attend the change? The Queen will be excommunicated; the French will renew the war at the behest of the Pope, invading through Scotland; the Irish may rebel; and the papists at home will make trouble. Moreover, when the subsidy is granted there will be discontent, and more ardent Protestants will gripe that the Queen's reform is but a 'cloaked papistry'.

Outlining solutions to these threats, such as making peace with France and enacting penal laws to force people to adhere to the new religion, the 'Device' arrives at its most famous suggestion. Asking what changes ought to be made in religion (apart from restoring the supremacy), it urges that a committee of learned men should be assembled to 'review the *Book of Common Prayer*, and order of ceremonies, and service in the Church', settling on a uniform order of worship. There is no evidence that such a committee ever met, but the plan suggested by the 'Device' was, at least in its vague outlines, followed in the ensuing months.[5]

Both documents agreed that the Queen faced a threat from the religious extremes, and she took steps to disarm them. Refusing to declare openly what she was going to do about religion, Elizabeth issued an accession proclamation which ordered her subjects to 'keep themselves in our peace, and not to attempt upon any pretence the breach, alteration or change of any order or usage presently established within our realm'.[6] Meanwhile her Council began to take steps to weaken the Catholic bishops: the commissions which had furthered the persecution of heretics were called in, and those jailed on suspicion of heresy were released. Fearing that Catholic clergy would foster revolt, Cecil took steps to curb their tongues, noting that a safe preacher had to be chosen for Paul's Cross 'that no occasion be given by him to stir any dispute touching the governance of the realm'.[7]

Ironically, the man Cecil chose, William Bill, the Queen's Almoner and a known Protestant, provoked one of the first instances of what Cecil feared. Responding to Bill's heretical sermon, Bishop Christopherson preached one that resulted in his imprisonment. His colleague Bishop White of Winchester took the opportunity of Mary's funeral to warn his audience against the wolves of heresy coming into the kingdom to prey on innocent English sheep, urging the clergy to resist them or be blamed by God for the slaughter. He too was arrested. As the new course of religion became clearer, news of other gestures of defiance trickled in from around the country. Perhaps the most frightening report was that a prebendary in Canterbury was arming people to resist religious change. Episodes such as this were met with quick action by the Council, which feared a Catholic revolt.[8]

The Protestants were causing trouble, too, though of a less dangerous kind. Assuming that the accession of a Protestant meant that they would be free to worship as they wished, they became impatient with the government's slow progress towards reform and, on Christmas morning, a London crowd broke into the church reserved for the Italian community. Ignoring the protests of the Italians, their leaders occupied the pulpit and began to preach, 'uttering a thousand ribaldries concerning the reign of . . . Queen Mary and of the Cardinal, and vituperating the people for the errors they had committed in believing their former teachers'.[9]

Such episodes, in combination with the Queen's pious desire to reform her chapel, led to a series of actions designed to reassure the Protestants while preventing dissent from the pulpits. Three days after Elizabeth strode out of her Christmas mass she issued a proclamation silencing all preachers, but giving hope to her Protestant followers by permitting them to use the English litany 'until consultation may be had by Parliament . . . for the better conciliation and accord of such causes as at this present are moved in matters and ceremonies of religion'.[10] Now the only sermons to be heard were those preached before the Court, and the preachers chosen kept up a constant attack on the Pope.

As the new government struggled with the problem of religion, it was in the process of establishing its position in the international system. Inheriting alliance with Spain and war with France and Scotland, the English had to stay on good terms with Philip II until the war was concluded. Beyond the issue of the Spanish alliance, however, were the twin questions of relations with the papacy and with the German Protestant states. On 1 February the Privy Council ordered the English ambassador to Pope Paul IV to come home 'in consideration there is no further cause why he should make further abode there'.[11] At the same time English representatives were sent to the German states, sounding out the possibility of alliances with them and telling them that Elizabeth accepted the Augsburg Confession – a useful though inaccurate claim that kept the Germans from mistaking her for a Calvinist and withdrawing their support.

England's relations with Spain presented a thornier problem. Allies in the war against France, they needed one another. Philip II and his counsellors were afraid that Elizabeth intended to lead her nation back into schism and heresy, but they were even more frightened that England was about to fall to a French–Scottish onslaught: if that happened, they believed, the Spanish Netherlands, cut off from Spain by hostile fleets in the Channel and North Sea, would succumb too. They would rather support a Protestant England than let that happen. For the same reason they were driven to prefer Elizabeth to the next, Catholic, claimant to the throne, Mary Stuart, wife of the Dauphin of France. If Elizabeth died or was excommunicated and overthrown, the Spanish nightmare would become a reality: a French–Scottish–English power block. This lively obsession dominated Philip's international relations into the 1580s and gave England considerable room in which to manoeuvre, preventing Elizabeth's excommunication for eleven years after she showed herself a heretic.[12]

Even before Mary had died, Philip's ambassador was assuring Elizabeth that Spain would not conclude peace with France unless the English were satisfied with the terms. The Queen's reply foreshadowed the policy which was to so frustrate the French and Spanish in the coming months: speaking of her representatives at the negotiations, she 'made it very clear that she would have them beheaded if they made peace without Calais'.[13] Her resolve in this was strengthened by Philip's assurances of friendship and support. Elizabeth and Cecil became convinced that Philip dared not abandon England and that they could use his fear of France as negotiating leverage. Sheltering under the wing of the great power without having to bow to it, Elizabeth therefore took a stubborn, independent course, refusing to make peace with the French until her demands were met. At the same time, her officers in the north were working to stir anti-Catholic and anti-French sentiments in Scotland.[14]

King Philip's worries about a possible loss of England to his enemy, combined with his deep piety, prompted him to propose marriage to Elizabeth in hopes of keeping England within Spain's orbit and the Roman Church. Decency demanded that he wait a short time after his wife's death before declaring himself to Elizabeth, and when he did he found the field already full of candidates. Besides Philip himself, the pro-Catholic, pro-Spanish party hoped she would accept one of Philip's relatives, the Archduke Ferdinand or his brother Charles. Protestants set their hopes on the Duke of Holstein, or the Lutheran King of Sweden, who had been ardently wooing Elizabeth. Home-grown contenders included Sir William Pickering, for whom Elizabeth was thought to have affection, and the Earl of Arundel. Robert Dudley, though already conspicuous in the royal Household, did not emerge as a favourite until the spring of 1559.

The hopes of these candidates were turned to England's political advantage by Elizabeth's refusal to choose among them. The frustrated Spanish ambassador blamed her indecision on the Devil, but thoughtful Protestants might have credited it to God, since it bought the new queen breathing-space in which to carry out her religious reform. So long as there was a hope that she might marry Philip or his relatives, the Spanish were not going to support internal dissent or papal interference.

III

Meanwhile Elizabeth instructed her Council to prepare for a parliament. The most pressing reason was financial: in order to carry on the war and pay the Crown's debts, she had to get a new subsidy from her people. Tied to this was the need for formal ratification of her right to collect the customs duties that traditionally were granted to the monarch. Moreover, she had to have parliamentary recognition of her right to the crown, which included restoring her mother's legal status. Just as urgent as all these was the question of religion. Elizabeth could not and would not change the national faith without Parliament's assent, and rapid change was necessary to forestall further disturbances. The writs for Parliament were issued less than a month after Elizabeth acceded, and it assembled in Westminster on 25 January 1559.

As freely elected as any in the sixteenth century, the new House of Commons was composed of a mixture of courtiers, clients of great men such as the Earl of Bedford, country gentry, and merchants and lawyers from the boroughs. 27 per cent of them had previous parliamentary experience – which was average for the mid-sixteenth-century parliaments. Most of the Commons were Protestants or were at least willing to follow their sovereign into Protestantism, though there were a few ardent Catholics in the House.

In the Lords the picture was different. Nicholas Throckmorton, in his advice to the Queen in November 1558, had with good reason recommended her to make 'you a better party in the Lords' House of Parliament'. Mary's bishops, twenty of whom were alive when Elizabeth acceded, could block the passage of reforming legislation through the Upper House. Allied with conservative laymen they were a threat to the

Queen's religious policy, and, despite deaths and ill health, their resistance nearly scuttled the Act of Uniformity.

As the members of Parliament gathered for the opening of the session, the Queen gave further indications of her religious intentions. Elizabeth absented herself from the traditional mass of the Holy Ghost, and when she was met at Westminster Abbey by a procession of monks with lighted tapers, incense and holy water she cried, 'Away with these torches, we see very well.'[15] After she had taken her place under her canopy at the high altar, Richard Cox, a returned religious exile, lambasted the monks for their part in the heresy persecutions and exhorted her to destroy idolatry – Catholicism – in England.

After the long sermon, the peers and Commons moved to the House of Lords, where Lord Keeper Bacon addressed them in the Queen's name. Calling for the 'uniting of these people of the realm into a uniform order of religion', Bacon warned them to avoid opprobrious words, such as 'heretic' and 'papist', and urged that they proceed with care toward the abolition of idolatry and superstition.

Once the formalities of the opening had been completed, Parliament settled down to business. On 9 February the Commons heard the first reading of a bill to make Elizabeth the supreme head of the English Church. When it reached its second reading a long debate ensued, ending three days later, when it was committed. That same day, 15 February, a bill 'for order of service and ministers in the Church' was heard, and on the 16th a bill entitled 'The book for common prayer and ministration of the sacraments' was ready. Thus by the middle of February there seem to have been three bills for the reform of religion. One was straightforward: though we do not know its content, it certainly was designed to re-establish the monarch as head of the Church in England, breaking once again with Rome. The other two bills, both connected with the establishment of a Protestant form of worship, have been the focus of much historical debate, but the best guess is that they were part of the government's plan to restore English worship to the standard of 1552 by imposing the second prayer-book of Edward VI and, perhaps, restoring his ordinal to use.

Whatever these bills contained, they were all lumped together in a new bill, introduced on 21 February. If it had been enacted, this compound would have made Elizabeth supreme head of the English Church and changed the form of its worship, but it was wrecked. Approved by the Commons despite the protests of Catholics and perhaps a few Protestants, it was sent to the Lords, who, after hearing its first reading, reacted strongly against it.

Holding the balance of power in the Upper House, the bishops, together with the Abbot of Westminster and some lay supporters, began strenuous manoeuvres to stop the bill, which, if passed, would deprive them of their religious freedom and condemn their flock to either persecution or Hell. Their first action was to secure a condemnation of the attempted change in religion from the clergy's representatives assembled in Convocation. Confirming the dogmas of transubstantiation and papal supremacy, their protest was delivered to Lord Keeper Bacon to be read to the House of Lords, but he conveniently forgot to present it there.

When the bill for supremacy and uniformity was read for a second time, the Lords' minds had been softened by the anti-papal Lenten sermons at Court, but again they reacted violently, forcing its committal to fifteen peers, eight of whom would later vote against the supremacy. By the time they reported on the bill, they had altered it almost beyond recognition. The planned restoration of Protestantism had been removed, and, rather than recognise Elizabeth as the supreme head of the Church in England, the peers would only admit that she could take the title if she wanted it – but they would not accept the responsibility for giving it to her. The Lords passed the truncated bill, ruining the government's planned reforms and frightening its Protestant supporters.

The Lords apparently had refused even to repeal the heresy laws revived by Queen Mary. In the face of this the Commons, fearing retaliation by the bishops and knowing that Parliament would probably be dissolved before Easter (25 March), passed a bill declaring that 'no persons shall be punished for using the religion used in King Edward's last year'. They apparently believed that they could obtain toleration for Protestantism even if they could not see it made the only religion in England. They also passed what was left of the supremacy and uniformity bill, accepting the Lords' changes because they had no better choice.[17]

By 23 March, then, the Queen and Cecil, having badly miscalculated the strength of resistance to religious change in the Lords, found themselves in a difficult position. Never before had the bishops behaved in such a truculent manner. Previous alterations in religion had passed the Upper House easily, and the Elizabethan government, seeing its programme ruined, was taken off guard by the effective attack on its legislation. At first Elizabeth and her advisers were inclined to accept this *fait accompli*, dissolving parliament and making the most of what they had obtained. Thus they prepared a proclamation allowing the people to take communion 'in both kinds', but admitting that no other 'manner of divine service for the communion . . . (than that which is now used in the Church) can presently be established by any law'. Printed but never proclaimed, it was an admission of defeat. By Easter 1559, then, it appeared that England would remain hanging in a Henrician limbo, Catholic but not Roman Catholic.[18]

While the drama over supremacy and uniformity was played out, Parliament had been dealing with many other issues in keeping with its role as the high court and supreme law-making body of the realm. In particular, the Commons had been occupied with bills attempting to sort out the mess made by the Edwardian and Marian deprivations and restorations of bishops. Edward had removed conservative bishops and replaced them with more fervid Protestants; each Edwardian bishop had made grants of land, leases and other arrangements, all of which depended upon his legal authority as bishop. When Mary had restored the conservatives, she had declared the acts of the Protestants to be invalid, resulting in a terrible legal tangle. For many properties there were two or more sets of claimants, who now brought their cases to Parliament for settlement. Few of them were successful, in part because the bishops in the Lords had some leverage in the matter, but the bills absorbed an enormous percentage of the Commons' time, with the result that they had passed very little legislation by Easter.

IV

Although the disputes over religion in Parliament had an important bearing on England's diplomatic future, in the month before Easter the foreign issues of most immediate concern were the treaty negotiations to end war with France and the preparations to resist invasion from Scotland.

When the negotiators reconvened on 10 February at a derelict château near Cateau Cambrésis they discovered that the only hindrance to a peace was Elizabeth's refusal to give up Calais, much to the frustration of the other nations' delegates. King Philip reminded her that without peace they would have to fight on, and neither of their countries was in a position to do so, but still she insisted on Calais. The French were equally unwilling to give a French city back to the English, but they too were desperate for peace: they tried all sorts of enticements to get it. Their first attempt was to break the Anglo-Spanish alliance, offering each country a separate peace; when that failed they looked for fictions that would give Elizabeth peace with honour and leave Calais in French hands. Elizabeth was not enthusiastic about their proposals, but she could not continue her bluff indefinitely. England needed peace as much as her ally and enemies, and the Queen gave her ambassadors secret instructions to get the best peace they could if it became clear that the talks were going to break down.

As February turned into March and the summer campaigning-season grew nearer, Elizabeth stepped up preparations for the defence of the north. Reports from spies in Scotland warned that 10,000 French soldiers were expected to arrive there after Easter, and that the Scots were increasing their forces on the frontier and making raids into English territory. The military situation was becoming so dangerous that the Earl of Northumberland warned that, without reinforcements 'ye shall in short time have the borders utterly destroyed'. In response troops and labourers were rushed to garrison and finish the new fortifications at Berwick, and Sir Thomas Gresham and his agents busily gathered munitions in Flanders – despite the Crown's lack of money to pay for them. Meanwhile Sir Henry Percy negotiated with the Scots, who were unhappy about the French presence in their country.

Urging them to join with the English against the Catholic French 'for maintainance of the Word of God', Percy and the Wardens of the Marches procured a ceasefire from 6 March.[19]

For a time it did not appear that the success with the Scots could be repeated with the French, and the negotiations at Cateau Cambrésis dragged on through March. Elizabeth had finally agreed to make peace on condition that Calais be returned later upon payment of an indemnity, but there was much haggling over the exact terms. Building on a French proposal, this route offered Elizabeth an exit from a very difficult situation. As she herself told her representatives at Cateau Cambrésis, 'The whole realm . . . lives in expectation of the recovery of the . . . town', so she could not surrender Calais without some face-saving expedient which left England in technical possession.[20] One doubts, however, that the English government expected ever to get the city back. As Philip's ambassador in London told the Spanish negotiators at the talks, 'the French will be quite willing to promise to restore Calais and then keep their word in their usual fashion', implying that the city was to remain in French hands, as it has.[21] Finally, on 2 April, peace was signed. France was to keep Calais for eight years, returning it at the end of that time if the English had done nothing to forfeit it. In the meantime, they agreed to pay an indemnity and to pacify the Scottish border. The war was over and Elizabeth had protected the national honour and proved her independence as a monarch.

Domestically, however, she was facing a very tense situation by Easter. The destruction of the bill for uniformity and supremacy by the House of Lords had left her in an untenable position. If she chose to dissolve Parliament before Easter, she would be forced to accept the retention of Catholicism as the national religion, doing violence to her beliefs and those of her most enthusiastic supporters. Recognising this, Elizabeth came to a sudden decision to continue it after the Easter Holy Week, opting to try again for a parliamentary sanction of the royal supremacy and a Protestant settlement, the necessary cornerstones of the policy she was pursuing.

The stumbling-block that had tripped her drive for a religious settlement was the power of the bishops and Catholic laymen in the House of Lords. The bishops were an especially difficult group to overcome because they were the official experts on religion, charged with its care and trained to defend it. As John Jewel explained two days after the Lords had finished mutilating the bill for supremacy and uniformity,

> The bishops are a great hindrance to us; for being, as you know, among the nobility and leading men in the Upper House, and having none there on our side to expose their artifices and confute their falsehoods, they reign as sole monarchs in the midst of ignorant and weak men, and easily overreach our little party, either by their numbers, or by their reputation for learning.

Another returned exile and future bishop, Richard Cox, reported that the bishops were effective in opposing religious change because in the Lords there were 'but few who durst even open their mouths against them'.[22]

Powerful and highly visible supporters of an ideology unfriendly to the regime, the bishops had to be discredited, and even before the final March vote on the supremacy and uniformity was taken in the Upper House the government was planning a public debate between Catholic and Protestant divines. A popular Reformation technique, the disputation was expected to show that the Pope's Church was in error, and that logic demanded the creation of a national Protestant Church in England. The Queen seized upon the disputation as a weapon to break the intellectual superiority of the bishops in the Upper House. It was to occur during Holy Week in Westminster Abbey, and would give the Protestant clergy a chance to show the lay peers how wrong it was to resist the intended reform of religion. The propositions for the debate were chosen with this in mind. They first asserted that it was against the Word of God to use a tongue unknown to the people in worship; second, that every Church had authority to change its ceremonies, so long as the changes were edifying; and, third, that 'it cannot be proved by the Word of God, that there is in the mass offered up a sacrifice propitiatory for the quick and the dead'.

Designed to support specifically political and clearly Protestant ends, these questions were propounded under a confused set of rules. The eight Catholic disputants requested that the

debate be in Latin and in writing, to prevent misunderstandings and misrepresentation, but the Queen denied their
request. Instead, she seems to have ordered that it be in English
with each side presenting a formal written statement, followed
by extemporised rebuttals. Accordingly, on the first day Dr
Cole read the Catholics' piece on Latin prayers, to be followed
by the Protestants' Dr Horne. Pointedly kneeling with his back
to the altar, Horne began with a prayer and followed it with
their 'book' on the question.

When the Catholic party rose to respond, Lord Keeper
Bacon, who was presiding, refused to allow it, and after some
wrangling Bacon conceded that they could make their response
on the next day of the disputation. When it dawned, however,
he ordered them to proceed to the next question; Bishop White
of Winchester, insisting that the Catholics be allowed to rebut
the Protestants on the first question, grew obstreperous.
Exasperated, Bacon instructed them to proceed to the next
question in the Queen's name, threatening that, if they would
not, he would end the debate. Uncowed, White replied,
'Contented, let us be gone; for we will not in this point give over.
I pray you, my lords, require not at our hands that we should be
any cause of hindrance or let to our religion, or give any such
evil example to our posterity, which we should do, if we gave
over to them.'[23]

Although both sides later claimed victory in the aborted
dispute, it is unlikely that it changed any votes, but it did
provide Elizabeth with an opportunity to alter the balance of
power in the Lords. Shortly after they left the Abbey, two
bishops were arrested and sent to the Tower, charged with
disobedience to common authority. By thus exercising its
political muscle, the Council helped guarantee the eventual
passage of the uniformity statute by reducing the number of
Catholic votes in the Upper House.[24]

V

As the Easter holiday drew to a close and Parliament reconvened, new bills for supremacy and uniformity were being
prepared for introduction. Because of the resistance to the

uniformity, each issue was to be dealt with separately, so the government would be assured of obtaining the supremacy, even if it did not achieve the form of worship it desired.

The new supremacy bill, which would become the statute, departed from tradition by giving the Queen the title of 'Supreme Governor of the Church', rather than of 'Supreme Head'. This was done in order to pacify Catholics and many Protestants, who had serious doubts about a human, and especially a woman, claiming to head the Church of Christ. John Jewel commended her new title when he wrote, 'She seriously maintains that this honour is due to Christ alone, and cannot belong to any human being soever . . . .'[25]

Regardless of the semantics of her title, the bill for supremacy would give Elizabeth as much power over the Church as any of her predecessors had enjoyed. Besides re-creating the supremacy and backing it with an oath for clergymen and royal officials, the bill repealed the Marian heresy laws, guaranteeing freedom of worship for Protestants in case the uniformity failed to pass, and provided for communion in both kinds by reviving a statute of Edward VI's first parliament, striking an oblique blow at the mass. Sure that the new supremacy bill would pass, Elizabeth and Cecil were slipping some reforms through on its coat tails, ensuring that, even if the uniformity failed, England would be more reformed than it had been on the death of Henry VIII.

The new supremacy legislation won the Commons' approval easily, though some members were surprised and confused by the change from supreme headship to supreme governorship. Predictably, when it reached the Lords it came under much heavier fire, and it was committed at the insistence of Archbishop Heath. Although unable to muster enough strength to wreck it as they had wrecked the combined bills before Easter, the conservatives were able to amend it in ways that gave them some protection. The most important of these changes was insertion of a statement that the Commission for Ecclesiastical Causes (the High Commission) created by the bill could not judge anything to be heresy unless it had been declared to be so by 'the authority of the canonical Scriptures, or by the first four general councils'. As Archbishop Heath argued it, the general councils of the early Church had approved the basic beliefs of the Catholics, and so the Commission could not declare Catholicism to be heretical. In the end the supremacy was approved by the Lords in spite of the united opposition of the bishops. Only one layman voted against it.[26]

The new bill for uniformity came much closer to defeat in the Lords. Designed to establish a uniform order of worship by imposing the *Book of Common Prayer* on the nation, it was disliked by a significant number of the lay peers because, although they were willing enough to break with the Pope, they could not reject transubstantiation. To ensure passage of the bill, the Protestants were forced to make some concessions to their opponents in the matter of enforcement, and even then the bill nearly failed. When the vote was taken, eighteen voted against it and twenty-one voted for it. If the bishops of Lincoln and Winchester had not been in the Tower, and if Abbot Feckenham of Westminster had not been inexplicably absent, England would not have had a new religious order.

The Act which now formed the foundation for the Church of England was, in almost every way, a compound of the two Edwardian Acts of Uniformity. It borrowed most of its form from that of 1549, while its substance came from that of 1552. Reimposing the *Book of Common Prayer* established by the 1552 Act, it required its use in all churches and set up a system of punishments for those who failed to use it or who publicly objected to its use. Ordering everyone to attend church on Sundays and holy days and to participate in the services using the new book, the Act declared that any who refused to attend would be fined a shilling each Sunday. The only important departures from the precedent of 1552 were the change in the words of institution (said by the priest as he consecrated the bread and wine) and a section which became known as the 'ornaments rubric'. This provided that the ornaments of the church and the dress of the clergy should be as used in the second year of Edward VI's reign 'until other order shalbe therein taken by the authority of the Queen's Majesty', and gave her the right to order 'such further ceremonies or rites as may be most for the advancement of God's glory, the edifying of His Church, and the due reverence of Christ's holy misteries and sacraments'; it was meant to establish a legal norm for ecclesiastical ornamentation. Presumably the Queen hoped thereby to short-circuit the iconoclasm and bitter division over externals to which Protestant communities were prone. As far as she was concerned, all externals were unnecessary for salvation and could, therefore, be regulated in the interests of peace and good government. Ironically, Elizabeth, reluctant to allow any change from the standard now established, was to impose conformity to this provision upon her clergy, thereby provoking the first major outbreak of clerical Puritanism, the vestments controversy.

The change in the words of institution may also have had a political foundation. By taking the 1549 formula and joining it to that in the 1552 *Book of Common Prayer*, the new language brought Elizabeth's book closer to biblical purity, perhaps in an attempt to silence criticism from both Catholics and Protestants by providing words which could fit any eucharistic doctrine. It was probably hoped that this intentional ambiguity would let people of several religious opinions commune together within the national Church.[27]

The Acts of Supremacy and Uniformity laid the foundations for later religious developments, but they did not complete the royal platform for reform of the Church. As her father and brother had done before her, Elizabeth set about securing the wealth of the Church for the use of her government. One of the Crown's earliest actions in this regard was the introduction of a bill which took the ecclesiastical taxes known as First Fruits and Tenths into the Queen's hands. Henry VIII had appropriated these to himself, and Mary had returned them to the Church, losing in the process thousands of pounds in annual revenues. Elizabeth needed those revenues badly and saw to it that they were restored to the Crown. The members of her Parliament, bishops excepted, approved, since this helped solve the Crown's financial problems without increasing the laity's taxes.[28]

In her enthusiasm for restoring Catholicism Mary had also re-established a few monasteries, while some of her subjects had founded chantries to provide prayers for the dead. As a Protestant, Elizabeth did not believe in either monastic vows or purgatory and so a bill was launched that would dissolve the monasteries and chantries, transferring their property to the

Crown. In the process she confirmed the validity of Henry VIII's actions against the monastic establishments and Edward VI's dissolution of the chantries, reassuring her subjects that their title to Church lands was secure. Besides being an affirmation of Protestantism, the appropriation of the religious foundations brought several thousand pounds into the Exchequer.[29]

By the time Parliament closed in mid May 1559, the Elizabethan religious settlement had taken its permanent legal form. Not everyone was satisfied with it, however. The Catholics, of whom there were many, could hardly like it, although, because of their bishops' resistance and the Queen's fear of religious revolt, they were not to be seriously persecuted under the new laws. Moreover, they were confused. Because of Spanish diplomatic pressure the Pope failed to make it clear to English Catholics where their duty lay, permitting them to live with the new regime and even serve it without betraying their own religious feelings. This gentleness toward the Catholics and the Queen's preference for more traditional ornamentation in her churches was already worrying some leaders of her new Church, who feared that the new religion would be laxly imposed and treated as a tool of policy instead of a command from God. As John Jewel, soon to be Bishop of Salisbury, expressed it, 'Others are seeking after a *golden*, or as it rather seems to me, a *leaden* mediocrity; and are crying out, that the half is better than the whole.'[30] This mediocrity, celebrated as the *via media* of Anglicanism, seems to have become the policy of Elizabeth's government. When Lord Keeper Bacon – whose personal motto was *Mediocria firma* – spoke to the members of Parliament at its close, he urged them to maintain the uniformity of religion they had just established, warning them against radical Protestants as well as Catholics.

And here great observation and watch should be had of the withdrawers and hinderers thereof; and especially of those, that subtly, by indirect means, seek to procure the contrary. Amongst those I mean to comprehend as well those that be too swift, as those that be too slow; those, I say, that go before the laws, or beyond the laws, as those that will not follow; for good government cannot be where obedience faileth, and both these alike break the rule of obedience; and these to be those, who in likelihood should be beginners, and maintainers, and upholders of all factions and sects, the very mothers and nurses to all seditions and tumults, which necessarily bring forth destruction and depopulation . . . .[31]

VI

As Bacon was stating this sixteenth-century political truth, Cecil was in the process of using religious faction as a weapon against England's enemies. Although a peace had been signed with France and Scotland in early April, he and his fellows were not comfortable with the situation in Scotland. That nation's queen, Mary Stuart, was married to the Dauphin of France, and was represented in Edinburgh by a regent, Mary of Guise. Thus tied to the French throne and garrisoned by French troops, Scotland was restless for religious reasons too, and when John Knox arrived home in May 1559 he crystallised Scottish nationalism and fervent Protestantism into a revolt against the French led by the Lords of the Congregation.

For Knox the revolt was a religious crusade, but for Cecil it was a Heaven-sent chance to exert English hegemony over Scotland, drive out the French, and spike Mary Stuart's claim to be the rightful Queen of England. The situation was further inflamed in July, when Henry II of France was killed in a joust and Mary's husband became King Francis II. This put the ambitious and expansionary Guise family in control of France and Scotland, and English statesmen feared that they would attempt, for reasons both political and religious, to put Mary on the throne of England as the only legitimate, Catholic claimant. When the French royal couple began sporting the arms of England on their dinner-ware, it confirmed England's fears and angered Elizabeth.

In the crisis which followed, Elizabeth's councillors came to be dominated by Cecil more clearly than ever, but only after he nearly fell from grace, and they learned how cautious and conservative their Queen was. From the beginning Cecil tried to persuade her that money and even troops should be sent to aid the Scottish rebels and oust the French, but he was fighting an uphill battle. She had a deep antipathy to subjects who revolted against their lawful monarch, and a lively hatred of John Knox, whose ill-timed attack on the 'regiment' of women and calls for the assassination of ungodly rulers had made him *persona non grata* in England; it was with the greatest difficulty that she was persuaded to send treasure, in French coins, to the Scots in the autumn of 1559. The failure of the rebels to overcome the French garrison at Leith prompted her to send weapons, and by the spring of 1560 she had concurred in the despatch of an English army. It failed as the Scots had failed, but Cecil was able to win an important diplomatic victory, securing a French withdrawal. From the Scottish adventure he emerged the clear leader of the Privy Council – though he was to face serious challenges – and the Queen, probably to her horror, emerged as champion of the international Protestant cause. Cecil's successful conclusion of the war with Scotland showed how a small state could protect itself from larger ones by stirring and supporting dissent within its enemy. Used in Scotland, this technique was shortly to be employed against the French and later against the Spanish in the Netherlands.

The realisation that Mary, Queen of the Scots and the French, was the next in line for the English throne appalled patriots and Protestants alike, spurring the nation's lively concern about their Queen's barren spinsterhood. Important as her marriage was in terms of international politics, it was even more important for her people, who feared that, unless she married and produced an heir, foreign domination, the Roman inquisition or civil war might come to England. Parliament gave voice to these concerns in the first week of its 1559 meeting, petitioning her to take a husband. Elizabeth's answer was gentle and elegant: if God willed that she marry, she would; if he did not, 'it is not to be feared but he will so work in heart and in your wisdoms as good provisions by his help may be made in convenient time, whereby the realm shall not remain destitute of an heir'. For herself, she said, it would be sufficient that in the end 'a marble stone shall declare that a Queen, having reigned such a time, lived and died a virgin'.

Though besieged by suitors of royal blood, neither Elizabeth nor any of her subjects would have been betting in favour of their success late in 1559. By May of that year it had become clear that she had fallen in love with her handsome Master of the Horse, Lord Robert Dudley, and for a time she lost some of her political discretion. 'Lord Robert', noted the Count of Feria, 'has come so much into favour that he does whatever he likes with affairs and it is even said that her Majesty visits him in his chamber day and night.' The rumours about their relationship began to fly, given impetus by the fact that Dudley was already married to Amy Robsart, and by the end of the year the scandal was the talk of Europe. Through it all Elizabeth insisted that she had remained virtuous, but her enthusiasm for Dudley embarrassed her councillors and created political difficulties. Lord Robert's influence with Elizabeth made him one of the most powerful men in the kingdom, against whom even Cecil could hardly stand. After the bubble of the affair burst in September 1560, when Amy Robsart was found dead at the bottom of a staircase (a probable suicide – though rumour said she was murdered so her husband could marry the Queen), Dudley remained a pole of influence and power for the rest of his life.

From the diplomatic romances and her genuine affection for Dudley, Elizabeth learned lessons that were to pattern her diplomacy and life at her Court. The marriage negotiations with the Habsburgs had shown her the value of diplomatic dalliance, to woo allies and frighten enemies. The bitter moral of her blind affection for Dudley was that if she was to be an effective queen she could not give free reign to her passion. Conversely, however, she also realised the value of making all her courtiers pay her suit, providing a vocabulary for the Court of a queen without a consort. However, no matter how Elizabeth thought of marriage, her marriage and the succession question would be a major political concern for years to come.

VII

All the issues in diplomacy and domestic politics were related to England's change in religion, and much of the government's effort in 1559 was devoted to the establishment of the reformed Church mandated by Parliament. From the Feast of John the Baptist, 24 June, the nation was to use the new *Book of Common*

Prayer, and shortly thereafter the Queen issued commissions for visitors to travel throughout the country taking the oath of supremacy from clergy, cleansing churches of papistical ornaments, and ensuring that services were properly and respectfully performed. Since it was clear that royal authority could not be successfully imposed on the Church unless those controlling ecclesiastical jurisdictions were willing to support the new settlement, the Privy Council and the visitors had to see to it that the archbishops, bishops, archdeacons, vicars-general, deans and parish clergy were willing to conform. Elizabeth had hoped that some Marian bishops might transfer their allegiance to the new Church as many of them had done during the religious vacillations of her predecessors, but all but one refused to take the oath of supremacy; she was forced to deprive them of their offices and replace them with trusted Protestants under the leadership of Matthew Parker as Archbishop of Canterbury.

By midsummer the Catholics had been deprived, but Elizabeth delayed the consecration of Protestant bishops-elect, choosing to keep their bishoprics vacant until her officers could, under the authority granted by the Act of Exchange, inventory and transfer to the Crown the temporalities of the sees. As a result, most of the new bishops took up the power of their offices only in December 1559 or early in the succeeding year. Elizabeth's desire to acquire more Church property upset her clergy, though it was in keeping with the attitudes of most Tudor laymen, and the refusal of Crown and Parliament to improve the financial position of a Church whose clergy seldom had adequate incomes was an important source of discontent in the coming years.

Equally scandalous to the godly was the shortage of properly qualified clergymen. During the religious confusion of the 1550s the number of ordinands had decreased sharply, creating a scarcity that was aggravated by the deprivations of recusant clerics during the visitations in 1559. In their rush to provide the people with spiritual services, the new bishops indulged for a short time in mass ordinations of deacons and priests, accepting men who could only read English and who had testimonials to their virtuous lives. This policy shortly backfired, however. The presence of these poorly trained clerics upset the serious Protestants because they believed that one of the marks of the true Church was the proper ministry of the Word: men who could read only English and who were not licensed to preach could not perform the role established by God for the Church. Like the Church's poverty, the number and quality of its servants was to become the focus of much criticism.

By the middle of her second regnal year Elizabeth could congratulate herself on having safely navigated the dangerous shoals of governmental transition, religious change and international reorientation, laying a course that she was to sail for years to come. Her government had taken shape around William Cecil, whose hand remained on the helm almost as long as Elizabeth's, and around Robert Dudley, whose influence was an important factor in national politics for thirty years. By then, too, the Privy Council had stabilised into a small, efficient working-group which had come to understand the cautious, conservative, and sometimes truculent nature of their mistress. In addition, Elizabeth had made it clear that she was not going to be ruled by her Council and that she, though a woman, was going to act like a prince.

Devoted to what she considered the concomitant ideals of the royal prerogative and the reformed religion, Elizabeth had set out to return England to the legal religion of Edward VI and had succeeded, aided by some careful politics and much luck. The death of many of the Marian bishops helped her obtain the reforms she sought, but the Catholics in the House of Lords nearly ruined her programme, demonstrating the hold Catholic theology, if not the papacy, had on England. Achieving the formal recognition of her supremacy over the Church and the imposition of a new, uniform order of religion, she did not have to face what she and her councillors feared most. The Catholics of England did not immediately revolt, remaining passive, confused by the lack of direction from their leaders, and lulled by the gentleness of their queen's settlement. Her Protestant subjects had united behind her in their desire to rid the realm of the Pope and his mass, but after the settlement had been enacted some of them began to find fault with the way it was carried out. Elizabeth, refusing to permit further changes, was to frustrate some and drive them into opposition to certain portions of the settlement, giving birth to the Puritan movement.

In international relations too, her experience in her first year set the pattern for her future policy and created some of her future problems. Having projected herself as the leader of international Protestantism, people expected her to act like it, but she was always reluctant to do so. Instead she clung to the lessons of her early years and refused to see that the political world was constantly in a state of flux.

In the last analysis Elizabeth's first year is the keystone of the history of her reign. Conservative, cautious and imperious, Elizabeth had made the change-over from Catholicism to Protestantism and had reasserted the Crown's authority over the Church in her first parliament. Forever after she refused to budge from the *status quo* of 1559. In 1559 she collected a set of councillors who would remain her councillors for years to come, and in the same year she established herself as an independent princess in international affairs, as well as giving the first hints of her spinsterhood. In many ways the political history of the next forty-three years of her rule is the story of her defence of the course she charted in the first months of her reign.

2. Eliza Enthroned? The Court and its Politics

SIMON ADAMS

IT is one of the curiosities of recent Elizabethan scholarship that the localities have received much more attention than either the Court or the central government. While counties and towns have been the subject of an impressive series of sophisticated monographs, research on the Court has stagnated. The standard account of its institutional structure was written by Sir Edmund Chambers some sixty years ago as an introduction to his work on the Elizabethan stage: since then we have had only the valuable, yet impressionistic, essays, of Sir John Neale, Professor Wallace MacCaffrey, Professor G. R. Elton and, most recently, Dr Penry Williams. Lacking is either the major survey of its personnel that Professor G. E. Aylmer has provided for the reign of Charles I, or the sustained analysis of its institutions that Dr David Starkey has undertaken for the earlier Tudors.

The politics of the Court retain, therefore, an enigmatic quality. Many key episodes – the approaches made by Lord Robert Dudley and Elizabeth to Philip II in 1561, the attempted overthrow of Sir William Cecil in 1569, Leicester's acceptance of the governor-generalship of the Netherlands in 1585, or Essex's return from Ireland in 1599, to cite but a few examples – still await adequate explanation. Most accounts of the Court have tended to emphasise factional strife and a vicious atmosphere of place-seeking, enmity and competition surrounding an alternatively goddess-like or hag-like queen. It has been easy to paint the picture in the most lurid colours. Yet, as I have suggested elsewhere, much of the evidence for factional strife has been drawn from the 1590s and by no means reflects the reality of the previous decades.[1] The Court was never completely free from conflict, but such conflict was less the product of faction among courtiers than of disputes between an able, charming, yet imperious and idiosyncratic queen, and councillors and intimates who generally shared a high degree of social, political and cultural homogeneity. Whatever Elizabeth may have desired, even her closest servants could not be isolated from outside pressures, whether the more immediate ones of family or clients, or those arising from the wider concerns of the post-Reformation world. Our primary concern here will be, therefore, to assess the impact of such tensions on political dynamics of the Court. It is to its institutions and personnel that we should turn first; then to the social and political composition of its membership; and finally to a more specific examination of its relationship to the Queen.

I

'The Court', declared Sir James Croft (Comptroller of the Household, 1570–90) in 1583, 'is divided into two governments, the Chamber and the Household.' It is similarly described in the only full source for its permanent membership, the surviving subsidy assessments of the Household.[2] The ambiguous nature of this description becomes apparent, however, when it is observed that not only were two other major departments – the Stables and the Privy Chamber – subsumed within the Chamber and the Household, but also such civil servants as the Principal Secretaries of State, the clerks of the Council, the signet and the privy seal, and the French and Latin secretaries were included among the members of the Chamber. There are fundamental difficulties in defining the boundaries of the Court, and a clear distinction between the courtier and the bureaucrat is almost impossible to draw.

Further ambiguities emerge when the more mundane aspects of the Court's domestic economy are considered. Overall expenditure ranged between £70,000 and £90,000 a year, but further accuracy is almost impossible. The spending of certain departments varied from year to year, each department accounted separately to the Exchequer, and certain minor items such as the annuities of the gentlemen pensioners or the annual Christmas present of £100 to the grooms of the Chamber were paid by the Exchequer directly.[3] Furthermore, it is particularly difficult to assess the overall impact of the Crown's various economy drives: a steady inflation-led increase in expenditure should not be assumed. The largest department was the Household, presided over by the Board of Green Cloth or Compting House. It received a statutory annual assignment of £40,027 in 1563, but its expenditure rose from £45,000–50,000 a year in the first half of the reign to £50,000 – 60,000 at the end. The largest part (usually in excess of £40,000 per annum) was taken up by the diets provided for those in attendance, bouge of court, and the wages of the Household and Privy Chamber.[4] Second in rank was the Chamber, whose Treasurer received annual assignments of about £15,000, from which he paid the wages of members of the Chamber, the yeomen of the guard and such miscellaneous servants as the Queen's boatmen, mole- and ratcatcher, together with her alms and the expenses of messengers and diplomatic couriers.[5] For the third great department, the Stables, there are no surviving accounts prior to 1638, but its running-costs cannot have been less than £5000 per annum.[6] Lesser departments – the Wardrobe, the Revels or the Works – spent more erratically: the expenses of the Wardrobe, for example, depended very much on the ceremonial engaged in during the year. Finally there was the Privy Purse, of which the account of only one of its three keepers – John Tamworth (1559–69) – survives. He received a total of £26,675 and disbursed £26,701. His functions, however, were still undefined: apart from providing for items of immediate personal use – the Queen's lute-strings for example – Tamworth occasionally paid wages within the Privy Chamber, and once channelled a loan of £5000 to the Earl of Moray.[7]

The Household was the largest regular spending-department of the Crown, and its expenses were the subject of constant review by Queen and Council. Economy campaigns took place at regular intervals, but particularly in 1564, 1569, 1576, 1582–3, 1589–90, 1598 and 1602. The primary targets were its basic running-costs, especially the diets and bouge of court. Both the Household officers and Lord Burghley appreciated that inflation was making an impact upon the price of foodstuffs, but the Queen was less easy to convince. At the end of 1602 she claimed to her Clerk Comptroller that the increase in Household expenditure was primarily due to excessive dining at her expense:

> I was never in all my government so royally with numbers of noble men and ladies attended upon, as in the beginning of my reign . . . and all those then satisfied with my allowance. . . . And shall these that now attend and have the like allowance not rest contented? I will not suffer this dishonourable spoil and increases that no prince before me did, to the offence of God and great grievance of my loving subjects . . . .[8]

The issue had, however, been repeatedly discussed in the past. The book of diets had been drawn up in 1560, and extensive comparisons with current costs (together with those of the reign of Henry VIII) made in 1576, 1583 and 1591. In 1576 it was observed that the annual cost of diets exceeded the authorised scales by £6000, and in 1583 Croft reported that the annual expenditure on food and other commodities had risen by £10,000–12,000 since the beginning of the reign. Moreover, despite the increased cost of living, the wages of the ordinary staff had been frozen, which had led to exploitation and embezzlement. Only the Yeoman of the Guard and the Stables staff are known to have received any increase in wages during the course of the reign.[9] The quality of the food served in the Hall did not help: 'for almost few or none in this house . . . likes their ordinary diet, for that they are grown to such delicacy that no meat will serve them but that which cometh from her Majesty's board'. The result was much dining in private chambers on food from the Queen's kitchens, while Hall food was wasted. The reforms that Lord Burghley proposed, however, verge on the comical: he wished to see room service terminated at eight o'clock, a halt to the filling of private bottles at the Buttery and measures to prevent the removal of the Queen's crockery from the Hall.[10]

Yet two more significant problems were less easy to remedy. The first was that the Queen herself, whatever her fussing, was the chief offender. Her own diets had increased more than anyone else's, while she was primarily responsible for another major source of expense: the annual summer progress.[11] Elizabeth did not invent the royal progress, but she always enjoyed playing to the crowd and she employed progresses in a striking manner. The impact on the nobility and gentry has been the subject of much recent comment. Less noted (except by Dr David Palliser) has been the fact that each progress usually contained at least one entry into a major corporate town. There she would be greeted by cheering, if well staged, crowds: to them, as at Worcester in 1574, she responded 'with a heartiness that did her honour, [and] threw up her cap and said "I say God save you all, my good people"'.[12] The cost of transporting the Court fell on the Crown: in 1576 Burghley noted that the last 'overlong progress' had cost an extra £2000, and he also complained of the expense incurred through the Queen's frequent changes of itinerary. It is probable that attempts to economise on progresses lay behind their relatively limited range (one to York was certainly planned in 1574 and 1575), and their suspension between 1580 and 1589.[13]

II

'Hard to be observed' was Burghley's comment on possible solutions to the other great problem of the Court economy: lack of control over the numbers living there, particularly the servants of noblemen and gentlemen in attendance. The reiteration of this complaint was a reflection of the fact that the Court was (to paraphrase Conrad Russell's now-famous description of Parliament) almost as much an event as an institution, and that its population fluctuated from week to week. At the centre of the Court were the Queen's servants, who swore an oath to her and took her wages. Yet (in the absence of the archives of most of the major Court officers) they are difficult to identify with assurance.[14] While the Household subsidy assessments provide the best overall guide, we possess an annual record of the permanent waged members of only one department, the still-mysterious Privy Chamber. But even this does not establish its full membership. The waged servants of the Privy Chamber consisted of a limited body of women, ladies or chamberers, of whom the four senior were known as the Bedchamber, and a smaller group of men, either gentlemen or grooms. Yet we know of a further group of women – among them Lady Mary Sidney, Anne, Countess of Warwick, and the two marchionesses of Northampton – who did not receive wages, but were also members of the Privy Chamber, personally close to Elizabeth and in frequent attendance. Of these women, however, there is only one complete list: the Coronation roll of 1559, which identifies them either as 'the Privy Chamber without wages', or 'extraordinary of the Privy Chamber, when the queen's majesty calleth for them'.[15]

On a more significant level, the composition of the Court remains difficult to define because its structure was still fluid and determined more by certain idiosyncracies of the Queen than by any formal hierarchy. It is true that Elizabeth made only minor changes in Court organisation – distinguishing the Bedchamber from the Privy Chamber in 1559 and abolishing the Henchmen in 1565 – but this static structure reveals little about the actual functioning of the Court.[16] Nor does the book of officers and fees, often cited in the past, provide an accurate guide to its personnel: it is simply a copy of the Edwardian survey of 1552 made in 1576–8.[17] A central defining idiosyncracy was the Queen's extremely conservative attitude towards office and rank, which can be seen very clearly in her reluctance to expand the peerage. Equally conservative was the composition of the Court. In its lower posts the Household possessed a recognised internal system of promotion (to the level of cofferer) and there was an established body of Household families whose position Elizabeth did little to disrupt. The same also appears to have been the case with the personnel of the Chamber and such attached bodies as the gentlemen pensioners: the one Elizabethan esquire of the body whose career has been studied – Roger Manners – had been appointed by Mary.[18] Among the senior personnel, there was only one purge of significance, and that followed her accession in 1558.[19] Thereafter men and women served until removed by death or incapacity. New blood entered only when vacancies were created, and the Court aged steadily with the Queen. The key to the process was Elizabeth's use of office as a reward rather than as a means of advancement: service was not dependent on office-holding so much as award of office followed on years of service. Croft could therefore defend the private sale of a recently awarded Household office on the ground that, since the recipient had obtained his reward, it did not matter in which form he received the benefit. Men such as Charles Howard of Effingham and Thomas Sackville, sons of councillors and major office-holders, spent long years at Court before receiving any significant office themselves. Moreover, Elizabeth's loyalty to 'old servants' (whether her own or those of her father, mother and brother) was pronounced, although it was also a widely respected social convention. Thus Bishop Cox was told in the midst of his disputes with Lord North in 1575 that 'she hath borne with me and put up with many complaints against me, in consideration of my age and for that I was her father's and brother's servant'.[20]

The static nature of the Court was further compounded by Elizabeth's tendency to leave offices vacant or held jointly by one person for long periods of time. The most striking instance was the vacancy in the Secretariat between the death of Sir Francis Walsingham in 1590 and the appointment of Sir Robert Cecil in 1596, but further examples are plentiful. No Lord Privy Seal was appointed throughout the reign, while the mastership of the Court of Wards was granted to a favoured existing office-holder: in turn, Sir Thomas Parry, Sir William Cecil and Sir Robert Cecil. Sir Francis Knollys, Sir Thomas Heneage and Sir John Stanhope all combined at some stage the offices of Vice Chamberlain and Treasurer of the Chamber, while Knollys and Sir Christopher Hatton combined the vice-chamberlaincy and the captaincy of the guard. Walsingham, Heneage (possibly the greatest pluralist of the lot) and Sir John Fortescue all held the chancellorship of the Duchy of Lancaster in conjunction with another office. Lord stewards were rarely appointed: Leicester (1584–8) alone made any impact on the Houshold, and his reforms were limited by his simultaneous employment as Master of the Horse and Captain-General in the Netherlands.[21]

The consequences of the system were significant. First, competition for a tightly restricted range of office became an issue in its own right and the Queen's parsimony with office as well as land and money was repeatedly commented upon. Secondly, a vast gap was created between those, such as Burghley, Leicester, Hatton and – on a lesser scale – Heneage, who received the full benefit of the Queen's favour and those who did not. For most servants reward took the form of grants that did not place a direct burden upon the Queen's purse: customs concessions or farms, wardships, leases in reversion, and a variety of licences were most commonly employed; in the late 1570s patents and monopolies became favoured. As their use expanded, such grants became increasingly controversial and by the 1590s were very much a public issue.[22]

A further consequence of the structure of the Court was the effect on its relationship with the Privy Council. Elizabeth's privy councillors fall into three distinct groups: the major officers of the Household, the major officers of state, and a more amorphous body of men not holding office of importance. For those in the first two categories appointment to the Council was practically *ex officio*: only the two masters of the Horse, Dudley and Essex, had to wait several years for membership. Other offices – the captaincy of the guard, or the regional lord presidencies, for example – did not involve automatic membership of the Council. In some cases appointment to the Council followed; but this was not (as with Sir Henry Sidney or the Earl of Warwick) necessarily a consequence of the office held. There was, therefore, always a group of men prominent at Court who were not members of the Council, while some councillors, particularly in the first decade, were hardly important men at Court (Dr Nicholas Wotton and Sir William Petre fall into this category). Only one leading Court figure – Sir Walter Ralegh – was never appointed to the Council, but several had to wait for some time: the Duke of Norfolk was not appointed until 1562, the Earl of Sussex until 1570, Hatton until 1577, and Heneage until 1587.

These considerations therefore raise the very important question of how far the politics of the Court were subsumed within those of the Council. The Council clearly regarded consideration of matters of state and the Queen's business as its concern. Burghley was very unhappy about public discussion of affairs of state within the Court, while Leicester warned Francis Walsingham in 1573 not to discuss his negotiations in

France with others 'being no councillors'.[23] Yet the Council had no power to enforce its monopoly and its success in so doing lay in the fact that within it there was a distinct inner ring of councillors who were also the leading members of the Court. The key figures were Burghley and Leicester. Burghley's genius lay in his ability to expand his position as the Queen's man of business to approach in stature the great ministers of Henry VIII. His power did not come from his offices; rather, his personal relationship to the Queen extended their potential functions. Unlike his predecessor as Lord Treasurer, he did not operate within a relatively restricted sphere. Burghley displayed little hesitation in supervising the reform of the Household, an area where Winchester, in common with other officers, was markedly reluctant to intervene.[24]

Yet Burghley's pre-eminence was not total. Until 1588 it was always limited by the influence of Leicester, and it is revealing that the clashes between them arose in the main from Leicester's resentment of Burghley's monopolistic tendencies.[25] Yet a sustained struggle for power was prevented by their similar outlook in religion and agreement on most matters of state, together with a mutual appreciation of their joint intimacy with the Queen. About them existed a group of councillors who were clearly more deeply involved in matters of state than others, and who can legitimately be characterised as an inner ring. Once again office was of less significance than personal relationships both to each other and to the Queen. During the 1560s the inner ring included Sir Thomas Parry (until his death in December 1560) and, intermittently, Sir Nicholas Bacon, Winchester and Pembroke. From the mid 1570s to the end of the 1580s the pre-eminent members (together with Leicester and Burghley) were Walsingham, Hatton and (until his death in 1583) Sussex. At the end of the reign the key councillors were clearly Robert Cecil, Buckhurst and Nottingham.[26] Only in the mid 1590s was the composition of the inner ring in any real dispute; and it was on this issue that the great faction fight between Essex and Cecil centred, a struggle which was fought out in both Court and Council.

III

The tightly restricted nature of the Court's inner circle and its close relationship to the structure of power within the Council raises several important questions about its composition and recruitment. Was it as representative of the nobility and upper gentry as Professor Elton and Dr Williams have suggested? Was it a meeting-place for divergent views and interests? Were there, as Dr MacCulloch and Dr Williams have proposed, 'more than one road to Westminster'?[27] Such a picture of the Court rests, however, on the assumption that there was a fairly constant balance of factions there throughout the reign, which in turn permitted a certain religious diversity. This assumption should not be accepted uncritically: a more complex situation is revealed when we examine the relationship between changes in personnel and major political debates of the day. The most dramatic aspect of the post-accession purge of the Court was the transformation of Elizabeth's previous household. On her accession, Elizabeth's servants and friends were already a well-defined and closely knit group, as the frequent references to her 'old servants' and the 'old flock of Hatfield' make clear.[28] As had been the case on Mary's accession, the women became the new Privy Chamber and the men received their reward in appointment as officers of the Court and Household: Sir Thomas Parry as Treasurer of the Household and Master of the Court of Wards, Sir Thomas Benger as Master of the Revels, Sir William St Loe as Captain of the Guard, Sir John Fortescue as Master of the Wardrobe, and John Ashley as Master of the Jewels. The creation of the new Privy Council was a more complicated process. The Council in 1559 consisted of nine (originally eleven) former Marian councillors and nine new men, several of whom had previously served on the Council of Edward VI. The surviving Marians had also been councillors of Edward, but, more importantly, they appear to have intervened on Elizabeth's behalf at some point in Mary's reign. This was clearly the case with the one Marian Household officer – Sir John Mason (Treasurer of the Chamber, 1557–66) – to be retained in post.[29] The new men were a more disparate body, but the majority were either members of her household, relatives, or men with an existing personal connection. There is

only one apparent exception: the former member of Edward
VI's Privy Chamber, Sir Edward Rogers (Vice Chamberlain
and then Comptroller of the Household to 1568), the nature of
whose earlier association with Elizabeth remains unclear.

Both Court and Council were thus bound to the new queen
by direct personal ties, an aspect of the Court which was to
remain a constant feature throughout the reign. Yet such
connections could not fully resist the impact of political debate.
The first cracks appeared in 1559. Two members of the Council
(Winchester and Shrewsbury) voted against the Act of
Uniformity and several (Winchester again, Arundel, Sir
Nicholas Bacon, Petre, Wotton and Mason) opposed the
intervention in Scotland, although only Arundel remained
adamant. The Queen began to conduct her affairs with the
assistance of the inner ring (Cecil, Parry and, possibly,
Dudley), a course which drew further complaint from the
excluded councillors. Conciliar opposition to the Queen's
policies in turn provoked criticism from the more radical
Protestants.[30] At this stage the radical wing of the Protestant
laity was composed of former Edwardians, who sought restoration to office lost in 1553, the settling of old scores with their
political enemies, and a more actively Protestant policy. They
looked for leadership to Cecil and Dudley, the son of their old
patron. For reasons that have never been entirely clear, a
number of the older Edwardians (Sir Peter Carew, Sir William
Pickering and Sir Nicholas Throckmorton, for example) did
not receive the offices they might have expected, but the
younger men soon became diplomatic agents and officers of the
major military operations, beginning with the Newhaven
Voyage of 1562 and Sir Henry Sidney's expedition to Ireland in
1566.[31] Simultaneously, age took its toll, particularly among
the former Marian councillors, while others retired from the
Court. Arundel resigned as Lord Steward in 1564, while Petre
stopped attending the Council in 1567. The Crown also carried
out one further purge: the removal of the Percies and the
northern nobility from offices of military or political importance, undercutting their local power base in the process. A
more difficult problem was posed by the Duke of Norfolk, who
preferred a domestic life to that of the Court, but expected
deference to his rank and disliked the trend of Elizabeth's

policies. His promotion to the Privy Council (though not to major office) simultaneously with Dudley in the autumn of 1562 was engineered by Cecil – despite the Queen's reservations – probably as an act of pacification when Norfolk opposed the expedition to Newhaven.[32]

During the mid 1560s the underlying political tension came to focus on the settlement of the succession, the question of the Queen's marriage to the Archduke Charles, and further intervention in Scotland. It took its most dramatic form in the running battle between Norfolk and Sussex on the one hand and Leicester on the other through the winter of 1565–6, in which Cecil and the Queen attempted to maintain a mediating position.[33] The collapse of the negotiations with the Archduke in 1568 – which ended any hope of obtaining a conservative king and a moderating influence at Court – together with the arrival of Mary, Queen of Scots, in England triggered the major eruption of 1569. This confused series of events was the product of the interaction of three overlapping political groupings: the Percies and their allies among the northern nobility (who had been pushed so far that plotting the overthrow of Elizabeth had become their only hope); a wider body of semi-Catholic nobles led by Arundel and Lumley, who wished to see Cecil dismissed for risking a war with Philip II through the seizure of his treasure-ships; and a party headed by Leicester and Throckmorton who sought (with Cecil's knowledge) to compensate for the Queen's hesitation over the fate of the Queen of Scots by arranging a Protestant marriage with Norfolk. The failure of their allies at Court to alter the Queen's policies led to the desperate rising of the northern earls, which in turn compromised the wider body of conservative nobles irretrievably.

The drift toward more open ideological confrontation was further impelled by the publication of a papal bull of deposition in 1570, Norfolk's participation in the Ridolfi Plot of 1571 and then the massacre of St Bartholomew's Day of 1572. Appointments to office and the Council in these years gave both Court and Council a more distinctly Protestant tone, beginning with Sir Walter Mildmay and the veteran Sir Ralph Sadler in 1567, Sir Thomas Smith in 1572, Leicester's brother Warwick and brother-in-law Sidney, together with Walsingham in 1573 and then Dr Thomas Wilson in 1577. The only exceptions to the trend were the more ambiguous Croft and Sussex in 1570, and the Queen's cousin Lord Hunsdon and Hatton in 1577.

From the early 1570s both Council and Court thus displayed a degree of political homogeneity previously unknown. The religiously conservative nobility no longer played any role there and, hamstrung by the conflict of loyalties created by their rank, either retired to their houses, went into exile or dabbled hesitantly in the plots of the early 1580s. This new wave of plotting was, however, in part a response to the new question that came near to dividing the Court itself: the long debate over intervention in the Netherlands from 1572 (or possibly more accurately 1576) to 1585, to which the clashes over the proposed marriage to the Duke of Anjou were closely related. The most outspoken opponent of intervention was Sussex and the issue revived the older tensions between him and Leicester (the leading interventionist): disputes between them became particularly marked in the early 1580s.[34] Burghley, trapped between his basic sympathy for Protestant politics and his equally fundamental dislike of military overextension, played a more cautious role as a councillor than heretofore. The decision to intervene in 1585 did not, however, bring the debate to an end; rather the years of Leicester's governor-generalship in the Netherlands (1586–7) created a novel dual focus for Elizabethan politics and brought to the surface the ambiguities of Elizabeth's foreign policy. Elizabeth reacted very strongly to rumours that Leicester was establishing an alternative court at the Hague, while the military and political failures of the expedition encouraged the anti-interventionists at Whitehall. Whether or not Burghley employed Leicester's absence to strengthen his own position, the appointment of new anti-interventionist councillors at beginning of 1586 (Archbishop Whitgift, Buckhurst and Lord Cobham) marked a reversal of the trend of the 1570s.[35]

The 1585 intervention did, on the other hand, precipitate the war that dominated the remainder of the reign. Elizabeth and Burghley were united on a cautious and largely maritime strategy; after the deaths of Leicester in 1588 and Walsingham in 1590, the spokesman for the continental strategy and the heir of the old interventionist party was the much less powerful Essex. Their agreement with the Queen over strategy gave the

Cecils (Burghley and his son Robert) a stonger hold over the Court and the Council than they had previously possessed. Essex's attempts to wrest control of the Court from them during the mid 1590s and then his attempt to appeal to the country against the Court merely made his position worse: the Court became a battleground for factional struggle, and his efforts to obtain office for his allies and followers were almost uniformly unsuccessful. Elizabeth, aging unhappily and increasingly withdrawn, resented Essex's 'presumption' and gave Robert Cecil a control over access not previously achieved by any other councillor.[36] The anti-Essex coalition was led by Cecil, Nottingham and Ralegh (united by their shared interest in a maritime war as well as by personal enmity to Essex), while the leading Court officers of the period were drawn from the established Court families. The old courtiers Nottingham (Lord Admiral since 1585, Lord Steward from 1597) and Buckhurst (Lord Treasurer in 1599) were now those closest to the Queen. Established Household officers such as Heneage (Vice-Chamberlain and councillor from 1587) and Fortescue (Chancellor of the Exchequer and councillor from 1589) rose to prominence, while sons of earlier courtiers – George, 2nd Lord Hunsdon (Lord Chamberlain from 1597), or Sir William Knollys (Comptroller of the Household from 1596, Treasurer from 1602) – succeeded their fathers. Only one new family entered: the Stanhopes, who had been associated with the Cecils since the protectorate of the Duke of Somerset. Sir John Stanhope became Treasurer of the Chamber in 1596 and then Vice-Chamberlain in 1601; his brother Michael was appointed a gentleman of the Privy Chamber in 1598. Against this solid phalanx, Essex could count on few allies: his uncle Knollys (fitfully) and the elderly ex-friend of Leicester, Roger, lord North (Treasurer of the Houshold, 1596–1600). Even allowing for his paranoia, his claim that the coup he attempted in 1601 was mounted against a Court dominated by his enemies was not without justification.

IV

Given this pattern of Court politics, certain conclusions can be drawn. Faction needs to be much more closely defined. Too much has been made, for example, of the enmity between Leicester and Sussex; there were bitter disputes in the mid 1560s and early 1580s, but during most of the 1570s their relations were quite amicable. Even their disputes cannot accurately be termed factional, because there never was a Sussex faction of any size.[37] Indeed, until the Essex–Cecil struggle of the 1590s, politics could be said to have intruded into the Court rather than extruded from it. These intrusions took either the form of major questions of state – generally of foreign policy, with ideological overtones – or else of local squabbles among the clients of great men, which then ran back up the ladder of clientage to the Court. In this context the barriers between 'Court' and 'country' were very slight indeed: when Croft penned a long defence of his conduct as Comptroller of the Household in 1587, he spent the greater part of it attacking his enemy in Wales, the 2nd Earl of Pembroke. Usually these local quarrels could be mediated informally by leading councillors, though often it was necessary to proceed more formally through the Court of Star Chamber. On rare occasions the Queen herself would act as arbitrator, as she did in the long-running soap opera of the Earl of Shrewsbury's divorce, which one wit wagered would outlast the Dutch Revolt.[38] Leicester very specifically defined his role as that of honest broker: 'I have never been willing to make quarrels in this Court nor to breed any. Mine own honour and poor credit always saved, I neither have nor will be a peace breaker but a peace maker.'[39]

The relative internal cohesion of the Court to a large extent prevented debates over policy or disputes over clients from developing into true factionalism. With the exception of Arundel, Norfolk and the brief appearance of the Earl of Oxford in the mid 1570s, few members of the older noble families played even a minimal role there. Almost all its members came from established Tudor Court families, and the web of intermarriage and family connection was extremely tight: they were practically all each others' cousins in the most literal sense. Even the apparent shift in the ideological outlook of the Council in the 1570s took place within a comparatively narrow compass; it was accomplished mainly through the promotion of several of Leicester's relatives and protégés. The succession of fathers and sons in office, or mothers and daughters in the Privy Chamber, is striking. The sons of Cecil, Sir Richard Sackville, Lord William Howard of Effingham, Hunsdon and Sir Francis Knollys, who had been among Elizabeth's first appointments or creations, all obtained major office by the end of the reign. Hunsdon's daughter Catherine, who married Lord Charles Howard, the later Earl of Nottingham, was the senior lady of the Privy Chamber throughout the 1590s. Both Essex and Sir Philip Sidney were to some degree surrogate sons of Leicester.

By contrast, only two real outsiders were able to break into the Court's upper ranks: Hatton and Sir Walter Ralegh. Hatton, from a minor-gentry family without previous Court connections, came to the Queen's notice, we are told, during the Inner Temple Revels of 1561; only in 1577 did he become Vice-Chamberlain and a member of the Council. His steady but slow rise appears to have been without immediate political significance; he did not participate in a major debate prior to the negotiations over the Anjou marriage in 1578–9, and there was never a Hattonian faction. His career was solely owing to the Queen's personal favour – as the frequent sneers about the 'dancing Chancellor' make clear – yet when he entered higher Court circles he was on equally friendly terms with Leicester, Sussex, Walsingham and Burghley. His success at Court may be attributed simply to his good nature and easy manners: Burghley informed him that 'I find you readier to change offence taken than any other with whom I have had like occasion.'[40] The rise of Ralegh was equally solitary (there was no Ralegh faction either), but meteoric by comparison. He also came from a minor-gentry family and in 1581 was still an officer of the Irish garrison; in 1587 he was appointed Captain of the Guard. His rise was due to his concentrated assault on the Queen, but his manner of proceeding was bitterly resented and Ralegh uniformly disliked.[41] He survived until 1603, despite his bitter vendetta with Essex, through a mixture of effrontery and ability.

The two outsiders were *sui generis*, yet their prominence has always provided evidence for those who have wished to portray the Court as a meeting-place for divergent opinions. Their religious views in particular have suggested that the Puritan patronage of Leicester, Walsingham and Burghley was by no means shared by the Court as a whole. But to portray this as religious factionalism is to overstate the case. A basic confusion has been caused by the Queen's comparative liberalism or agnosticism. Apart from the oath of supremacy, she always resisted pressure from Parliament and Council for the establishment of a narrower religious test, so it remained possible for a religious conservative such as the 4th Earl of Worcester to progress at Court. Yet even he took the supremacy oath 'on his knees' on appointment as Master of the Horse in 1601.[42] There were a few conservative councillors (the ex-Marians or the more ambiguous Croft, Hatton and Norfolk) and looser connections (the second Keeper of the Privy Purse, Henry Seckford, was the son-in-law of the Marian Vice Chamberlain, Sir Henry Bedingfield), while several women of the Privy Chamber married men of conservative outlook (Margaret Willoughby and Sir Matthew Arundel provide one example), yet these hardly amounted to a coherent conservative party.

The perspective shifts, however, if the attitude towards Puritanism is taken into account. When portrayed as the factious and nonconformist proceedings of the lower clergy, Puritanism certainly created enemies at Court. Here the lines were drawn between those, such as Leicester, Walsingham and, less clearly, Burghley, who were prepared to overlook the preciseness of 'godly ministers and the queen's best subjects' and those, such as Hatton, who shared the views of the archbishops Parker and Whitgift that the maintenance of order was the first priority. Thus there were always potential pro- and anti-Puritan parties at Court; but their influence depended on the Queen's attitude at the time.[43] While she could be panicked into a crackdown on nonconformity, she was also receptive to godly preachers and numbered such Puritan patrons as Leicester and the Countess of Warwick among her intimates. It has generally been agreed that Puritanism lost its foothold at Court after the deaths of Leicester and Walsingham, but the promotion of so many of Leicester's former chaplains and clerical protégés to bishoprics in the 1590s suggests that the strength of the reaction can be overplayed.

V

If the social and political homogeneity of the Court shaped one dimension of its political dynamics, the relationship of the Court to the Queen created the other. There was never any doubt as to who was the dominant personality: Elizabeth's notorious vanity permeated all aspects of Court life. Her sexual jealousy not only embittered her relations with women of royal blood (Mary, Queen of Scots, the Countess of Lennox or Lady Catherine Grey) and made the lives of her gentlewomen miserable, but also threatened the careers of favoured men when they made marriages of which she did not approve.[44] Her vanity also affected her attitude towards the public position of courtiers: she alone could play to the crowd. Essex's attempts to cultivate his popular standing in the mid 1590s only worsened his relations with the Queen. Leicester had been more cautious, but when he played the role of popular political leader in the Netherlands the effect was equally disastrous.[45] Elizabeth's influence was more than merely emotional, however. Some features of the Court can possibly be attributed to a sense of feminine identity: her fixation with Household management may reflect a conception of good housewifery, while foreign envoys commented upon the prominence of women at formal diplomatic receptions.[46] The Court also reflected her intellectual and artistic tastes. The influences of her education – a mixture of early Italianate Court humanism and Protestant evangelism – created a distinct cultural context. Together with her pleasure in music and the dance, she took her scholarship seriously. In the 1590s her favourite reading is said to have been Seneca, while in 1593 she had it recorded that she had translated Boethius's *De Consolatione Philosophae* in a total of twenty-four hours.[47] Under her encouragement, therefore, spread the Elizabethan fascination with allusive prose, poetry and pageantry. After 1580 Court culture entered a particularly intense phase, coinciding both with the spread of the Gloriana cult (and her own acceptance of the role) and the growing formality of ceremonial. Under the auspices of Sir Henry Lee (Master of the Armoury from 1580) a particular form of entertainment, the Accession Day tilts, developed from comparatively informal jousts to elaborate rituals and pageants, while foreign ambassadors in the period were struck by the careful staging of receptions by ranked members of the Court in the various chambers leading to the Presence Chamber.[48]

Yet essential to Elizabeth's self-image were also the vision of herself as the Senecan princess and her own application to the business of state. Central to the conduct of affairs was – as the more sophisticated students of the early modern Court have noted – the question of access. It was widely recognised – not the least by Elizabeth herself, who considered the privilege part of their reward – that those in immediate personal attendance, however humble their rank, had the greatest opportunity to advance suits.[49] In earlier Tudor reigns this opportunity had led to the increased importance of the Privy Chamber; but under a female sovereign, a Privy Chamber staffed by women became an inner sanctum impenetrable to most of the Court. Elizabeth's careful choice of personal friends and established servants further strengthened the barriers. No foreign ambassador was able to penetrate her Privy Chamber in the way Thomas Randolph did that of Mary, Queen of Scots, in 1565.[50] Yet the women could not be completely isolated: the great majority of them were connected by marriage or family to the leading men at the Court. That they provided Elizabeth with information is clear. In 1569 Leicester complained of the leaking to the Queen by 'some babbling women' of news of the proposed marriage between Norfolk and Mary, Queen of Scots.[51] There is also considerable evidence that members of the Privy Chamber could do their friends favours, either by providing them with access (as William Killigrew did for Sir Robert Carey in 1597) or by advancing their suits (as the Countess of Warwick did for John Dee in 1592). But whether this amounted to political influence is another question. Here we possess a categorical statement by a knowledgeable witness: Rowland Vaughan, the nephew of one of the most long-serving women of the Privy Chamber, Blanche Parry. When complaining of the Court of James I, he noted that

> I remember in Queen Elizabeth's days, my lady of Warwick, Mistress Blanche and my lady Scudamore in little lay

matters would steal opportunity to serve their friends' turns
. . . because none of these (near and dear ladies) durst
intermeddle so far in matters of commonwealth.[52]

The Queen's toleration of personal patronage by members of
the Privy Chamber should therefore not be construed as an
acceptance of independent political involvement on their part.
On this issue Elizabeth had made her position clear in the early
years of the reign. The complaints of her newly appointed
gentleman usher, Dru Drury, and his brother Sir William
about her relations with Lord Robert Dudley at the end of 1559
earned them both a spell of imprisonment. A milder form of the
same punishment was suffered by her favourite gentlewoman,
Catherine Ashley, and her husband for their assistance to the
suit of Eric XIV of Sweden in 1561 and 1562. Yet only
Catherine Ashley appears to have had such confidence in her
knowledge of 'her highness nature by long continuance of time';
after her death in 1565, none of the other gentlewomen
displayed a similar initiative.[53] So the influence of the Privy
Chamber could be discounted by the Queen's leading ministers, confident that their monopoly over the conduct of affairs of
state would be upheld. Even the success of the complaints of
William Carmarden against Customer Thomas Smythe in
1589 may owe more to the recent appointment of Fortescue as
Chancellor of the Exchequer than, as often claimed, to
Elizabeth's receptivity to backstairs criticism.[54] Nor, unlike in
the previous and the succeeding reigns, did foreign ambassadors play much of a role at Court. The only continuous
embassy was that of the kings of France, and until 1587 French
ambassadors were compromised by their function of protecting
the interests of the Queen of Scots. Spanish ambassadors were
distrusted and kept at arms length: in 1562 the Bishop of Aquila
defended his reliance on Catholic informants on the ground
that the Queen and Council would tell him nothing of
importance.[55] Protestant envoys, with the possible exceptions
of Paul Choart de Buzenval, agent of the King of Navarre in
1586–7, and Noel de Caron, Dutch agent from 1586, generally
held too low a status and too brief a commission to exert much
influence.
  Yet Elizabeth's dealings with her councillors were never

entirely straightforward. She rarely attended Council meetings and was more than willing to delegate minor and routine matters to them. Major questions were reserved for discussion with the inner ring of councillors, and there is considerable evidence that she enjoyed playing them off against each other. Their opinions were sought individually and then relayed to the others.[56] It was widely known that she could not keep a secret: in 1587 Thomas Wilkes was worried that Walsingham would impart his criticisms of Leicester's government in the Netherlands to Elizabeth, 'who as your honour knoweth can hold no secrets'. Burghley provides further evidence of her tactics. When Leicester accused him of going behind his back with complaints over financial maladministration in the Netherlands, he protested that 'her Majesty many times chargeth me that I conceal, I flatter, I dare not speak anything that you should mislike'.[57]

Yet Elizabeth's playing off of councillors against each other had its limits. The comparative unanimity of the inner ring of councillors provided for a basic political consensus, and maintenance of a common front against the Queen became a pronounced feature of the Council's advisory function. Thus Cecil advised Sir Henry Sidney in 1566 that, while persuasion might take some time, 'I have good hope that her majesty will, with the good importunity of her Council, stick at nothing devised in this behalf.'[58] The correspondence of Leicester, Burghley and Walsingham in the 1570s and 1580s is very much concerned with their attempts to concert their approaches to Elizabeth and then to hammer away at her. Here they were rarely successful, as the long debates over intervention in the Netherlands, or the execution of Mary, Queen of Scots, show. Frequently the Queen would simply lose her temper and the matter would rest in suspension. A very revealing picture of the Elizabethan government at work in the early 1580s is provided in the report of the agent sent by the city of Geneva to negotiate a loan in 1582. His initial contacts were with Leicester and Walsingham, but Walsingham advised waiting for a more propitious moment because Elizabeth was presently averse to spending more money on the Protestant cause. He spent a year in London and, in the end, despite the sympathy of the Council and the support of the Puritan nobility, gentry and clergy, never saw the Queen and only received permission to raise a voluntary collection through the Church.[59] What would spur Elizabeth in action – temporarily – was less pressure from her councillors than a panic or an emotional reaction, but for such a reaction a sufficient danger was necessary. It was for this reason that the uncovering of the various Catholic conspiracies of the 1570s and 1580s became an essential feature of the campaign to persuade Elizabeth to reach a decision over the fate of the Queen of Scots.

On the other hand, attempts to maintain a common front against the Queen did not amount to an independent position for the Council. The reign saw at least four major attempts to play off the Council against the Queen in order to force her into agreeing to measures she opposed: the parliamentary appeal for the establishment of the succession in 1566; Archbishop Grindal's refusal to co-operate in the disbanding of prophesyings in 1576; Leicester's acceptance of the governor-generalship of the Netherlands in 1586; and William Davison's dispatch of the warrant for the execution of the Queen of Scots in 1587. In each case those responsible knew that they were in some sense defying the Queen, but expected that the backing of the Council would cause her to retract. In none of them were they successful, though her initial anger may have been moderated by the Council's stand.

The tensions that doing business with Elizabeth created fed the recurrent complaints against the Court. Backbiting, 'whereof that place indeed is too full', was constantly complained of, yet apparently universally practised. Much of the leading councillors' time was spent in protecting their absent friends and clients, particularly those (such as the lord deputies of Ireland) conducting expensive military operations. It is not surprising to find some of the strongest criticisms of Court life from men at its centre.[60] Yet compared to that of Henry VIII Elizabeth's governance was, without flattery, mild and merciful. Leicester commented during his quarrel with Sir John Norris in 1587 that 'in King Henry the 8th's time his doings for sure would have cost him his pate'.[61] Elizabeth may have been imperious, vain and sharp of temper, but she was unwilling to go to extremes, as her agonising over the executions of Norfolk and Essex revealed. For those who experienced it, the Court of

Elizabeth I, like the Queen herself, evoked an ambiguous response. In 1602 her godson, Sir John Harington, looked forward to the imminent accession of a king instead of 'a lady shut up in a chamber from her subjects and most of her servants, and seldom seen but on holy days'; yet, as his sardonic account of the drunken shambles that attended the reception of Christian IV of Denmark in 1606 and his later affectionate portrait of the aged Queen show, his mood soon turned to nostalgia.[62]

3. Parliament

G. R. ELTON

IT is at present particularly difficult to give an account of the role and history of Parliament in the reign of the first Elizabeth. The last three generations have seen two well entrenched interpretations shattered, one after the other, and we are still in the process of putting the new insights together.[1] Until about sixty years ago it was generally held that in the sixteenth century Parliament played very little part in a system of government which centred on an exceptionally strong, even autocratic, monarchy. Parliaments were thought of as 'subservient'; the Tudor period supposedly formed an interruption in what was regarded as the normal and proper development of England – the subjugation of the Crown to the representative assembly. As recently as 1964, this medievalists' view, which treated the Tudor age as a retreat from the position achieved under the Lancastrians, could be defended against the newer theories of Parliament's novel political importance in the sixteenth century.[2]

This newer view, although adumbrated already by A. F. Pollard, became dominant through the work of Sir John Neale and was orthodoxy until very recently. Neale believed in a markedly evolutionary scheme for the history of the Tudor Parliament, a progress from underdeveloped beginnings handed on by the Middle Ages to 'maturity' under Elizabeth – maturity in procedure, privilege and political role-playing. To him, the reign of Elizabeth witnessed the rise of the Commons, just in time to get ready for the battle with the Stuart kings. Indeed, he thought he saw Elizabethan rehearsals for that political conflict. Neale discerned an eager interest (which he thought novel, though it existed in the fourteenth century) among the gentry in parliamentary representation; he argued for a steady rise in education, experience and eminence among the members of the Lower House; and he discovered there a powerful group of assertive men, able and willing to challenge the control which the government normally exercised, directly through privy councillors and the Speaker and indirectly through the messages and inspired rumours with which the Queen tried to suppress unruly thoughts and actions. For these difficult men he identified an ideology: they were Puritans – that is, men anxious for drastic changes in Church and religion who used Parliament to promote their ambitions, attacked the Queen's policies when these seemed to threaten the future of the reformed faith, and worked in harness with the Puritan clergy outside. Neale thus presented a coherent story of loyalty and conflict expressed in the workings of an institution which both offered opportunity for opposition and, in turn, learned through opposition to develop claims and machinery to make it effective. Neale's Parliament – or, rather, his House of Commons – fitted neatly into the received story of a growth from the supposedly acquiescent assemblies of Henry VIII's reign to the supposedly recalcitrant assemblies of the early seventeenth century.

Of this picture and story so little now remains that I must first emphasise the need to remember that Neale got some things right. His narrative of parliamentary events is quite often correct in detail, though often also falsely slanted in interpretation. His analysis of the expansion of constituencies and election disputes appears to be still acceptable. He was also right in his analysis of knights and burgesses: the reign of Elizabeth did witness the final culmination of a process by which the gentry came to take over a proportion of parliamentary seats four times larger than under the qualifying laws they should have held, at the expense of genuine townsmen. However, Neale misunderstood the political consequences of this by ascribing the growing independence of the Commons to this influx of men of standing. It is true that the Commons thus acquired a social homogeneity which made them more representative of the political nation as a whole, but the gentry did not so much free the House from outside influence as introduce into it the politics of the shire and the royal Court –

politics themselves dominated by the nobility also present in the Lords. It was the normal political involvements of the age that this influx of gentlemen carried with them, and those politics had little to do with parliamentary affairs and nothing with institutional independence.

The work of major revision is still very much proceeding, and at present no new comprehensive analysis and reconstruction presents itself for summary. This account, therefore, must to an extent rest on unfinished and unpublished labours. It may, however, make the discarding of the old interpretation more persuasive if reasons can be shown to explain what it was that put Neale on so wrong a track. At heart he simply accepted a highly traditional general scheme which read the history of Parliament as one of conflict between Crown and Commons, regarded the Commons' role as pertaining solely to the control of the Crown, and was always aware of the breach of 1640–2, which was treated as conditioning all that went before and came after. Neale's originality lay in his fitting the Elizabethan phase more neatly into this whiggish outline. Yet of late all the components of this hoary myth have been shown up for what they are: a mixture of political conviction and of tendentious misreadings of selected evidence. Since the notion of an independent, anti-government, opposition has had to be abandoned for the reigns of both Mary I and James I,[3] it is the less necessary to look, as Neale did, for an Elizabethan House of Commons which will not disturb the line of development. Directed by prevalent interpretations to a false approach, to which he adhered throughout his life, Neale then found what he was looking for by three heuristic devices which have little virtue in them. He assumed the role of the Upper House, a part of Parliament on which he did no work, to be that of assisting the monarch against a rising House of Commons; once assumed, the point was never investigated. He took over from Wallace Notestein evolutionary theories according to which developments in procedure helped the Commons to freedom from official control, and he added his own mite to all this evolution by treating the Commons Journals as having developed from primitive to accomplished, a view resting on false assumptions and arguments from silence. Lastly, he identified as Puritans and as members of a consistent and cohesive policy-making group a number of men who were neither of these things.

A word is needed to substantiate this critique. Touching the Lords, the record makes it very plain that they were not only an active part of the Parliament, deeply engaged in the work of legislation, but also by no means united and quite capable of going counter to the Queen's wishes. It was members of the Upper House who opposed the religious settlement of 1559,[4] and it was the bishops quite as much as ardent Protestants in the Commons who, in the face of Elizabeth's disapproval, kept trying to use statute for the improvement of Church and clergy.[5] The social pre-eminence of the peers, and the close relations between noble courtiers and particular men in the Commons, are well documented in the correspondence of the day, though these things still require the sort of study which factional influences have been receiving in the next two reigns.

With respect to the record – Journals and the rest – what we now have is known to lack some material once extant, and Neale introduced a wrong note when he called the Commons Journal of Elizabeth's first two parliaments more primitive than the later ones.[6] He mistook a change of clerk for a significant change in procedure, compared a fair copy with a rough draft, and supposed that recording speeches in the House proved 'maturing' when it is more likely to be connected with Cecil's move into the Lords and his need for written information. The keeping of parliamentary diaries seems to have begun in 1571, the year of the Lord Treasurer's elevation. Those materials, which have never received really critical attention, need to be studied without the tacit conviction that they reflect a growth in the Commons' self-esteem, powers or procedural advance. Indeed, the whole notion that developments in procedure measure a rise in independence has been convincingly demolished:[7] in so far as procedure developed – and the very term is suspect – it did so under the pressure of business and demonstrably on the initiative of the Council, who were forever seeking ways of speeding the handling of bills; for the Queen's distaste for parliamentary meetings always threatened premature prorogation or dissolution. In the Lower House, business was managed not only by the Speaker and clerk, with the assistance of privy councillors, but also by 'men

of business' – that is, men without official positions but active as
Council agents. Thomas Norton, famous in his day as a
parliamentarian and to Neale a leading Puritan proponent of
the Commons' independence, has turned out to be such a
conscientious labourer on behalf of Council and Queen.[8]

Furthermore, the whole notion of a Puritan opposition group
rested on two unfounded assertions. Neale supposed that in
1559 more extreme Protestants exercised a powerful influence
on the Church settlement; however, ingeniously as he argued
his case, it has turned out to be contrary to the facts.[9] And a
squib of 1566, listing some forty-odd members of the Commons
of very varied views but all active in the succession agitation of
that year, was read by Neale to comprise a hard-core body of
Puritans, so that whenever men there mentioned afterwards
occur in the story he smelled out opposition tactics and
manoeuvres employed by a Puritan opposition. He employed a
circular argument: without good grounds, leading members of
the House were identified as Puritans, so that what leading
members did became Puritan activities, and when something
happened that might be connected with reformist views in
religion the notional Puritan group was alleged to be behind it.
In fact, the members of that 'choir' formed no party and few of
them were Puritans; the actions and opinions of those supposedly part of it cannot be assessed from that accidental
listing.[10]

One example shall be cited to show how preconceived
notions misled this historian. Among the bills for religion put
up in 1566 there was one for enacting the Thirty-Nine Articles.
It is agreed that the Queen heard that the bishops had been
active in promoting it, read the riot act to some of them, was
assured that those present had not been responsible, and a few
days later received a petition from fifteen bishops (including
some involved in that audience) asking that the bill be allowed
to pass. The obvious, and correct, conclusion is that the
original report told something like the truth, though face to face
with their angry sovereign the prelates prevaricated a little.
Since Neale, however, had convinced himself that the bill came
from a Puritan (anti-episcopal) quarter, he ascribed the report
of the bishops' initiative to 'some mischief-maker' (uniden-
tified), accepted their denial before the Queen, and could offer

no explanation for the subsequent petition, which yet he dutifully mentioned. His one footnote reference does not support the crucial details of his reconstruction.[11]

It has been necessary to spend so much time in discussing Neale's work because, expansive and cohesive as it is, it naturally has a firm hold: denying him outright, as I have been obliged to do, will not be acceptable unless reasons are given. Now that the ground is clear, we must see how the next generation of historians are likely to replant it. As has already been made plain, much of what must be said constitutes a preview of work in progress.

II

The Elizabethan Parliament was in one way a very ancient institution, in another of quite recent origin. As Tudor antiquarians never tired of pointing out, its history vanished into the mists of time, even if they erred in supposing that it had existed from the beginnings of that time. That history is sufficiently continuous from the late thirteenth century onwards, and the Elizabethan Parliament is in some respects identical with its medieval predecessor. On the other hand, the Parliament had undergone something like a transformation roughly between 1484 and 1540, a time during which the two Houses moved from inferiority/superiority to institutional equality, the Crown turned from the owner of a high court into a member of the parliamentary trinity, legislative procedure was settled, statute acquired both omnicompetence and a kind of legal sanctity as the Crown lost the power to amend it unilaterally, and the keeping of records was systematised.[12] In spite of a paucity of records, enough survives to support the conclusion (also reached by Arthur Hall, Elizabethan burgess for Grantham[13]) that the shape of the Elizabethan (and therefore the later) Parliament was effectively established in the long Reformation Parliament of 1529–36. The better documentation of Elizabeth's reign enables us to trace further changes in practices and attitudes, but nothing happened then to justify talk of transformation. For instance, we can be confident that a record was kept in the Commons before the accidental date (1547) from which the Journal now survives. A 'clerk's book' is mentioned authoritatively in an act of 1515, and no one looking at the seemingly scrappy first surviving volume can fail to note the air of established practice that hangs over that record as it registers bill proceedings, licences for absence and orders touching privilege. The Lords Journal underwent no changes after 1536, from which session the first complete and separate volume happens to survive, until exigencies of politics led to a different format in the 1620s. Though, naturally, the forty-five years and thirteen sessions of the Queen's reign do not depict a static condition, the parliaments of 1559 and 1601 are the same sort of institution and do not testify to institutional development. In all that governed their work, their rights and their accepted claims, 'maturity' – as Sir Thomas Smith's description, written in the early 1560s, testifies[14] – had been achieved by the beginning of the reign. Furthermore, the Parliament was an institution, not just a succession of occasions, and this despite the long gaps between meetings and the less than three years altogether in forty-five that it sat. This shows clearly in the regularity of all the arrangements which governed meetings from the opening day to the close, and in the continuity of business across the gaps. It needed only the push of a button – the writ of summons – to activate this institution in full and familiar detail. Routine, not improvisation, governed all the meetings of the Parliament, and while the roots of that routine went back into the fourteenth century its Elizabethan form and substance had been shaped by what had happened under Henry VIII.

The Parliament consisted of three parts – prince, Lords and Commons. By 1559, the King-in-Parliament as a sovereign lawmaker had replaced the King's High Court of Parliament. The new concept was first spoken of round about 1530 and had been endorsed by Henry VIII in 1542. Occasionally the older doctrine of three estates assembled in Parliament to assist the prince can be found, but the dominant doctrine, as stated by Lord Burghley himself,[15] identified the three estates with the three parts of the Parliament, jointly able to make laws. In that respect all parts were equal: unless all consented no law could be made. But, of course, equality is not really the right word for a relationship in which one of the partners alone could decide whether and when the partnership should come to life and again retire into a suspended state. At the same time, it should be remembered that the Queen did not have total freedom in her role as the convenor and terminator of parliamentary meetings. Since there were things that she could do only in Parliament, she had to call it when she wanted to tax the realm or have new laws for its defence, and since both needs occurred regularly in the reign it would be a mistake to suppose that the sometimes lengthy intermissions signified the possible end of Parliament. No one in this reign considered a government without it.

The possibility was the more remote because in this reign neither Lords nor Commons constituted any sort of threat to the Crown. We have heard so much about the rising power of the Lower House, or alternatively about the political strength collected in the Upper, with its complement of locally dominant men, that it comes as something of a surprise to discover how little real power the Commons especially possessed. By comparison with such late-medieval assemblies as those of Aragon or Sicily, or with the contemporary provincial and general States of the Netherlands, the English Parliament – that is, Lords and Commons without the monarch – was really quite weak; more precisely, it was strong, indeed very strong, only when acting in unison, for of its component parts only the Crown had strength of its own. Each House exercised various constitutional powers over its members, and both at times, with limited success, tried to extend these over outsiders, but the reality is well exemplified in the fact that when the Commons, asserting themselves, sent a man to the Tower they could get him out again only by relying on the Queen for his release.[16] What from the first marked the Commons in the Long Parliament as so revolutionary was the manner in which they acted on all sorts of issues by their own authority – actions for which there were no precedents at all. In constitutional fact, the Elizabethan Commons were weak, not strong.

Yet that weakness, in its turn, demonstrated the real strength of those parliaments. Since they could not threaten the rule of the monarch even if they had wanted to, they could but be useful to him – and so they were. In the sixteenth century, as it always had been and nearly always was to be in future,

Parliament formed a component in the system of government, not an agent outside and possibly in opposition to it. In order to carry out its role in government effectively and usefully it needed management – instruction, guidance, control. After all, when we speak of co-operation between the three parts we really mean co-operation among potentially more than 500 individuals. These individuals' interests might very easily conflict among themselves, and these individuals were liable to hold widely different views on the issues of the day, large or small; if it is wrong to interpret events from the assumption that conflict between Queen and Commons directed them, it would be as wrong to suppose that general agreement came naturally, perhaps by the dispensation of providence. By the reign of Elizabeth, the techniques of management had become well understood – mainly, it would seem, as the result of the feverish activity of the years 1529–59. During those thirty years the Lords and Commons had again and again been involved in the highest of high politics and very explosive issues: of course they had to be guided, and the standards of managerial practice first established by Thomas Cromwell had become routine in the hands of the Privy Council. They included not only the preparation of official bills (though it is an ancient error to suppose that the bulk of public bills came from the Council) and the steering of them, but also the organisation of useful patronage and the reasoned persuasion of doubters. No detail could safely be overlooked: thus Francis Bacon was quite right when in 1615 he ascribed recent failures to the incompetence which had started sessions without providing something for members to do apart from voting money.[17] Much depended on councillors' manners: neither Lords nor Commons contained an 'opposition', but both contained (as all of Elizabethan England did) touchy men likely to stand on their dignity. A parliamentary session meant intensive work for the Council, and the brevity of meetings owed something at least to the difficulties they created for men who had to govern the realm, conduct foreign policy, supervise religious conformity, oversee the administration of justice, not to mention lead private lives and run their own affairs, while giving time and thought to the often capricious behaviour of Lords and Commons in Parliament. There has never been a time when the ministers of the

Crown have not welcomed the parliamentary recess with sighs of relief; in the reign of Elizabeth such recesses, while very much longer, were equally welcome.

Ordinary members of either House, not compelled by managerial duties to attend with regularity, avoided the burden of attendance with respectable readiness. For the Lords we possess presence lists, and they are revealing. No peer could ignore the summons without permission, but permission was often granted and every session saw the presentation of numerous proxies. However, the purpose and meaning of proxies, never, apparently, used in votes and occasionally entered by peers who attended, remain very obscure. Generally speaking, the spiritual peers proved more conscientious than the temporal. Take the Parliament of 1571, an averagely busy one which sat for just about eight weeks, an averagely normal length of a session.[18] That year the Upper House consisted of twenty-four spiritual and sixty-four lay peers, but of the latter three were under age and thus disqualified from sitting. The total, therefore, was eighty-five. On the formal opening day, with the Queen present, fifty-nine attended (17 + 42), some of them persons who had given proxies. Just over halfway through the session, on 8 May, when the much contested treasons bill was passed, the numbers though not the people were still exactly the same. Attrition set in as the session wore on. A week before the close, when pressure of business compelled afternoon sittings, even the bishops' resolution faltered: in the morning of 22 May there were altogether fifty-three members present (14 + 39), but by the afternoon they had dwindled to thirty (10 + 20). Even the closing day, when the Queen again came into the House, could not restore the original zest: though the eighteen bishops present formed the largest spiritual contingent of the session, only thirty-three lay peers bothered to come, the decline being particularly marked in the higher ranks of the peerage.

Nevertheless, proportionately the Lords did much better than the Commons, whose members notoriously included many for whom Parliament time offered the opportunity to come to London on business or pleasure. While we have no attendance lists for the Lower House, we know that it frequently got so seriously depleted that a call was threatened for the next sitting – a roll-call of the membership which involved fines for absentees if fewer than forty answered it. Our only figures come from the very occasional divisions which, by definition, occurred on contested matters when one would expect attendance to be larger than usual. In 1571 the clerk lets us down completely. The House divided four times in the session but the only figure recorded is a majority of thirty-six on the first occasion.[19] That clerk's predecessor – damned by Neale as 'more primitive' – kept a more businesslike record, so that we have information for the very active and allegedly very disturbed session of 1566, during which the House also divided four times. On those four days, 160, 133, 136 and 158 of its approximately 400 members were in the House – the last occasion being the vote that dashed the bill for renewing expiring acts, a move that has been read as expressing the resentment of 'the House' at the blocking of 'Puritan' bills in the Lords.[20] Ordinarily, we may well suppose, even fewer members attended. Seeing that St Stephen's Chapel contained only about 450 feet of seating-space in its four rows around two sides, and remembering that many members wore swords in the House, one can imagine the embarrassment that a full attendance would have caused; even when far from complete, the House could be stiflingly overcrowded, and, despite efforts to keep the door clear, members unable to find a seat quite often blocked the Speaker's view of the bar.[21] Regular absentees deserved some gratitude.

A thin presence could work both ways. It might easily assist oppositionist moves by real zealots whom one would expect to be more assiduous, but it could also reduce the burden of management. Our patchy evidence gives grounds for thinking that one feature familiar from later days may well already have been characteristic of Commons' debates: it looks as though just about all the talking was done by a hard-core group of regulars among whom the official element – office-holders and men of business – predominated. Since diarists cannot be expected to give a full tally of speeches and might well prefer those that agreed with their own views, it may be dangerous to rely too trustingly on the record of debate we find in private diaries, but the extant evidence (at present available only for the years 1558–81[22]) suggests a quite balanced coverage. The

number of frequent speechmakers is really quite small: Francis
Alford, Robert Bell, John Dalton, William Fleetwood, Sir
Francis Knollys, Thomas Norton, Richard Onslow, John
Popham, Robert Snagge, Thomas Williams, Christopher
Wray. Of these men five served as Speaker: Williams (1563),
Onslow (1566), Wray (1571), Bell (1572 and 1576), Popham
(1581). For the last three, the record includes their activities as
private members. Even though at times they may not have seen
eye to eye with Council policies, they were obviously accom-
modating enough to satisfy the Crown and must throughout be
reckoned as essentially official. Knollys was the only privy
councillor among them, seemingly the most talkative of the
councillors, though William Cecil would probably rank high in
the list if we had evidence of debates during his time in the
House. Norton, much the busiest of the lot, we now know to
have been the Council's most energetic assistant, and Fleetwood, a Cecil client, is emerging as such another.[23] That leaves
only three frequent debaters outside the obviously managerial
ranks: of them Alford leant towards conservative views in
religion and politics, Dalton may be called a true Puritan, and
Snagge tended to a prudent middle way – an admirable
balance. It is clear who pre-empted the time and dominated the
business of the House.

Management was not necessarily concerned with assuaging
or suppressing opposition; the task of getting the business
through could be impeded by much less spectacular difficulties,
such as the whims of private members promoting private
causes, or those sudden rushes of blood to the head for very
small reasons to which the House of Commons has always had
an inclination – a not unnatural result, perhaps, of those 'idle
heads' (to use Elizabeth's description) in close proximity and
only half aware in all that to-and-fro of what was going on. A
very experienced parliament man has left us his thoughts on
what hindered business, and he knew nothing of principled or
Puritan opposition. He embodied his experience in a long note
of advice, written in 1572 for the benefit of Sir Christopher
Hatton, who in that session took on the management of the
House for the Council and needed instruction; the writer may
just possibly have been Thomas Norton.[24] The paper deals
with two issues and adds an afterthought. It first discusses what

sort of person should be considered for the speakership and advises against a member of the Privy Council, chiefly on the grounds that 'being Speaker [he] loses his voice, which will be no small hindrance to her Majesty's service'. Councillors, that is, must be available as debaters and voters. Secondly, and mainly, the advice reviews the best ways of fulfilling the Queen's desire for short sessions and comes up with six 'things that lengthen the session'.

There are, first, too many private bills for individuals, but the adviser deprecates any direct order from the Queen to restrict them, 'for so would by and by be raised some humorous [obstreperous] body, some question of the liberty of the House and of restraining their free consultation'. Instead he prefers broad hints in the speech from the throne – references to the approaching summer with its threat of plague – and suggests appointing committees to select the more urgent bills from among those delivered into the House. Secondly, delays arise from the mass of bills promoted by trading and manufacturing interests 'and especially the bills of London': these could be cut down by consulting with the members for the City and referring items to the Common Council there. Thirdly he turns to 'motions without book for matter whereof never questions arise', that is motions moved on the spur of the moment with no intention to proceed to any decisions. These would be best handled by the Speaker's asking the mover to prepare a written motion in association with everybody else who showed signs of wanting to speak on the matter. 'The more committees [committee members] that you make . . . the longer it will be ere the matter come in again, specially if you will appoint lawyers in term time' – when, he implies, they have other calls on their time. Fourthly there are the big and unavoidable issues, 'matters of long argument' (in 1572 he would have had the previous session's treason act in mind, a government bill which had given much trouble); these should be raised only 'towards the rising of the House'. He agrees that this will particularly test the Speaker's skill, in case he seems to deprive the House of liberty, but thinks that a 'discreet interposing of committees' plus the postponing of the further reading of bills 'that have been found at first and second reading to be so large walking fields' should do the trick. Fifthly he draws attention to the tactic of securing a longer session by dragging out whatever business the Queen regards as the principal issue of the session, mostly the subsidy: he advises careful preparation and presessional drafting of the bill. Lastly he regrets the increase in conferences with the Lords, a device which, though often useful, had grown too common and occasioned much delay. By way of an appendix he warns against upsetting the tender feelings of the House by 'hard messages': they lead to 'speeches, questions, petitions and great delays'. When the Queen's desires are to be conveyed, it is best to tread warily and use very conciliatory language. His objection is not to the political dangers of 'opposition' but to the loss of time needlessly caused by provoking the principle-hunters.

The chief purpose of management, therefore, was to smooth the paths of legislation – to get bills through and cut down on speeches. The adviser of 1572 would have agreed with the clerk of the House who told an investigating committee in the early nineteenth century that sometimes there was 'a cessation of business, in consequence of the House being in debate for many hours'.[25] Now, getting bills through is not the sole purpose of parliamentary meetings, but (as John Pym noted in 1621) 'bills are the end of a Parliament',[26] and thinking of them first approaches from the right angle the question of why parliaments are held. The making of acts, or indeed the blocking of undesirable bills, constituted their chief function in the administrative and social system of England, and every member of the body politic had or could have an interest in what Parliament produced.

The Queen's first interest concerned the granting of supply; she sought and obtained subsidies in all but one of her thirteen sessions, and since each grant was always spread over several collecting years few of her years of rule were entirely free of the activities of subsidy commissioners. The conventional notion holds that Parliament's strength, indeed its chance of survival, rested in this power of the purse, but the facts do not fit the theory very well. Subsidies were always forecast in the opening address and always started early in the session. There were certain decencies to be observed. In form, the initiative lay with the Commons and until 1576 the first move there came from some private member, put up for the purpose and backed up by official members who explained the Queen's needs. After that date this rather pointless pretence was abandoned in favour of letting the Chancellor of the Exchequer both lay out the necessity and move for a grant. The House then appointed a committee to draw articles and, after these had been reported though rarely debated, to prepare the necessary bill; in fact, the Council was usually ready with the former and commonly with the latter also. Virtually always the bill passed all its stages without trouble, except in 1566 when the subsidy got involved in manoeuvres designed to force the Queen to listen to petitions about the uncertain succession. For the years 1559–81, when the survival of the Journal makes it possible to do the calculations, we can say that the bill was not much used to protract the session, nor did its passage immediately lead to the close. Only in 1566, for the reason just stated, did the bill take a long time; usually it passed in anything between two weeks and four, and only in 1563 were there less than two weeks left of the session when the Commons had done with it. The Lords always despatched it very swiftly. Thus it would not seem to have been the case that the Lower House tactically exploited the Queen's needs or that she took care to end the session the minute she had her money. Nor did anyone seriously invoke the famous principle, 'no supply before redress of grievances', which seems to have been quite unknown in the sixteenth century, or indeed later. The supply of 1571, which has been supposed to have occasioned the appointment of the first committee of grievances, has been quite misread. The Council did lose control momentarily at the start of the session and was late in introducing supply, as a result of which certain grievances raised ran parallel with the money bill, but the grievances in fact dwindled into Council measures and supply went on on its own.[27] The one thing that roused the Commons, always aware of the taxpayers back home, was any attempt to enlarge the customary size of the grant, but the war years after 1588 saw ever larger sums voted readily enough – except in 1593, when the government tactlessly used the Lords in an effort (ultimately successful) to increase the money grant. One really cannot tie any sort of constitutional history, touching the rise of the Commons or the weakness of the Crown, to the history of parliamentary taxation in this reign.

Much the largest part of any parliamentary session was occupied with bills intended to become acts, and, though some of them concerned the Queen sufficiently to compel her to call Parliament, the bulk came from the country in one way or another. Far more bills were promoted than seems generally realised. The thirteen sessions of the reign passed 433 acts, an average of just over thirty-three – just under two public acts for every private one. Averages mislead because they do not show the legislative slump between 1584 and 1593, both years of active lawmaking, or the relatively greater number of private acts in the first three sessions of the reign, but they may be used to assess the fact that in every session anything between sixty and eighty additional bills failed to make it to the statute book. A small number passed in one House only to fail in the other, sometimes by formal rejection and sometimes through lack of time; a still smaller number passed both Houses but were vetoed by the Queen.[28] A great many received only one reading in either Commons or Lords, mostly the former: this signifies a kind of kite-flying rather than a proposal seriously meant. Bills that failed in one Parliament, having yet got some good way towards completion, not infrequently appeared in another and sometimes passed. Two kinds of bills stood the best chance of success: those promoted by the Council, and private bills for individuals. A general impression is that among those seriously pursued without success bills concerning the manufacture and sale of cloth fared just about worst: they came from interests that faced far too many rivals.

Bills could start in either House, though more started in the Lower, and there seem to have been few conventions in this matter, except that reversals of attainders, usually signed by the Queen, were regularly introduced in the Lords and bills for naturalisation in the Commons. Government bills tended to start in whichever House contained the leading manager of the legislative programme; thus Cecil's transformation into Burghley is reflected by the move of the main official measures from the Commons to the Lords in 1571. Though at times, especially for private individuals' bills, one can guess at the initiative behind a measure, the life histories of bills are often so complicated – major amendments during passage, replacement bills drawn in committee, and so forth – that only detailed study of each example can hope to identify origins, and in many cases this may remain forever obscure. On several occasions, failed private initiatives were later taken up and pushed through by the Council. Only one thing is quite certain: the ancient supposition that in the sixteenth century almost all legislation originated with the government is totally wrong – except perhaps in the age of Thomas Cromwell.

III

This very general summary is all that in the present state of research, or in the present compass, can usefully be said. It should, however, suffice to indicate the very heavy burden of potential legislation that occupied these parliaments, as well as the very wide range of people or groups of people who sought to tap the legislative authority of Parliament. When a meeting was announced, interests ranging from the Privy Council, through shire and town authorities, economic pressure-groups, reforming lawyers and reforming Protestants, to the heirs of persons attainted, estate-managing landowners and merchants of foreign origin (to name but a selection) prepared their bills for the Parliament, most of which obtained at least one reading. Private bills could take up an inordinate amount of time because both Houses, anxious to prevent fraud or collusion, encouraged parties to appear with their counsel; very soon these investigations, which usually produced a satisfactory settlement, were transferred to the committee for the bill, but the outcome had still to be reported to the House and sometimes led to further argument there. It is no wonder that the Journals of both Houses are essentially registers of bill-proceedings: that was the main business before them and one so crowded and complex that only a careful record could prevent total confusion. As it was, errors touching the number of readings and suchlike slipped in once in a while. When Burghley moved to the Lords he complicated the Commons' clerk's life further by asking for frequent statements concerning the present state of bills there. Those lists testify both to the Lord Treasurer's primary concern during a parliament and the clerk's efficiency in keeping up with the flow.

The history of legislation disposes of the view that an

ever-likely opposition in or by the Commons was held in check through the Lords and ultimately blocked by the veto. Both these devices of control did occur, but exceedingly rarely. The normal relations over business are not comprehended in a notion of obstreperousness on the one side and supervision on the other; and the vast majority of bills vetoed had nothing to do with the interests of the Crown. Instead we find private promoting-interests clashing with private opponents and the consequent arguments being fought out at every stage of a bill. If one side won in the Commons, the other might contrive to block the bill in the Lords; and interests defeated in both Houses, or perhaps too late alerted to what was happening, on several occasions secured the intervention of the veto, intended to provide the opportunity for further local negotiations.[29] In the vast majority of cases, the politics of bills and acts were peculiar to those bills and acts; they arose at local or sectional level, not between Parliament and Crown, between Lords and Commons.

It would, however, be wrong to suggest that those who have spread themselves on great principled conflicts between Queen and Commons – on all those occasions of sharp words, ruffled feelings, high-sounding assertions, elegant pacifications – have talked of only imagined things. Conflicts and arguments, even quarrels close to real rifts, do appear in the record, even if they do not signify nearly as much in terms of time spent or passions roused as the standard accounts might lead one to think.

From the first days of the Parliament, in Edward I's day, the writ of summons had always mentioned the need to consult over the affairs of the realm, and matters other than legislation had regularly been thrashed out in those asemblies, though until the Reformation Parliament the usual venue had been in the Lords. The Lord Keeper drew explicit attention to such wider purposes when, in 1559 and 1572, he mentioned the need to settle religion and to deal with Mary, Queen of Scots. Elizabeth, however, faced the problem that on several hotly debated issues she wished to avoid action while other people wished to see it taken; in particular, this applied to the question of her own succession and marriage, but also to the further reform of the Church. Her sister had set a precedent in 1553 when she furiously rebuffed a petition not to marry a foreign prince, but her father's precedents, which had demanded parliamentary initiatives in the attack on Rome and the settlement of the Crown, worked the other way. She therefore worked out what in effect was a new constitutional rule, according to which issues debated in Parliament fell into two categories – matters of the common weal, to be raised by anyone, and matters of state, which could be discussed only if she invited the Parliament to do so. At this level of principle, this rule clashed with the demands made by Paul and Peter Wentworth for full liberty of speech, meaning the right of the Commons, defined (another real innovation) as themselves a council of the realm, to initiate debate on whatever they wished.[30] Even though on occasion other members of the House recalled forty years of active participation in, for instance, religious changes and wondered how the Queen could now inhibit them from talking about those things again, the Wentworths' position met with no general acceptance; on the contrary, when Peter made his great plea for free speech in 1576, he was explicitly disavowed. The House took a much more mundane view of what privilege involved; to them privilege meant the right enjoyed by members and their servants to avoid arrest or summons in a private suit. Liberties to them were the technical rights involved in bill-proceedings – freedom to amend any bill even if signed by the Queen, or to refuse an invitation to a conference with the Lords touching a bill in the Commons because such an invitation had to come from the House that held the bill. The history of the Commons' privileges in Elizabeth's reign testifies neither to any growth in power nor to the forging of weapons for a fight; it records only the exploitation of immunities against legitimate claims by persons outside, and a sense of self-importance directed against the Lords.

Secondly, though this is often forgotten, it is obvious that in matters of high policy, as in commonwealth matters, the House of Commons formed no monolithic entity. Parliaments (both Houses) were entirely the proper place for discussing such issues, whether or not one accepted the Queen's insistence on royal initiative, but in that arena all sorts of opinions made themselves heard and agreement for or against the official line was rarely complete. The arguments ran between different individuals, not between institutional components of the Parliament. While debate could signify disagreement it did not always mean conflict, least of all conflicts in which 'the House of Commons' as a body attacked Queen and Council. Parliament existed for, among other things, the airing of opinion – as a sounding-board to assist government, not as an instrument of opposition endeavours to subjugate the Crown – and only total peace, total absence of argument, would have been a cause for disquiet.

It is against this background that the clashes of the reign need to be judged. They arose over religion, the Queen's marriage, the safety of the realm, and prerogative practices allegedly harmful to the subject, but there is room here for only a few words on each. In matters of religion it has now been clearly shown that the 1559 settlement took the form intended by Queen and Council; it was not troubled by opposition in the Commons, and opposition in the Lords failed to modify it. Later moves to improve the manners of the clergy, the government of the Church or the piety of the people came from several quarters but quite as much from the bishops as from ardent Protestants dissatisfied with the established order. Thus the religious bills of 1566, revived in 1571, had episcopal support, though most of them failed because the Queen, better gauging opinion in the country, regarded them as too likely to disturb the peace. The appearance in the seventies of 'the platform' – a coherent presbyterian programme for reform of the Church – did produce a Puritan agitation in the country which tried to exploit the occasions of parliamentary meetings (the 1571–2 Admonitions, and Cope's Bill and Book in 1587),[31] but in neither the country nor the Commons could that agitation gain any significant support. A general disquiet over the state of the Church and the threat to the Protestant religion was not the property of Puritans determined to form an opposition in the Commons; it was shared by concerned men in the Queen's government, by councillors and bishops, who deplored the Queen's own insouciance and expressed their view in Parliament without dreaming of opposition or seeking power for the Lower House, but rather in the hope that such quasi-public pressure might change Elizabeth's refusal to encourage reform.

The agitation over the Queen's marriage and the uncertain succession even more clearly demonstrates the real meaning of protest in Parliament. In 1563 and 1566, led by councillors despairing of any chance of pressing their policy in Council, both Houses were mobilised to urge the Queen to act, and the disapproval that expressed itself in the years when Elizabeth seemed likely to marry a French prince was egged on by Court factions opposed to such a marriage. Similarly, the pressure for the executions of Norfolk and the Queen of Scots (1571, 1572, 1587) exhibits not the opposition of religious extremists but a rift within the government itself, as some courtiers and councillors, having failed at Court, tried to use Parliament to press their policies upon the Queen. As for prerogative devices resented by those who did not benefit from them, they could indeed rouse majority protests in the Commons but also tended to reveal differences within the normally dominant element of officialdom in either House. In the best-known manifestation of this grievance – the campaign in the nineties against mono-polies – members in the Commons rightly responded to pressure from their constituents (an element in the equation which, though hard to document, should never be forgotten) while the Crown in Parliament stood in some disarray because too many of its agents there profited from the practices attacked. There had been a rehearsal of these fumes in 1571, when Robert Bell, one of the Council's managers, got out of step with his conciliar bosses by questioning the granting of monopolistic licences, but on that occasion the issue was not sufficiently alive to cause a serious rumpus.[32]

Anybody who was there could use Parliament to promote his policies or air his grievances, but on most occasions it was quite evidently the leaders of Parliament, the Queen's councillors fighting out the unfinished business of Court and Council politics, who so employed the institution. This could, of course, produce awkward moments, such as those so manifest in Cecil's efforts to hide from Elizabeth his share in the agitation of 1566.[33] Such a use of Parliament, whether by official or unofficial promoters of causes, could also get out of hand. The presence of a few genuinely independent agitators could embarrass the majority by giving the Queen a chance of branding more responsible men as disloyal, and Elizabeth's inclination to lose her temper over all that unsolicited advice, however well meant, did not help matters. As the adviser of 1572 so rightly pointed out, 'hard messages' needlessly caused friction with members 'so disposed to love her Majesty', and it was unfortunate that some of the Council had a way of irritating the House. Not every official manager was good at the job. Council and Court factions, clashing in the Commons and bringing *arcana imperii* into the open, exasperated Elizabeth into uncalled-for harshness, and though in the end she usually succeeded in smoothing ruffled feathers no one had done more than herself to ruffle them in the first place.

The Elizabethan Parliament was a working institution engaged in the manufacture of legislation by agreement and in the sorting-out of such matters as might cause disagreement. It was dominated by the Queen-in-Council, who guided business in both Houses and only rarely lost control; apparent loss of control either hid covert Council activity against the Queen or resulted from factional divisions among those she expected to act in unison. 'Opposition' is the wrong term to employ, and 'Puritan opposition ' an even more misleading concept. But all this still needs a lot of working out.

4. Government, Finance and the Community of the Exchequer

J. D. ALSOP

IN recent years, some of the most interesting and fruitful research into Tudor government and society has focused on the enforcement of Crown policies and interests. The prevailing concern for the themes of political stability, religious orthodoxy, and social-economic regulation has emphasised particular aspects, not least the relationships between the monarchy and the political and social élites. In consequence, our knowledge of the operation of the political system – its character, effectiveness and limitations – has been greatly enhanced through the study of Parliament, the Privy Council, the royal Court, and the county and borough communities. Rather less consideration has been devoted to the regular instruments of national administration: the institutions of the central bureaucracy. These agencies were central to some of the principal functions of the early modern state, not least justice, finance and defence, and their proceedings and management reveal much about the nature of Elizabethan government. This investigation is intended to introduce this topic from the perspective of one of the largest and most important of these institutions: the Exchequer.

No single department can be considered typical of the late Tudor bureaucracy as a whole. From what is known about the other sectors of the administration, there was a considerable common ground in relation to general conditions and patterns of office-holding, remuneration, working-practices, and so forth. Earlier assessments of a unique and distinctive Exchequer character have been overdrawn. Nevertheless, each institution necessarily possessed its own administrative qualities, conditioned by its past and by its role within the Elizabethan polity. In particular, each had a relationship with the Crown (the monarch and the Privy Council, or portions thereof) as befitted its function in the royal service and as developed from the myriad of personalised connections serving to bind together the Tudor state. In regard to this relationship between the bureaucracy and the superior power, a special insight may be acquired by focusing upon the Exchequer. For almost a century after the amalgamation of the revenue courts in 1554, this department dominated the management of government finance, and, since the authority for all fiscal policy and virtually every decision on the expenditure of even trivial sums of money rested in the Crown, the Exchequer had a regular interaction with both the Queen and the Privy Council. Moreover, the monarch had a clear vested interest in finance (in a way not true, for example, of justice), and the concentration of royal finance in one agency facilitates an appraisal of the impact which a particular administrative system had upon a single, very important, priority of the Elizabethan state.

I

One might begin with a question which is rarely asked of central government: how 'royal' was the royal administration? The bureaucrats and underlings of the Exchequer were all representatives of the Crown in that they exercised their authority in the Queen's name. Many were deemed to be her servants, although this only encompassed those on the 'establishment'. The approximate number of posts on the payroll of the department at the beginning of Elizabeth's reign was twenty-two in the Receipt, or Lower Exchequer, and fifty-seven in the Upper Exchequer, or Exchequer of Audit. These ranged from the Lord Treasurer of England down through the institutional subdivisions – the judicial officers, the auditing staff, the tellers, the messengers, the archivists and the various functionaries – to the humble porter of bags and rolls. All these totalled less than half of the individuals connected with the central Exchequer at this time. The substantial numbers of private or semi-private clerks and deputies who assisted the officers or substituted for them accounted for most of the remainder. Appointed privately, on terms of employment decreed by the individual officials, and paid by their employers (either in cash or, more commonly, in a proportion of the fees and gratuities leviable upon the public), these administrators had no direct link with the Crown. Through ability, connections, service or purchase, many did eventually secure offices in their own right, and by the nature of the recruitment procedures a large number were already related to the incumbents in the Exchequer or other departments of state. But these individuals, an important component of the bureaucracy, were merely private agents whose allegiance to the Queen was no greater than that of any other English subject and who, while usually industrious, competent, and considerate of their duties, naturally paid close attention to their own and their employers' interests.[1]

Additionally, a number of subordinate Exchequer staff were on the establishment but not on the payroll. In this category may be placed, for instance, the clerks of the parcels, the attorneys in the Pleas Office, and at least some of the porters. Indeed, it is an oversimplification to include the eight ushers and grooms and twenty-four junior clerks, divided between the offices of the Queen's and Lord Treasurer's remembrancers and the Clerk of the Pipe, as being in receipt of salaries. Combinations of remuneration for working-expenses, diets, liveries and occasional rewards were here even more common than elsewhere, and the modest wage components which had crept into the calculations were still regarded as somewhat irregular. This does serve as a reminder that central, as well as local, government possessed unsalaried servants. The modern concept of a single 'living' wage, intentionally designed to provide full sustenance for an official and his family, was unknown to Tudor government. Quite apart from inflationary pressures, it was traditionally accepted by all parties that a major proportion of an official's income would come from fees for services to 'the public', the miscellaneous and often plentiful profits of office, and from personal sources such as landholding, commerce, or positions elsewhere in public or private administrations.

Of the established staff, the monarch held the right to appoint to twenty-nine of the approximately ninety-four places. This was itself a substantial improvement over the medieval period. Piecemeal, the Crown had acquired since the late fourteenth century (mostly at the expense of the Treasurer) the selection of the second Chamberlain, the Under-Treasurer, the Lord Treasurer's Remembrancer, the Clerk of the Pipe, the four tellers and four messengers, and all the auditors of the Upper Exchequer. By Henry VIII's death it monopolised appointments to all the most important offices and many others. Although each instance requires individual study, it is unlikely that the acquisition of patronage was inspired by conscious royal desire to control the institution. Such a design would have been foreign to the widespread acceptance of 'mixed' government lasting well past the end of Elizabeth's reign. Rather, it appears that as offices became more important, better established in departmental routine, and less intimately attached to the original patrons, there was a general tendency for the sovereign to assume responsibility. This process was fragmented and incomplete. The three deputies to each of the two chamberlains always remained in the gift of the latter, although by the Tudor period the chamberlainships were largely inactive sinecures. The original rationale still retained some validity in other areas, as in the personal selection of the two secondaries (chief clerks) and numerous under-clerks in each of the offices of the Queen's Remembrancer, Lord Treasurer's Remembrancer and Clerk of the Pipe by the heads of the sections themselves.

The Lord Treasurer's own patronage remained significant: in the Receipt he appointed the Auditor, the Clerk of the Pells, the Tally-Cutter, and probably an usher; in the Audit he assigned the Foreign Apposer and the Clerk of the Estreats, and recommended to the Queen the auditors. Of these, the most prominent were the Auditor of the Receipt and the Clerk of the Pells, who either jointly or independently dominated the day-to-day administration of the entire Receipt. Both of the great Elizabethan lord treasurers, William Paulet, Marquis of Winchester (in office 1550–72), and William Cecil, Lord Burghley (1572–98), took care to engage personal servants and clients and to retain intimate links with them. This need not have been to the Crown's disadvantage, but neither were the appointees necessarily the most appropriate in the circumstances. Winchester's Clerk of the Pells from 1560 to 1570 was the noted recusant Robert Hare, later accused – by a biased party – of serious misconduct in office and described as 'a man devoted to popery and therefore not without suspicion'. More straightforward was the case of Winchester's Auditor of the Receipt, Humphrey Shelton, who fled abroad in 1569, in debt to the Crown, and was henceforth referred to as 'Shelton the fugitive'. Other important, autonomous posts which remained independent of the Crown were the Clerk of the Pleas, Controller of the Pipe, and Clerk of the Nichils (all in the gift of the Chancellor of the Exchequer), the two clerks of the parcels (Chief Baron), and the Marshal (Earl Marshal of England). Influence, though, was frequently just as meaningful as formal patronage rights, and this could work in many ways. The Lord Treasurer, in particular, normally possessed considerable influence with both the sovereign and his inferior officials in the department, the Exchequer staff interacted amongst themselves, and the persuasive power of the Queen was very considerable, should she choose to exercise it. The last, however, was largely a latent force, except when set in motion by individual suitors.

All royal appointees, and at least the important remaining administrators, received formal patents of office, in the first case from the Crown and in the second from the individual patrons. It is probable that all incumbents, even the non-established clerks and deputies, were employed upon specific terms, but information is scanty at this level. The patents of appointment were legally enforceable documents, and – unless technically invalid – could not be altered or superseded. The most common form of tenure, particularly in the middle ranks of the hierarchy, was for the life of the patentee. This was true for both royal and private placements. The implications are obvious; Lord Treasurer Burghley was throughout his twenty-six years in office encumbered, for better and for worse, with Winchester's last appointee as Clerk of the Pells, Chidiock Wardour (1570–1611). One teller placed in the Exchequer by Queen Mary remained there until 1598, as did one of the messengers. It is just as well that the Lord Treasurer's

Remembrancer, Peter Osborne, got on well with the Elizabethan establishment, because he held this responsible post for forty years from 1552. Many of the principal Exchequer supervisors waited decades before they could prefer their own nominees to places of trust under them. This rarely disrupted departmental administration noticeably, but it did severely limit the potential for innovation.

Even the offices granted in theory during pleasure or good behaviour were in practice customarily held for life. The deputy chamberlains and all the private clerks and deputies had security of tenure, at most, only during the incumbency of their patron. Their technical expertise, however, and perhaps a willingness to offer suitable remuneration meant that a substantial number survived to serve several masters. A renowned devotee of the institution's records, the deputy chamberlain Arthur Agard, held his position under seven successive chamberlains from 1570 until his death in 1615. William Stanton began in 1550 as a teller's clerk, but with the demise of his employer he moved five years later to be under-clerk to the Clerk of the Pells, and soon acquired a complementary ushership in the Receipt. He overcame the death of one Clerk of the Pells, but apparently not that of the next in 1560. Stanton remained Yeoman Usher until 1573 and in 1565 was appointed to a second establishment post as a deputy chamberlain. Thomas Borough entered the Receipt in 1545 at the age of fifteen; after several changes in position he was still there in 1591. Naturally, not every Exchequer office-holder was so fortunate or so inclined to stay put. William Walter appeared in the Exchequer in 1584 to advise on customary procedures; his own experience dated back to 1534, but he had severed his connection with the department in 1548. Men did enter and leave the Exchequer with some regularity; yet, in view of the rewards of office, the rather limited opportunities for advancement and the improbability of formal retirement, the chief factor governing this was mortality. The Elizabethan Exchequer had perhaps more than its fair share of geriatrics. Presumably Secretary of State William Cecil thought so in one instance; he had probably had his eye on the Lord Treasurer's place for some considerable time before Winchester finally expired, decrepit and deaf, in 1572 at an age of somewhere between eighty-six and 106.

Service for life – albeit sometimes in name only – was facilitated by the use of deputies. Within the Exchequer, as in other sections of the bureaucracy, this was an accepted privilege by Elizabeth's reign for most officers – apart from some possessing judicial responsibilities. It was a right guaranteed by patent and usually sanctioned by tradition. Although open to abuse, the system possessed advantages for the Crown and it is difficult to conceive of how Tudor government could have functioned without it. This is especially true in that authority and responsibility were still widely regarded as personally tied to individual officers, who, if they employed private assistants, were in effect delegating some functions to deputies. The privilege was utilised in ill health or old age, because of incompetence, disinclination to serve or the burdens of work elsewhere, and when the demands of the office exceeded the capacities of any single official. For the monarch, the principal disadvantage was that some of the most important administrative tasks in the state could be assigned to individuals who were not appointed or paid by, nor directly accountable to, the Crown. This undoubtedly worries historians more than it did contemporaries: however, it is a moot point whether it should have attracted more attention at the time.

Offices in Tudor England served purposes well beyond the simple task of governing the realm. They were bestowed, too, to meet the needs of politics and patronage, and as a method of indirect payment. In this system of personalised administration the use of deputies at least ensured a qualified replacement for any incumbent who was unable or unwilling to serve. Elizabeth's first Queen's Remembrancer was Sir Thomas Saunders of Charlwood, Surrey, in possession from 1549 until his death in 1565. He had a distinguished career in government dating back to 1540, was a friend of Sir Walter Mildmay, and was occasionally called before the Privy Council as a financial expert, but from the early 1560s he relinquished most of his duties as Remembrancer to a personal deputy. This was Henry Fanshawe, a long-serving attorney in the office, who had been promoted to Secondary and in 1561 secured from the Crown a patent in reversion to succeed Saunders. Similarly, during the last decades of Christopher Smith's long and tiresome service as Clerk of the Pipe (1548–89), he deputed functions to Thomas Morrison, a clerk in the office since at least 1548, the holder of the reversionary interest, and Smith's eventual successor. The Exchequer officials generally tried to select able, competent deputies and provide some measure of supervision. This was in their own best interests. There was as yet no sense of corporate institutional accountability; each official was personally responsible for the royal money or functions entrusted to him. Formal liability could only exceptionally be transferred to clerks and deputies. The limited alternative was the imposition of private financial safeguards in the form of bonds and sureties for good behaviour in office. These afforded some security for the Crown, but their main function was to protect the individual administrators. Sir Percival Hart was Gentleman Usher of the Receipt, 1553–80; this was traditionally a sinecure with effective direction assigned to the Yeoman Usher, the custodian of the premises. When several tellers' chests were broken into at Easter 1573 it emerged that the Yeoman Usher, William Stanton, was bound in the sum of £500 'to save him [Hart] harmless against the queen's highness for his said offices'.[2]

The only officers of the central Exchequer bound by the Crown itself were the four tellers, the department's receivers and paymasters. Even then, it was only in the 1560s, when several financial scandals finally stirred the government into action, that the practice was introduced. This was approximately a century after the tellers had taken effective custody of the cash, and over a decade since bonding had been recommended for the tellers by the royal commission's report on the revenue system in 1552, and imposed by statute in 1553 on other royal treasurers and receivers.[3] In the absence of bonds the chief restraint on the Exchequer personnel was their oaths of office, which were still taken seriously in this age. Clearly, an oath would not necessarily deter an unscrupulous individual, and it provided no means of recovering losses arising out of corruption or negligence. At most, it simply stressed the office-holder's personal obligation to the monarch and helped establish minimum requirements, the abrogation or neglect of which could give grounds for dismissal or imprisonment. Of course the swearing of oaths was restricted to the establishment. Moreover, it seems that oaths were inadvertently not always attached to posts instituted since the fifteenth century.[4]

II

In terms of the general conditions of office-holding, the Elizabethan period was primarily a time of consolidation or intensification of earlier trends. Possibly the most unsettling development was the reliance upon an increasing number of private clerks and agents, along with the piecemeal insertion of 'extraordinary' officers in preference to a more systematic overhaul of the bureaucracy. These processes can be viewed at the very top within the Cecil secretariat, in Chancery and elsewhere. It was the scale, rather than the existence of the practices, which was distinctive. Bureaucratic empire-building cannot be excluded, but greater weight should be assigned to two interrelated features of late Tudor government. The first, especially in the last decades of the century, was an increasing competition for offices and the rewards which they could provide in an inflationary era. Secondly, the demands of religion, foreign policy, war, judicial change and so forth significantly expanded the work of central government.[5] Both developments, however, took place when the Crown's policy towards central administration – to the extent that it could be said to have a policy – was essentially one of conservative retrenchment. Expansion was curtailed, delayed and diverted into devious channels – in part because of official concern over the expense of government in a period of continued financial strain. Certainly in comparison with the first half of the century, bureaucratic growth was very slow, and probably well below what was appropriate in the circumstances. Vested interests within the administration also modified and conditioned responses: the pressure of inflation (unmitigated by any general advancement of salary levels) operating within a state service of confined horizons made it essential for each official to hold on to what he had and lay claim to what he could. The flexibility of the Tudor system ensured that the important business of the realm and the necessity for reasonable patronage would be met, but the results were not always the most rational, consistent, or administratively and politically desirable in the long term.

Within the Exchequer itself several specific processes enhanced these trends. The amalgamation of the revenue courts in 1554 greatly increased the volume of financial work in the department. The 1552 royal commission had suggested that all revenue could be processed in the Exchequer with a very modest addition in personnel. This impractical proposal was ignored, but the staff transferred from the old agencies were insufficient. Prior to 1554 the four tellers performed all their duties (in person or by deputy) without clerical assistance; thereafter the workload was such that each required the aid of one or two private clerks.[6] The most noteworthy expansion took place at the top of the structure. After the appointment of Paulet in 1550, the Lord Treasurer assumed an active role in the operations of the institution, in contrast to his largely inattentive early-Tudor predecessors. Elizabeth's first Under-Treasurer, Sir Richard Sackville (1559–66), and Chancellor, Sir Walter Mildmay (1559–89), were also industrious administrators. Mildmay's personal unification of these supervisory positions in the Receipt and Audit after Sackville's death in 1566 set the pattern for the future, and consolidated the importance of the Under-Treasurer/Chancellor in departmental management. The earlier lord treasurers had occasionally utilised a personal servant in the Receipt, but the first regular private clerk was the future Clerk of the Pells Robert Hare, serving under Winchester by at least 1556 and later followed by Humphrey Shelton, Chidiock Wardour and others. Burghley continued the pattern: his client Vincent Skinner was private Exchequer secretary by the year 1575–6, almost two decades before his installation as Auditor of the Receipt in 1593. The first definite reference to a personal assistant to the Under-Treasurer is for 1561. Meanwhile, by 1560 Mildmay had a clerk and a keeper of the court seal, both non-established positions. The keeper was his relative and servant William Dodington. In 1564–5 he had another assistant, Robert Petre, whom he managed to advance to the auditorship of the Receipt (1569–93) in the aftermath of the Shelton scandal.[7]

The creation of clerical positions, particularly at this level, had a pronounced effect upon administration. The necessity for extensive assistance was clear and incontestable, yet the recourse to private retainers disrupted the already complex departmental hierarchy, further reduced the Crown's control of personnel and in many instances placed the burden of payment entirely upon the subject. The individual officers themselves would have welcomed a regularisation of the situation. Several succeeded in enlarging the establishment in their own interests. In the late 1560s the Clerk of the Pells used his favoured relationship with Lord Treasurer Winchester to get his personal clerk, acquired by the office soon after the reorganisation of 1554, placed on the payroll at the modest salary of £5 per annum. It was one of the few successes in an era of retrenchment.[8]

With existing places saturated and little likelihood of significant growth, aspiring office seekers had no alternative but to look to the future, while incumbents recognised the need to safeguard their own and their families' interests. The result was a noticeable rise in patents in reversion throughout Tudor government. The granting of future entitlements to Exchequer offices had been practised before the 1550s, but not as extensively as thereafter. This further decreased the Crown's freedom of action and correspondingly increased the ascendancy of administrators over individual positions. Some of the family successions are well known: Peter Osborne and his descendants were Lord Treasurer's remembrancers from 1552 until 1695 without a break; the Fanshawes and their relations held the post of Queen's (or King's) Remembrancer, 1565 to 1674; Chidiock Wardour in 1570 began a family control over the clerkship of the Pells lasting well over a century. This merely intensified the collective tendency of office-holding conditions to create and maintain tightly knit departmental social groupings.

Patronage patterns, if nothing else, ensured that there were close ties between the members of individual offices (the remembrancers', the Pipe and others). But friendships extended well beyond, crossing divisional lines – even that between the Receipt and the Audit – to provide a context for administration as real and important as the formal structure. The Elizabethan staff – especially those who were active in the institution – intermarried, transacted business together, bought, sold and enfeoffed property among themselves, exchanged medieval manuscripts, and chose their companions as executors, overseers and witnesses for their final testaments. A few illustrations must suffice: among the friends selected in 1566 by the Under-Treasurer, Sackville, to execute his will were the Chief Baron, Sir Edward Saunders, and the Chancellor, Sir Walter Mildmay; Winchester both supervised the execution of Sackville's will and married his widow; when, in November 1558, William More, the son of a previous King's Remembrancer (1542–9), required sureties for his good behaviour as sheriff of Surrey and Sussex, these were provided by Henry Fanshawe and the Clerk of the Pleas, John Brace; Thomas Felton, Auditor of the Receipt, 1550–66, witnessed the wills of two tellers and had business dealings with at least two others.[9]

Relationships were not always cordial – no dispute is as bitter as one between relatives, friends or neighbours – and this too left its imprint upon financial management. The same sources reveal that the Exchequer was very far from being a closed circle: intimate relationships existed throughout central government and well beyond. This is one reason why newcomers were so readily absorbed. Even when not related to existing members of the department, fresh appointees were hardly unknown to them. Thomas Argall had already served in the archbishop of Canterbury's administration for over thirty years and under the Crown for nearly twenty when he came to the Exchequer, late in his career, as joint Remembrancer of First Fruits following the reorganisation of 1554. He had, though, long been a client of Sir John Baker, then Under-Treasurer and Chancellor of the Exchequer. Argall's involvement in the institution came to an end with his death in 1563, but twenty-one years later, in 1584, his daughter selected as godparents for her third child the Lord Treasurer's Remembrancer, Peter Osborne, and Mrs Thomas Fanshawe, wife of the Queen's Remembrancer.[10]

The Exchequer staff worked, socialised and, when royal business required it, ate together. However, it would be completely inappropriate to describe them as an office-holding caste, alien to and divided from the rest of the nation. The bureaucrats and clerks who industriously applied themselves to financial operations were as likely to be landed gentry, retailers, or merchants, as to be the speculators in property and overseas enterprises or monopolists who are commonly associated with central government. A large proportion, at levels appropriate to their circumstances, were members of Parliament, justices of the peace or local officials, not least in the borough of Westminster itself.[11] Even at the end of the century it was not uncommon for personal and departmental affairs to be intermingled in correspondence, record files or individual memoranda.[12] In practice, 'public' and 'private' merged.

The administrative routine was performed within both the Exchequer premises at Westminster and private houses in London and its suburbs. Winchester and Sackville conducted business from their homes, as did the Auditor of the Receipt, some of the auditors, the tellers and the Queen's and Lord Treasurer's remembrancers. In the case of the Auditor of the Receipt, remembrancers and tellers, the authorities paid for the fitting-out of offices to hold the Crown's records and cash. Communications were necessarily retained with section supervisors, such as Felton and Fanshawe, when they devoted time to their country estates. Through a combination of illness and preference, Lord Treasurer Winchester transacted Exchequer business by correspondence from his seat at Basing, Hampshire, over long periods.[13] Meanwhile, Sir Walter Mildmay conducted operations from a house he had acquired within the Exchequer premises, later held by successive auditors of the Receipt. The Usher of the Receipt resided in the department with his family and servants, and for long periods in the sixteenth century the Usher of the Upper Exchequer possessed the Exchequer tenement named Heaven, which was alternatively used for domestic and public functions or let on lease.[14] Such behaviour was unremarkable in an age when buildings customarily served dual business and residential functions within the 'private sector'. There was little reason why conditions should have been markedly different within the 'public sector'. Indeed, the distinction is very much a modern one – useful for historical analysis, but imposed upon the early modern period with some risk of misrepresentation. Likewise, the more that is known about individual office-holders, the harder they are to typecast. To take an extreme illustration, Sir William More of Loseley, 'the perfect Elizabethan country gentleman', acquired a prestigious chamberlainship in 1591 at the advanced age of seventy-one, his only place in the central administration during nearly fifty years in local government. In view of his age, background and interests, and the decay of the chamberlainships, the assumption that the grant was a sinecure would appear eminently reasonable.[15] Regrettably, the records prove otherwise.[16]

The operations of the Exchequer were dominated by the middle-ranking administrators, particularly the heads of sections, such as the Auditor of the Receipt, the Clerk of the Pells, the three remembrancers, the Clerk of the Pipe and the Clerk of the Pleas. Over the preceding century or more, the main institutional subdivisions had developed into essentially self-governing, independent bureaux. These interacted with each other and with the chief officers, but day-to-day management was fully internalised. Throughout the sixteenth century each office was still led by an individual who, almost invariably, had spent many years, often his entire career, within the section and/or in related posts in the Exchequer. They were the real departmental experts. Even the presence within Elizabeth's Exchequer of three of the acknowledged work-horses of Tudor government – Winchester, Burghley and Mildmay – did not radically alter this state of affairs, although it did entail modification of internal procedures. The Exchequer representatives on royal financial investigations in the early 1560s were regularly Thomas Felton for the Receipt; the Lord Treasurer's Remembrancer, Peter Osborne; the Clerk of the Pipe, Christopher Smith; and the Secondary (and effective head) of the Queen's Remembrancer's office, Henry Fanshawe. These might be assisted by one or more others, from among the Remembrancer of First Fruits and Tenths, the auditors and tellers. By comparison, the Lord Treasurer, Under-Treasurer and Chancellor attended only intermittently, and occasionally all were absent.[17] It was the Auditor of the Receipt who reported on revenue and expenditure to the chief officers and the Privy Council, and the remembrancers who provided the gross financial figures and estimates of future receipts. The voluminous extant Elizabethan working-papers of the Auditor and the Queen's Remembrancer demonstrate their authority and proficiency. Nor was it accidental that Peter Osborne was the author of the definitive description of the institution, *The Practice of the Exchequer Court*, written in 1572 to guide Burghley on his appointment as Lord Treasurer, or that the treatise was later revised by Thomas Fanshawe to assist Burghley's successor, Lord Treasurer Buckhurst.[18]

In Elizabeth's reign the head officials were industrious and very far from being ciphers; but they remained almost wholly dependent on the bureaucrats (including their own appointees) for information and advice. The Chief Baron, Chancellor, Under-Treasurer and Lord Treasurer were always appointed from outside after Henry VII's reign, and the last three were invariably leading politicians or administrators. The almost total ignorance of departmental procedures of these Crown appointees and the knowledge they needed to acquire if they were to play significant roles in the internal routine, are demonstrated by Sir Julius Caesar's extensive researches on becoming Chancellor and Under-Treasurer in 1606. Winchester revived the Lord Treasurer's position but, to judge from the testimony of a contemporary chamberlain and the course of events within the agency, even he remained largely unaware of basic aspects of the Receipt for six or seven years after entering office. Likewise, in 1578, after six years as Lord Treasurer, Burghley lacked regular personal knowledge of important Exchequer concerns, such as debt collection or land exchanges and sales, and had apparently devoted little direct attention to key areas of income and expenditure management. Long before this, addressing himself to an equally illustrious Tudor administrator, a clerk with over thirty-five years' experience in the Upper Exchequer neatly summed up the situation. By 1540 Christopher More had known Thomas Cromwell for two decades and he respected Cromwell's achievements as Chancellor of a smaller, less complex Exchequer. But ultimately it was More who was the expert, 'your Lordship not being brought up in that court'.[19]

In these circumstances it is hardly surprising that the Lord Treasurer sometimes experienced difficulties in imposing his authority. An order written by Winchester and countersigned by Mildmay, issued to the Queen's Remembrancer in March

1562, commanded him to desist from making judgements on cases of disputed title between the Queen and private parties out of court. Precisely one year later Winchester and Mildmay were compelled to dispatch an identical command, commenting that, although the Remembrancer had been told on several occasions to cease, he had not yet complied. Allegations that individual officers exploited the dependence or ignorance of the head officials, including both Winchester and Mildmay, were commonplace.[20] Probably, though, each gave as good as he got, according to his abilities. A large institution such as the Exchequer contained a bevy of overlapping interest groups. The administrators might combine to oppose external threats to their privileges or positions, but just as frequently the disputes were internal. At various times Winchester fell out with both of his chancellors, Baker and Mildmay, to the detriment of administrative cohesion. In Baker's case, under Queen Mary, the dispute spilled over into the royal Court.

As Chancellor, Baker was also accused, with some justice, of exploiting his judicial authority for factional political ends against his Kentish rival, the former Master of the Rolls, Sir Robert Southwell. Winchester took an active interest in Exchequer business relevant to his circle of influence in Hampshire and his local clientage. Others, including the Chief Baron, Sir Roger Manwood, in 1581, were on various occasions charged with using their royal positions wrongfully to acquire lands and possessions – although, since the information almost invariably came from interested parties, each instance demands detailed examination.[21] All, Burghley included, ensured that their servants and dependants received favourable leases of Crown lands and places of profit in local revenue administration. This was unexceptionable. The Elizabethan polity expected that offices in both central and local government would provide for their holders influence and economic advantage. Illegality apart, complaints were special pleadings by the losing side. Conflict of interest was not always involved. The same individuals who spent decades in the laborious service of Crown finance were the ones who, when the opportunity or necessity arose, ensured that their unrivalled command of the system would be put to good advantage. Contemporaries also considered divided loyalties unexceptionable. The City of London invariably paid a yearly fee to a member of the Upper Exchequer to serve as its attorney and represent its interests in this court, as did other corporations and great magnates. This could rarely have benefited the state, as for example when the fee'd council and estate administration of the 4th Duke of Norfolk, in the years preceding his execution in 1572, included the Queen's Attorney-General, Solicitor-General, Master of the Rolls and Attorney of the Court of Wards and Liveries, the Queen's Remembrancer Thomas Fanshawe and several former Exchequer employees.[22] The problem went far beyond the deliberate exploitation of positions for personal and family profit. Most office-holders belonged to several communities, with overlapping responsibilities. When in 1586 property held by one Thomas Sisely was claimed for the Crown in the Exchequer as concealed land, his relatives naturally sought the advice of a close friend involved in the family's affairs. It so happened that this was that competent and trusted official the Lord Treasurer's Remembrancer, Peter Osborne.[23]

A comparison between the Exchequer and local government in the shires is not inappropriate. Each was dominated by an oligarchy of established families, bound together – in friendship and enmity – by ties of kinship, geography and mutual concern. In both cases royal administration was conducted in an intimate, highly personalised atmosphere. Neither was isolated nor altogether introverted, yet each was highly conscious of internal, often very localised, interests. Administration in both spheres was frequently vigorous, sustained and effective. At the same time it was self-interested, rarely susceptible to unwelcome external pressure, and on occasion wholly indifferent to 'national' requirements as assessed by the Crown. None the less, many of the principal explanations for local-government independence – most notably distance from the centre and a dependence upon unpaid amateurs – are clearly irrelevant to a Westminster institution composed of career professionals (in so far as this term is relevant to the sixteenth century), many of whom were paid directly by the state and all of whom were to a considerable degree dependent upon the profits of office.

Extremely few Exchequer officials were dismissed during the second half of the century. The most remarkable instance was in 1553, after Mary's accession, when Sir John Cheke, Secretary of State under Northumberland, was unceremoniously deprived of his positions, including a chamberlainship. Following the robbery of the Exchequer in 1573, Usher Stanton was removed: as a scapegoat, his negligence subsumed that of his superiors. Lord Treasurer Winchester voted against the 1559 Act of Uniformity in Parliament, was the leader and promoter of Catholic factional politics in Elizabethan Hampshire, and has been implicated in the 1569 plot against Cecil. His tenure in the Exchequer was marked, in perhaps equal measure, by an able attention to detail and impetuous favouritism combined with the stubborn assertion of his rights, even against the Queen. In Winchester's final years, it was later reported, his memory was so bad that he forgot to secure proper authorisation for the disbursement of royal money, but he died in office respected by many as 'the principal husband of this famous Realm under our royal and sovereign Princess'.[24] Winchester was exceptional merely in his prominence. Below him, the entire pattern of office-holding conditions served to insulate the incumbents against either removal or enforced compliance. A statement made in relation to local administration is equally applicable to the central bureaucracy: 'Elizabethan government was government by consent'.[25]

The royal commission of 1552 had recommended that the auditors in the Upper Exchequer be compelled to attend to their duties in person and cease to execute their places by deputy. Consequently, the articles annexing the courts of Augmentations and First Fruits to the Exchequer in 1554 – authorised by royal letters patent and a preceding parliamentary statute – ordained that the auditors must serve in person unless specially licensed by the Exchequer Court. This order was wholly unenforceable, because all the auditors held patents of office which specified their right to execute their responsibilities by deputy. The Exchequer records prove that both existing occupants and new appointees after 1554 continued for decades to employ deputies. This included John Hornyold, who was in Elizabeth's reign incarcerated in the Fleet prison over alleged partiality and corruption as auditor.[26] Reform, even limited and piecemeal improvement, could succeed only if the government demonstrated, as it rarely did, dogged determination and consistency. All too frequently, as in the introduction of tellers' bonds, the Crown simply reacted to events.

III

The Exchequer was on the very doorstep of the Privy Council, yet in a sense it was as distant as a midland shire. Individual councillors passed through it regularly, but few knew it. The department had its own 'resident' privy councillors in the persons of the Lord Treasurer and Under-Treasurer, who could at least serve as channels of communication even if their own attitudes to the institution and the Crown were often complex or ambiguous. With respect to financial information, the Council probably received from the Exchequer all that it required, or perhaps all that it could manage – which was little enough in relation to the wealth of statistical data which could have been provided. There was, however, little contemporary expectation that the government would necessarily employ a large volume of evidence in policy formation. Beyond this, the distinct impression is that the Council remained relatively unused to its role as the principal superintendent of state finance and was, moreover, beset by a wide range of difficult tasks in the administration of the realm. As with the problems of local government and other responsibilities, the Privy Council usually treated financial topics piecemeal, with little forward planning or even coherence.[27] None the less this generally sufficed, which, in view of the difficulties of the era and the exigencies of both peace-time and war finance, was a notable achievement. With financial administration it was different. There were no procedures by which the Crown might readily diagnose maladministration, corruption and anti-quated practices, or formulate improvements. If the Crown did not seize the initiative itself, it was (again resembling the relationship with the provinces) at the tender and restricted mercy of the busybody, the paid informer and the interested party. Indeed, all too often these were the sources of knowledge even for the Lord Treasurer.[28] This absence of informed knowledge was critical, and no less significant in restricting reform of the financial structure than the presence of a system of vested interests. The following case, which represents the Elizabethan state's only significant attempt at enforcing policy for the central Exchequer machinery, bears this out.

For a full half century from 1556 until after the accession of James I the Exchequer of Receipt was intermittently convulsed by bitter internal dispute.[29] The main rivals were the Auditor and the Clerk of the Pells, but in the course of the altercations Winchester, Burghley, Mildmay, the tellers and the chamberlains were all interested parties, and the Upper Exchequer and even the royal Court became involved. In a controversy of such breadth and duration the issues were numerous and the reasons for individual participation varied, affording the historian valuable insights into Tudor administration. Reference here is restricted to a few salient points. The basic issue was whether or not the Receipt should reintroduce the 'ancient course' – the administrative system which contemporaries all believed had been followed from the twelfth century until the beginning of the sixteenth. At the very least (the ultimate outcome) this entailed the installation of the Clerk of the Pells as an independent supervisor of the Receipt alongside the Auditor, with the restoration of medieval records and the establishment of new series overlapping with those already in existence. A more comprehensive approach would deprive the tellers of most of their control over royal funds, and beyond that would rehabilitate the chamberlainships, which had long been in decline. Yet contemporary understanding of the medieval history of the institution was faulty (especially in the perception of the details and duration of the 'ancient course'), and the process of conservative renewal, as is so often the case, created an unprecedented, novel system. Further, the new administrative routine was essentially unnecessary, more complex and time-consuming, and more costly to both monarch and subject.

The initiative succeeded because of the partisan encouragement it received within the department, particularly from the Clerk of the Pells, aided and abetted in the early stages by Lord Treasurer Winchester, and through the final direct intervention of the Queen. Elizabeth apparently first became aware that the Receipt had deviated from its time-honoured procedures near the beginning of the reign, when informed that the tellers were transacting business and keeping money in their private residences, and that two former tellers had left office indebted to the Crown. Her reaction in April 1562 was to command Winchester, Sackville and Mildmay to ascertain the correct ancient order of the Receipt by consulting the Exchequer officers and records, and then to implement it. The tellers in particular were henceforth to work in the department, and they were commanded to obey this instruction.[30] The royal initiative received derisory attention. The head officers were far from inactive in this period, but several years elapsed before the fringes of the subject were tackled, with belated consideration of the deputy chamberlains' controlment rolls. The medieval issue roll was reinstated in 1567, but being substantially copied from the tellers' accounts it served no productive purpose and was quietly abandoned in 1570. In 1567 the Exchequer was still openly paying the expenses of the tellers' operations in their London homes. Only internal reforms, culminating in the departmental regulations of 1571, helped bring the tellers back into the Receipt, and even then these measures were not wholly effective.[31] Meanwhile the internal dispute waxed and waned. Authoritative decisions by Exchequer committees proved ineffectual. Finally in 1589 the Clerk of the Pells, Chidiock Wardour, appealed directly to the Queen. Her predictable response was to order Lord Treasurer Burghley to oversee the immediate 'restoration' of the Clerk of the Pells's position. This command was met merely by further internal quarrelling, but Elizabeth did not follow up her action and apparently remained unaware of her royal impotency for almost eight years. In March 1597 she stridently repeated the command in a formal Privy Seal letter read in open court and placed on record in the Black Book of the Exchequer. This time Burghley complied, although the Auditor and the Clerk of the Pells continued to contest subsidiary points well after the death of both Burghley and the Queen. The entire affair highlights the difficulties experienced by the Tudor Crown in governing its own central bureaucracy. For a half century the principal Exchequer officials proved incapable of settling a disruptive administrative dispute. The monarch's direct commands were completely ineffectual for decades at a time. Equally unsettling is the realisation that these instructions were not merely sporadic and indifferently pursued, but essentially wrong-headed, being based upon a profound ignorance of the institution which the Queen was attempting to 'reform'.

IV

The Exchequer was staffed by a large body of reasonably capable and responsible administrators. It was fulfilling useful functions and, even in the midst of the Receipt controversy, was never in danger of collapse. Hence there was no administrative crisis which had to be met by the monarch and Privy Council. At the same time, the second half of the sixteenth century was an era of important change in the economy, society and government. If the Exchequer, as the principal element in the central financial structure, was to continue to assist in the achievement of the state's financial goals, then adaptation and innovation were in the long term essential. The Exchequer could, of course, adjust itself to changing requirements and had done so since the twelfth century. Internal innovation was effective, but it was limited and piecemeal, creating overlapping strata of fossilised, amended and sometimes confused duties and records. The Exchequer had thus far demonstrated an ability to cut through its own internal red tape and remain remarkably efficient. But the process could not continue indefinitely, particularly in the face of the conservatism within Elizabethan and early Stuart government. *Ad hoc* improvements were, moreover, as in the case of the Receipt, susceptible to reactionary or legalistic challenges from both within and without.

The greatest handicap suffered by internal reform, though, from the viewpoint of the polity, was that it was necessarily devised to meet the needs and the interests of the administrators themselves. While useful, this did not address the broader issues but tended to introduce additional complications. In a century of substantial price inflation, for example, official salaries in the Exchequer remained constant or rose only modestly – especially in Elizabeth's reign, when the main beneficiaries were the chief officers themselves or their personal appointees.[32] This was deliberate policy, but among the unforeseen consequences was an expansion in fees and gratuities which altered the relationship between the Crown and its bureaucracy and was to prove contentious within the polity. On the whole the Crown showed little perception of long-term trends, awareness of the tensions within its bureaucracy, or concern.

Effective government requires knowledge, interest and power. In its relationship with the central Exchequer the Elizabethan Crown displayed deficiencies in each. In consequence it was not in full control of this important area of national administration. The Exchequer was adrift, moving where the currents of economic change, vested interests, the blossoming patronage system, and so on, would take it. The monarch, Council and bureaucracy all exploited this situation, however imperfectly they understood it, for their own short-term advantages. Thus the Crown could manipulate features of the changing office-holding pattern to its economic or political benefit (the reliance on reversions being a case in point). In these circumstances the Exchequer was very much in danger over the long term of becoming more closely associated with the problems of government than with their solution.

5. The Crown and the Counties

PENRY WILLIAMS

I

WHILE the demands made by the first four Tudors had weighed heavily upon the officers of shire, hundred, borough and parish, the pressures of government increased markedly, sometimes alarmingly, under Elizabeth. The Crown tried to impose upon its subjects outward ecclesiastical conformity: the press was censored, the universities purged, pulpits tuned, bishops and clergy bullied from time to time into compliance; most remarkable of all, the adult population was compelled, at least in principle, to attend church services each Sunday. With a growing population pushing up food prices and intermittently bad harvests threatening serious shortages, the supply of grain had to be secured. Unemployment, vagabondage and endemic poverty led to firmer, more permanent measures than before for the suppression of beggars and the relief of the poor. Above all, war with Spain and rebellion in Ireland imposed heavy military burdens upon a state that was slenderly equipped to fight campaigns on land. The increase in governmental pressure came in two waves: during the 1570s new poor laws were enacted and greater vigilance exerted over vagabonds, while the Crown became nervously concerned about Catholic missionaries and recusants; then, after 1585, war, hunger and inflation compelled the state to lay still heavier burdens upon the localities.

Henrician government, however sophisticated its 'bureaucratic' resources may have become at the centre, relied for local administration upon sheriffs, justices of the peace and muster-commissioners, reinforced by the informal support of magnates and bishops. Its most dramatic and impressive acts of policy were usually carried through by special commissions, such as those which investigated and later dissolved the monasteries. Under Elizabeth there developed, in piecemeal fashion, more permanent or semi-permanent organs of local government. The Crown's response was essentially *ad hoc*: there is no sign of any systematic, reforming mind at work in the Elizabethan Privy Council. But, for all that, the English polity of the last quarter of the sixteenth century differed greatly from its predecessors. The judges of assize on their twice-yearly circuits conveyed the Crown's wishes to local governors, supervising their activities and reporting back to the Privy Council on the conduct of county business. Some judges interfered vigorously in the enforcement of the ecclesiastical laws, although in general prosecution, like so much else in Elizabeth's government, was sporadic. At the county level JPs were the traditional agents of government, and have usually been regarded as the foundations of the Tudor commonwealth, their backs bent under increasing tasks: 'it was in this age that they flowered in all the powers conferred by . . . "stacks of statutes that have . . . been laid upon them"', wrote Dr A. L Rowse. More recently Dr Peter Clark has affirmed this view of the JP as the 'keystone of Tudor local government', commenting that quarter sessions, 'already a lynch-pin of local administration in 1558', had by 1603 become 'the principal forum for county government', 'a self-conscious assembly of the county's ruling order'. But Dr Clark is also careful to remark that the county oligarchy 'was clearly centred around the lieutenancy'.[1]

The lieutenancy system represented by far the most important development in county administration during the sixteenth century. Commissions appointing lords lieutenant had been first issued under Edward VI, but for many years thereafter were made only in times of emergency. From 1585 every shire normally came under a lord lieutenant, responsible for its military affairs: supervising the musters, exercising the militia and trained bands, levying men for service abroad and establishing county armouries. To assist him the lieutenant had deputies – usually from two to six in each county – captains of companies and professional muster-masters. While the lord lieutenant was usually a privy councillor or grandee, often absent from the county, his deputies were drawn from the top ranks of resident landowners and were responsible for the day-to-day running of military affairs. With the realm continuously at war during the last eighteen years of Elizabeth's reign, their role in government naturally increased. In particular, they had to levy contributions for the supply of arms and armour, for coat-and-conduct money, for the salary of the muster-master and for the costs of coastal defence. Such financial authority greatly added to their power and sometimes to their unpopularity. Dr Hassell Smith has claimed that the lieutenancy system encroached upon the traditional system of county government, the quarter sessions. Whether that is so or not – and we shall return to the question later – there is no doubt that the lord lieutenant and his subordinate officers formed a command structure for military affairs which was entirely novel.[2]

The Crown issued many other commissions for enforcing specific aspects of policy at local level. Ecclesiastical commissions, containing both lay and spiritual members, were appointed in many sees. Their work was assisted in the latter part of the reign by recusancy commissioners, specially chosen to discover and interrogate suspected Catholics. After 1576 the government tried to secure the supply of corn by forbidding its export, and appointed commissioners for the restraint of the grain trade as part of the apparatus of economic regulation. To these examples one might add the commissioners for piracy, fen drainage, charities and debtors. New local officers appeared during the reign: provost marshals, long employed to discipline armies, were regularly appointed from 1588 in London, the home counties and the coastal shires for executing martial law upon 'masterless men, soldiers, rogues and others'. Initially charged with controlling disbanded soldiers, they came to assume responsibility for suppressing vagabonds and criminals. Overseers of the poor were established under the statute of 1597 for collecting the poor rate, setting the unemployed to work, apprenticing children and distributing relief to the 'impotent poor'. The Crown did not rely solely upon formally appointed officers and commissioners, and the attractions of private profit were used as an inducement to activity. Licences or patents were granted to individuals and syndicates for enforcing decrees and carrying out local tasks. For instance, Robert Kirke and Thomas Greene received letters patent authorising them to collect fines in East Anglia from all those who offended against the statute for the compulsory growing of hemp; and Sir Arthur Heveningham, a Norfolk landowner, obtained a patent for raising a county rate to repair the road across Attleborough Fen.[3]

One cannot of course measure the activity of ruling. But it seems indisputable that by the end of the sixteenth century England was more intensely *governed* than before. Although in practice many regulations were never enforced at all and others only spasmodically observed, more compulsion was being applied and more elaborate machinery employed for the purpose by a government which knew more about its subjects than had any of its predecessors. The state papers, with their lists of militiamen and trained bands, of missionaries and recusants, of creeks, havens and pirates, testify to that knowledge.

The pressure for more stringent control did not derive solely from the Crown. Urban oligarchs and village notables were also concerned to impose effective regulation upon the mass of the population. Boroughs were alarmed by the influx of beggars. London and Norwich raised compulsory poor-rates as early as the reign of Edward VI, and most large towns followed their example in the second half of the century. Alehouses were condemned as haunts of criminals and sources of immorality. However, local notables did not co-operate enthusiastically with the officers of the Crown in every parish: borough officials and village constables were often reluctant to offend their neighbours by enforcing the law too rigorously. Nevertheless, after about 1580 the local authorities in many communities were coming to share the concern of central government over the conduct of the poor. Theft, drunkenness, begging and the begetting of bastards all met with disapproval from 'respectable' merchants and yeoman farmers. Thus the intensification of governmental pressure came from above and from below, although the motives were not always the same, Protestant piety playing a role in towns and villages that is not very evident in the policies of the Privy Council.[4]

II

How effectively did the Elizabethan monarchy tap the resources of its subjects? What was their response to its demands? From 1585 until the end of the reign, heavy and continuous calls were made upon the counties for waging war at sea and in the Netherlands, Portugal, France and Ireland. 105,800 men were levied for service overseas in those years.[5] The soldiers had to be supplied with arms, with uniforms, or 'coats', and with their maintenance, or 'conduct money', to the port of embarkation. In theory coat-and-conduct money was raised locally and then recovered from the Exchequer; in practice reimbursement was always slow and often impossible. At the same time local authorities were responsible for providing and maintaining the stocks of parish arms and armour for the county militia; for building and repairing coastal forts; for paying the muster-master; and for providing beacons to warn of invasion. After 1588 the Queen demanded ships for naval service or money in lieu. The royal right to commandeer ships from ports had long been established; but the regularity of the demands in the 1590s and their extension to inland towns and shires was new.[6] While the burden of direct parliamentary taxation was relatively light in these years, thanks to totally unrealistic assessments, specific local levies bit more sharply. To begin with they involved substantial sums of money. In Northamptonshire £1056 was paid out in 1588 for coat-and-conduct money and a further £250 for a defence fund: this was said to be three times the yield of a single parliamentary subsidy. Norfolk's expenditure on coastal defences, coat-and-conduct money, weapons and other military supplies came to £4240 in the same year. 1588 was exceptional in many ways. But on the whole the costs of home defence and overseas expeditions tended to rise thereafter. Ship money weighed heavily on the smaller ports: King's Lynn and Yarmouth had to pay £3000 for providing two ships for Essex's expedition to Cadiz in 1596. London, having agreed in 1595 to produce twelve ships for that purpose, was faced with a demand for another three early in 1596 and a further ten in the following December.

These impositions encountered a good deal of grumbling,

procrastination and dispute. The very system for assessing the militia rates was guaranteed to call forth complaints. Based on an out-of-date statute of 1558, it ensured that the burden of local taxation fell unevenly on different parishes, often burdened the poor to the benefit of the rich, and eroded resources at a time when the need for them was growing. Those responsible for the militia were frustrated and disputes broke out between districts. Payment of salaries to muster-masters became a particular object of dislike. Up to 1588 these professional soldiers were paid by the Exchequer; but after that the counties were forced to pay from their own funds. Muster-masters were often appointed from outside the shire and seemed insensitive to local susceptibilities. The JPs of Cornwall so resented their muster-master that they offered him money to go away – unavailingly as it turned out. Ship money was a still more bitter source of contention. Opposition was strong enough in London for the Queen to drop her demand for ten ships in December 1596. The deputy lieutenants of Dorset reported that it would be impossible for them to collect the required sum of £700 without arousing great discontent and having to send many recalcitrants to London. The most persistent opposition to ship money, outside London, came from the West Riding of Yorkshire and from East Anglia. The Privy Council accused the JPs of the West Riding of having 'eluded our earnest discretion by dilatory, frivolous and framed excuses'. Some had evidently called in question the Crown's right to call for the levy.[6] In Suffolk the JPs peremptorily refused any assistance from the county to Ipswich and allegedly forbade the collection of ship money within the shire, 'aggravating the matter', in the words of the Privy Council, 'and dissuading the same by perilous arguments, meeter to move the people to discontentment than to concur in Her Majesty's service'.[8]

Money was not the only burdensome demand. Continuous requests for men to serve abroad drained the patience of deputy lieutenants and captains. While the county authorities were content to fill the ranks of the overseas levies with vagabonds and beggars, the commanders in the field naturally wanted better material. By 1601 shires and towns were appealing for relief from their burdens: the bailiffs of Colchester begged for mitigation of their quota of men and arms; Sir John Harington complained of the excessive demands made upon the impoverished county of Rutland.[9] The officers commanding troops destined for service overseas were gloomy about their levies, the Bristol commissioners protesting in 1602 about the new recruits that 'there was never man beheld such strange creatures brought to any muster. . . . They are most of them either old, diseased, boys or common rogues . . . .' Many deserted and others mutinied: there was a 'great mutiny' of the Gloucester levies on 26 May 1602 and in July a soldier stabbed his officer.[10]

The state papers and the correspondence of the Privy Council convey a powerful impression of growing reluctance in the shires to contribute to the needs of war. In 1591 the Council complained to the lords lieutenant of Sussex that 'by example of some few at the first and toleration of their undutiful obstinacy' many inhabitants of the shire were refusing contributions for 'martial services'. Similar reprimands were delivered to the authorities of Middlesex, Hampshire, Buckinghamshire and Yorkshire during the early years of the decade. Until 1598 refusal seems to have been sporadic; but in that year alone resistance was reported from Oxfordshire, Norfolk, Suffolk, Rutland, London and Coventry. The Council accused the muster commissioners in Suffolk of dealings which were 'full of careless negligence'.[11] During the last four years of the reign such reprimands and complaints were common form, with the authorities of Kent, East Anglia and London the most slack and recalcitrant. The Privy Council expressed particular indignation at the way in which the wealthy shifted the load to their poorer neighbours: 'it hath been noted', they wrote in 1598, 'that this burden [the subsidy] is laid on the meaner sort, who though they contribute small sums yet they are less able indeed to bear the burden'.[12] In no single year were the exactions very oppressive. But their constant repetition, year after year for eighteen years, made them increasingly irksome.

Apart from providing for the needs of war, Elizabeth's subjects were called upon to supply the royal Household, to subscribe to her ordinary revenue and to reward her servants. The burdens of purveyance, wardship and monopolies stirred up at least as much, probably more, resentment than did military levies. Purveyance was a long established right of the monarch, entitling agents of the royal Household to buy food and other provisions at less than the market rate. It imposed hardship on farmers, was fertile ground for corruption and had long been a source of grievance and dispute. A bill introduced into Parliament in 1589 for curbing the powers of purveyors was said to have 'much nettled all the officers of Greencloth' – the board responsible for provisioning the Household – and to have been disliked by the Queen. However, Elizabeth promised to devise the necessary reforms herself. A system of compounding was drawn up, by which each county agreed on a sum to bridge the difference between the market price and the 'royal' price for the goods it was required to supply. 'Undertakers', normally a group of JPs, levied the tax, bought supplies at the normal rate and sold them to the Queen's Household at the lower 'royal' price, recouping their expenses out of the composition money. This should have removed the worst features of the old system: the burden would be more equitably spread and the corrupt purveyors eliminated. But several counties declared themselves reluctant to enter into compositions. The amounts demanded from them varied wildly: Kent and Essex were assessed at £3000 per annum each; Norfolk at £1000; Yorkshire at only £495; and the whole of Wales at £360. The further a county lay from London the lighter its assessment. Even when compositions were agreed at county level the 'undertakers' found it difficult, sometimes impossible, to raise the money. In Norfolk the leading gentry were acrimoniously divided on the issue, some contending that 'this course of composition . . . is without the compass of the law'. After an initial refusal to compound, the Norfolk JPs were persuaded into an unwilling agreement, only to repudiate it in 1600. In many counties the purveyors, aided by royal pursuivants, continued to operate the system as they had done before, one writer complaining angrily that 'the perverse and crooked nature of this untoward cattle hath wasted with our laws and law makers many ages'.[13] A possible reason for dislike of the composition may have been provoked by the Privy Council's express desire that the new scheme should spread the burden more equitably between rich and poor: this hardly appealed to wealthy landowners. But however strong the opposition may have been the Crown could not afford to surrender so valuable a right: it was estimated in 1604 to be worth £50,000 per annum, though £37,000 may have been nearer the mark.

The royal rights of wardship had long been resented. The heirs and heiresses of tenants-in-chief of the Crown who were under age at the death of their father were taken into ward: the monarch received the profits of their lands and arranged their marriages. For the most part Elizabeth sold the rights over the lands, the choice of marriage partners and the guardianship of the young rather than directly administer affairs herself. Complaints against wardship were directed more strongly against lack of care in the upbringing of wards and in the selection of their spouses than against the Crown's profits, which, until Robert Cecil took over as Master of the Wards in 1599, were relatively small. The subjugation of an heir or heiress to the dictates of the market place was distasteful. Although some guardians, like Burghley, were conscientious in discharging their duties, others were less scrupulous. They had bought their wardships as an investment and were determined to exact a fruitful yield. When Burghley was Master, from 1560 until 1598, revenue from wardship averaged only about £15,000 per annum. Wardships were sold below their market rate and the major share of the profit went to the guardians. The system was valuable more as a means of rewarding courtiers and royal officials than as a direct source of income. Robert Cecil, on taking over from his father in 1599, issued instructions that wardships should henceforth be sold at their true value. Increasing the purchase price induced guardians to exploit their investments more rigorously. It is not surprising that the Apology of the House of Commons in 1604 should have attributed to wardship 'great grievance and damage', 'the decay of many houses' and the 'occasion of many forced and ill suited marriages'. Hostility to the system was not of course universal, since some men were enriched by it; but the large numbers of courtiers and Household servants among the beneficiaries helped to arouse animosity against the Court among the county landowners.[14]

Greater still was the resentment at royal patents for monopoly and other privileges. Originally intended to encourage enterprise and invention, monopolies had become, by the

1590s, primarily a means of gratifying courtiers and officials. Monopolists were a scandal: 'blood suckers of the commonwealth'. Bracketed with them as objects of detestation were patentees, who were granted the right to enforce and profit from certain statutes, and licensees, who were given exemption from specific economic controls. Sir Walter Raleigh, for instance, issued licences, at a price, for the keeping of taverns; the Earl of Leicester and other courtiers had licences, which they sold to merchants, for the export of undressed cloth. Indignation against monopolists and patentees had first been voiced in Parliament in 1571 by Robert Bell, a Norfolk lawyer, and complaints were made by various local authorities and town corporations over the next two decades. The main attack was launched in the Parliament of 1597, when Robert Wingfield, a Northamptonshire gentleman, nephew to Burghley, asked for a committee to be set up for enquiring into the 'sundry enormities growing by patents of privilege and monopolies and the abuses of them'. He got his committee, but Elizabeth promised reform of abuses before it could make any recommendations. However, the government's reforms were insufficient to prevent anger over monopolies from mounting during the next four years. Shortly before the next parliament assembled, in 1601, Buckhurst, the Lord Treasurer, told Robert Cecil that he had ordered a list to be made of existing monopolies and had thought most of them odious. He proposed that the most objectionable be revoked before Parliament met.[15] But nothing was done and monopolies became the centrepiece of debate in the final parliamentary session of the reign. Francis Moore, MP for Reading, asserted that monopolies brought 'the general profit into a private hand, and the end of all is beggary and bondage to the subject'. Richard Martin, member for Barnstaple, told the House that he spoke 'for a town that rieves and pines, and for a country that groans under the burden of monstrous and unconscionable substitutes'. If the blood suckers were not repressed, the fruits of the soil and of labour would be taken from ordinary subjects. No one defended monopolies: spokesmen for the monarch restricted themselves to warning members against interfering with the royal prerogative. In the end the Queen cancelled eleven of the most unpopular patents and referred the others to the test of the common law. The concession promised more than it achieved, for monopolies were again to provoke angry protests under James I.[16]

The monopolies issue has not always been accorded the importance that it deserves. Sir John Neale commented on the 1601 debate that 'the tone . . ., if earnest and critical, had on the whole been restrained, and certainly fell short of the passionate, rebellious mood when religion was the issue in earlier Parliaments'. He saw the predominance of economic issues as a consequence of 'the eclipse of Puritanism', after which 'a vacuum existed, into which rushed concern for the economic disorders of the day'. This is a strange metaphor, suggesting some misapprehension about the earlier religious debates. Many of those classed by Professor Neale as passionate Puritan rebels, members of an opposition 'choir', emerge on fresh reflection as loyal subjects, anxious above all to protect their sovereign and her Protestant settlement.[17] The attack on monopoly was not of course an attack upon monarchy, for the critics carefully protested their loyalty, but some of them bravely attributed the odious grants to the Queen herself. The Puritan campaign was the work of a small minority in the political nation; its most passionate advocates were far too extreme for most members of Parliament. The issue of monopolies touched the lives of many: landowners, lawyers and merchants, as well as poorer men who never aspired to Parliament. It reflected a general and growing indignation against abuses of the Court and of government officers.

The debates were certainly taken very seriously by Robert Cecil, who had been shocked by the appearance outside Parliament of 'a multitude of people who said they were commonwealth men and desired [the House] to take compassion of their griefs'. Later he upbraided his fellow MPs for discussing parliamentary affairs outside the House: 'we are not secret amongst our selves. . . . Whatsoever is subject to a public exposition cannot be good. Why, parliament matters are ordinarily talked of in the streets.' Riding in his coach he had heard men say 'God prosper those that further the overthrow of these monopolies!' In a great rage he urged the House to take note 'that the time was never more apt to disorder. . . . I think those persons would be glad that all sovereignty were converted into popularity. . . . The world is apt to slander, most especially the ministers of government.' Cecil's almost hysterical outburst was an excessive reaction to the criticisms of monopoly: it may be that the Essex revolt earlier in the year had made him unduly nervous. But his speech reflects, not only some remarkable views on the proper relationship between Parliament and the public, but also the fears and suspicions of a government subjected to mounting criticism and resistance.[18]

III

Turning to examine the effects of Court politics and governmental pressures upon the administration and politics of the localities themselves, we at once confront the concept of the county community. Led by Professor Alan Everitt, many historians have viewed the county not only as a convenient unit for study, which undoubtedly it is, but also as the fundamental organic unit of local culture and politics. For Professor Everitt and others the counties in the early seventeenth century were the primary areas of allegiance for the landed classes. English gentlemen had become more isolated in their outlook than before, in spite, or perhaps because, of the growth in central power and the attractions of the universities and the inns of court. Quarter sessions and assizes were the rallying-points of political consciousness; JPs and MPs were more concerned with their 'countries' – as the counties were usually called – than with issues of national politics. Lately this perspective has been questioned.[19] Many counties were far from being organic units: Warwickshire, for instance, was divided into a predominantly pastoral region in the north and a corn-growing area in the south. Landowners were often more strongly drawn to small districts, hundreds or parishes, than to their counties. Many of them also looked beyond the boundaries of the shire to London, even to Ireland and the New World. To the great indignation of Elizabeth the gentry were increasingly tempted to stay in London – attracted by the royal Court, the law courts, the theatre, and the social life of the metropolis – instead of remaining at home in the shires, ruling their 'countries'. Their correspondence shows a lively concern for affairs beyond the

county borders, and their attitude is typified by a Gloucestershire gentleman, Sir Charles Percy, marooned at his home in
Dumbleton: 'I am so pestered with country business', he wrote
to a friend in town, 'that I cannot come to London. If I stay here
long, you will find me so dull that I shall be taken for Justice
Silence or Justice Shallow; therefore take pity of me and send
me news from time to time . . . .'[20]

Yet the county boundaries were no mere artificial divisions.
The devotion of men such as William Lambarde in Kent,
Richard Carew in Cornwall and George Owen in Pembroke-
shire to the antiquities and topography of their shires testifies to
a deeply felt loyalty. The county maps of Saxton and Norden,
printed and widely sold, were a new development in cartogra-
phy: inspired at first by the government's need for local
knowledge, they quickly appealed to the literate classes.[21]
Quarter sessions might not meet very often and assizes might
be the instruments of direction from central government, but
both were occasions of some ceremony, drawing together the
leading men of the shires; and there was no intermediate
assembly between quarter sessions and Parliament. The truth
is that most men of worth and importance belonged to several
communities: to parish, hundred, county and nation.
Allegiance was not single and undivided. Mostly the central
government regarded the county as the primary unit of local
administration: it addressed its commands to the lord lieutenant, the JPs or the sheriff. The great bulk of criminal cases were
heard at quarter sessions or assizes. Local political rivalries
generally revolved around control of the lieutenancy and the
commission of the peace. For all those reasons the county
remains more than a convenient unit for research: it was *a*
principal arena of administration and politics, commanding
the loyalty, though not the exclusive loyalty, of its landowners.
But there are real dangers in exalting the county community
above all others. The concept itself may encourage excessive
attention to the upper élite of local society, to the detriment of
lesser gentlemen, townspeople and yeomen, whose allegiance
was probably devoted to smaller areas. Second, the idea of the
county community suggests an isolation and localism among
the ruling caste which was uncharacteristic of all its members.
Third, there is in the phrase a hint of an harmonious

neighbourliness which was seldom present. Counties and county societies were without doubt important; but the word 'community' has overtones which can be misleading.

Dr Hassell Smith has argued, albeit with careful and scholarly qualifications, that in the later years of Elizabeth's reign a 'conflict between "court" gentry and "country" gentry' opened in Norfolk as a result of the Crown's desire for 'more dynamic and efficient administration' and of the 'legalistic conservatism' of the 'county opposition'. He believes that the emergence of this conflict can be linked with the 'development of the lieutenancy into a permanent feature of military administration in 1585' and suggests that the deputy lieutenants and patentees represented the Court, while quarter sessions defended the interests of the county. He also intimates that the 'county opposition' was linked with the 'Puritan ethic'. Dr Peter Clark has reached similar conclusions for Kent, presenting quarter sessions as the conscious representative of the county community.[22] Were such reactions typical of English counties under the pressure of war in the late sixteenth century? Was a 'country opposition' beginning to appear in the last years of Elizabeth?

As Dr Hassell Smith himself remarks, protest and resistance in the face of royal demands were most marked in the coastal shires of eastern and southern England, upon which the burdens of levies and taxation fell most heavily. Elsewhere, for instance in southern and western Wales, royal orders seem to have been placidly accepted. But grumbling and procrastination were one thing; the emergence of a conscious 'county opposition' quite another. I do not find convincing Dr Clark's evidence for his belief in the leadership of the quarter sessions in county affairs: it played that role in 1640–2, but there is little or no sign of such conscious activity in the sixteenth century. Nor was the pattern of lieutenancy *versus* JPs repeated in other shires. In Suffolk opposition to ship money in the 1590s was led by the deputy lieutenants themselves. In Wiltshire the Lord Lieutenant, the Earl of Hertford, was thoroughly disliked by the leading gentry, and the principal contest was fought out between the Earl and his own deputies, who combined with the JPs to protest against the method of raising the muster-master's salary – described by one of the deputies as 'exceeding distasteful'. In Northamptonshire the principal deputy lieutenants, Sir Richard Knightly and Sir Edward Montagu, interceded with Sir Christopher Hatton, the Lord Lieutenant, to secure a reduction in the county's assessments for troops and money. The quota of foot soldiers was lowered from 1200 to 600 and that for the forced loan of 1589 from £5000 to £3000.[23] A successful lord lieutenant mediated between the county and the Court; intelligent deputies worked to secure the best bargain for their shire, knowing that they would then be better placed to collect what was required. A division between Court and county damaged the interests of the shire because it narrowed the opportunity for bargaining and mediation. Landowners needed friends at the centre to bring them royal patronage and to maintain their local influence. From every point of view negotiation, balancing and contact were better than confrontation. Of course these were not always successful and disputes occurred. The patterns of relationships between centre and localities were many; but usually the Crown and its agents maintained a posture of dialogue rather than conflict. Norfolk seems to have been exceptional in the sharpness of its divisions.

The burdens of war were not the only sources of division. The imposition of the Elizabethan settlement and the contentions between Catholics and Protestants, moderates and radicals, were also potentially disruptive. Both Catholics and Puritans resisted the Crown's demands for conformity; and factions often formed, however loosely, around conflicting religious loyalties. In the early years of the reign Catholic resistance to the Elizabethan Church was passive rather than active; but most counties contained a conservative element among the gentry. There were, for instance, strong Catholic and Puritan groups in East Anglia. From 1560 to 1575 the Catholics and conservatives were on the defensive against the vigorously Protestant Bishop of Norwich, John Parkhurst. But they survived his assaults in sufficient strength to counter-attack when he was succeeded by Edmund Freke, a determined opponent of the Puritans. Neither bishop was entirely successful in his endeavours. Recusant families such as Cornwallis, Jerningham and Drury survived with diminished influence, protected in some cases by their links with the Court: Whitgift was told by the Privy Council in 1589 that he should not insist upon the appearance in London of Sir Thomas Cornwallis, he 'being a very old man and one that beside the matter of his religion hath not been known to have intermeddled in causes of the state'. Similarly, Puritan ministers were defended by Lord Burghley and by Robert Beale, Clerk of the Privy Council, against persecution by Freke and the assize judges.[24] Sussex was also divided by religious faction: the eastern part of the county was predominantly Protestant, even Puritan, the western was Catholic well into Elizabeth's reign. The principal contention broke out when the zealous Bishop Curteys of Chichester summoned several leading gentlemen, suspected by him of recusancy, to a public appearance in the cathedral. Their petition to the Privy Council produced a response which drove Curteys into making a submissive apology: he regretted that his 'dealings have bred great offence' and offered 'recompense . . . according to the judgements of the councillors'. In Hampshire there was serious faction fighting early in the reign between the predominantly Protestant followers of Bishop Horne of Winchester and a more conservative group led by William Paulet, Marquis of Winchester. Although kinship may have been as important as religion in the bonding of these factions, it is noticeable that all Horne's friends were Protestant, while Paulet's included some Catholics and several lukewarm conformists. Eventually, the impact of central government severely reduced the number of Catholics on the commission of the peace as well as the strength of the Paulet faction, so that after 1568 Hampshire was politically dominated by Protestant gentry.[25] Similar results were achieved in Suffolk: religious disputes exacerbated faction fighting until the 1580s; but thereafter religion ceased to be divisive as the Protestant group emerged supreme. The central government tried both to enforce uniformity and to prevent overenthusiastic bishops and gentlemen from offending against local susceptibilities. At the level of outward conformity it was broadly successful in most counties, with the conspicuous exceptions of Lancashire and the shires on the Welsh border. Protestant gentry were usually supreme in county affairs by the end of the reign; and, although some of them were too zealous for the liking of Elizabeth, the Puritan gentlemen of the 1590s were devoted to maintaining the social and ecclesiastical order, in no way fanatics or rebels.

While the Crown had managed, by the beginning of the final decade of the century, to quieten the discords provoked by religious dissension and the imposition of the Elizabethan settlement, the same could not be said of the faction fighting which stemmed from divisions within the Court itself. Indeed these conflicts grew sharper and more disruptive after 1590. Until then the rivalry of Court factions had been relatively muted and the divisions between them blurred. The Earl of Leicester had certainly built up regional followings, especially in the west Midlands and in north Wales; and his activity aroused resentment among some local landowners. But divisions at county level reflected only very dimly those at Court.[26] With the deaths of Leicester, Walsingham and Hatton, Burghley insisted on the right to exclusive control of patronage, provoking the jealous hostility of Robert Devereux, Earl of Essex, the Queen's new favourite. The intense competition between Essex and the Cecils, in particular their unremitting efforts to secure offices for their friends, disrupted the politics and government of many shires, exacerbating local hostilities. In Kent the contest between Cecil's ally, Lord Cobham, and Essex's brother-in-law, Robert Sidney, centred on the lieutenancy of the shire and the wardenship of the Cinque Ports. In the event Cobham succeeded his father in both posts after some delay; but shortly after the fall of Essex he broke with his Cecilian allies and tried to establish a personal dominance in the county. The consequence was a bitterly contested parliamentary election in 1601 and savage in-fighting until Cobham's overthrow during the early months of James's reign.

The destructive force of faction is clearly visible in Wales, where Essex consolidated his inherited landed influence in the south-west and extended his patronage to the gentry of the northern counties. His fixed determination to place kinsmen and followers – especially young soldiers who had campaigned with him abroad – into positions of local power brought him into acrimonious dispute with the Earl of Pembroke, Lord President of the Council in the Marches of Wales. Allegedly, Essex received Pembroke's recommendations for the deputy lieutenancy of Radnorshire with 'scoffing laughter'. Pembroke, convinced that his position should give him the prime voice in appointments, complained against the exclusion of his own nominee, John Bradshaw, writing that 'I am very sensible of the unkindness lately offered unto me by the refusing an honest gentleman whom I did recommend and in naming another whom I do not like'. A strong-willed lady from Carmarthenshire rebuked Essex for allowing his men to oppress the Queen's subjects: 'most of them that wears your honour's cloth in this country is to have your honour's countenance . . . everything is fish that comes to their net'. In Denbighshire Essex attracted support in areas where Cecilian influence was weakest and imported the rivalries of the Court into the affairs of the county. In Wales and the Marches the repercussions of courtly faction fighting undermined the authority of the 'provincial governor', Pembroke, and damaged the fabric of county government in more than one shire; similar consequences can be observed in Kent and may perhaps be discovered elsewhere.[27]

IV

Did the links that joined central government to the localities weaken in the last years of Elizabeth's reign? While the chains of government were more numerous than in the early years the burdens put upon them were greater. War, inflation, bad harvests and faction fighting severely strained the system: some historians have written of 'The Crisis of the 1590s'; Dr Hassell Smith has argued that conflicting views were emerging in Norfolk about the innovations in local government, leading to the appearance of a county opposition. The reactions of Robert Cecil to the parliamentary debate on monopolies in 1601 certainly suggest that Elizabeth's ministers themselves feared that their authority was under attack. Within the counties factional rivalry disrupted the patterns of authority, while the attractions of the Court drew some magnates and landowners away from their shires. By the early years of the seventeenth century the Earl of Arundel had left the Sussex gentry to look after their own affairs, while Sir Robert Sidney had shifted his attention from Kent to London. The circle of courtiers was becoming narrower and less closely in touch with the shires; at the same time authority in many counties was becoming more widely diffused among the middling gentry. Whether this increased the difficulties of governmental control is hard to say; but the local concentrations of power seem in many places to have been breaking up.[28]

Yet, under Elizabeth, even in her later years, the Privy Council gives the impression of a tightly organised body, working effectively to secure compliance. True, its reactions were sometimes excessively nervous. The pathetically feeble rising in Oxfordshire in 1596 provoked intensive investigation, combined with all the horrors of torture. Yet only four men had appeared at the rendezvous, while six others were implicated and a further eight suspected. But if the Council overreacted, the utter failure of these 'rebels' at a time of appalling dearth is evidence of general quiescence in the country. The Privy Council under Elizabeth was, by contrast with its successors under James I and Charles I, firm in handling resistance to its demands for men and money. Subjects reported as 'backward' in their response were ordered to appear before it. Not that the councillors relied entirely upon coercion: as we have seen, they were prepared to bargain and to concede; but in the last resort they demanded obedience. It is impossible to assess at all precisely the extent of its success in meeting targets for taxes and troops. Obviously it did not obtain as much money or levy as many men as it demanded; but it can hardly have expected that. By and large it secured enough revenue and as many troops as were required to achieve its military ends.[29] Professor Conrad Russell has implicitly suggested that the governmental system of the late sixteenth and early seventeenth centuries was incapable of waging war: 'a successful war could not readily be combined with the local self-government which was the tradition of the English counties'. While this may have become true by the early years of Charles I, it was not so under Elizabeth: large-scale war, of the kind waged by Philip II, was far beyond the reach of the English Crown; but limited war could be and was successfully conducted by Elizabeth's government for eighteen years. Aid was given to the Dutch and the French; the country was defended against invasion; the

Irish revolt was extinguished; and the cost to the English economy was much less damaging than were Philip's campaigns to the Spanish.[30]

Faction fighting in the counties and at Court was certainly disruptive. But the Council tried, on the whole successfully, to calm the conflicts over religion, so that during the last third of the reign it had ceased in most shires to be a serious cause of dissension. The rivalry between Essex and the Cecils was perhaps more dangerous. Had Essex been more restrained and less intemperate he might have polarised both Court and counties. As it was, his behaviour was so extreme that all but his most hot-headed followers dropped away from him during the last eighteen months of his life. His fall produced only sporadic and ineffective protests from his friends; the Essex faction had no existence beyond the life of its leader. The most remarkable tribute to the Elizabethan political system was the untroubled accession of James I. In spite of the legal obstacles to his inheritance and the notable absence of any recognition by the Queen of her heir, the King of Scotland entered his new kingdom without a voice being raised in protest; his predecessor's principal adviser, Robert Cecil, remained in charge and consolidated his position by abruptly removing Ralegh and Cobham from political life. Cecil's intrigues do not make a pretty sight; but the smooth transition from one reign to another is evidence that the political system had been little disrupted either by the antics of Essex, the failings of the aging Queen or the strains of war. Tarnished and corrupt it may have been; brittle it was not.[31]

In conclusion it is worth attempting a brief comparison between the English and continental systems for securing local compliance to the will of the central government. The French monarch was served by some 40,000 paid officials in the early seventeenth century, most of them proprietors of their offices. There were perhaps ten times more French bureaucrats in proportion to the population than there were English. But the French kingdom was morcellated into separate regions with varied systems of control, much less effectively centralised than the English. In the *pays d'états* the provincial estates combined with royal officers to assess and collect taxes; in the *pays d'élections* — and in some *pays d'états* – this work was performed by bureaucrats known as *élus*. But the machinery was varied and complex, with no single pattern for each type of *pays*. Furthermore, during the second half of the sixteenth century its working was fatally disrupted by civil war. With the restoration of royal power under the Bourbons, efficient control over the provinces was eventually secured by circumventing the venal officers through the employment of special commissioners, later to be known as *intendants*. But the workings of Valois government give the strong impression that a large bureaucracy, especially one in which offices were bought, sold, and inherited, might obstruct as much as it helped the implementation of royal policy.

The Iberian kingdoms of Philip II and Philip III were even more divided and fragmented than those of France. At the pinnacle of the system authority was tightly concentrated into the hands of the monarch himself; in the provinces it was widely diffused, with urban oligarchies and landed nobles possessing great influence and power. Philip II attempted to control tax collection, borrowing, recruitment of troops and military supply by direct administration through royal officers. Where he succeeded in this, the results were at best unimpressive and at worst disastrous. However much the King and his councillors disliked managing affairs by contract, or *asiento*, with entrepreneurs, after 1580 they were gradually forced, much against their will, into reliance upon private individuals for collecting taxes, providing credit, manufacturing armaments, building and manning ships: contracts were certainly cheaper and probably as effective as direct management. Recruitment and command of troops was increasingly handed over to the towns and the great nobles, whose regional power grew in extent and in strength. Under Philip II and his successors the absolute, bureaucratic state was a myth: it was attempted, but never became an effective reality. True, the future lay with his sort of state, which emerged triumphant in the later seventeenth and eighteenth centuries. But at the close of the sixteenth that future was a long way off.[32]

One other comparison must be made: with the kingdom whose ruler was to mount Elizabeth's throne in 1603. Scotland at the birth of James VI was a very different state from its southern neighbour. The central institutions of government were very little developed, local ones hardly existed. There was no regular taxation and the King ruled by personal contact with the magnates who dominated their regions. During the long reign of James the machinery of central government was extended and offices proliferated, while laymen replaced clerics as the principal administrators. Taxation became a normal part of royal revenue; commissioners were established for enforcing policy in the localities; about a quarter of Scottish shires had justices of the peace by 1625; and officials of the central administration came to exercise greater authority on the borders. In other words Scottish monarchy was slowly coming to resemble the English model, but was still, in 1603, much more personal and informal in its workings.[33]

The Elizabethan polity lay somewhere between the elaborate bureaucracy of France and the undeveloped informality of Scotland. It had many agencies of enforcement, but still depended substantially upon co-operation with nobles and other landowners, blending personal contact, conciliation, persuasion and coercion. Its arrangements were often casual and *ad hoc*; but in this it differed less than might be supposed from France, Spain and, at the other extreme, Scotland, while centralisation of its territories provided it with great advantages over the Valois and the Habsburgs. By comparison with modern state machines, even with those of the eighteenth century, such a system seems ineffective. By the standards of the sixteenth century it was at least adequate; and Elizabeth avoided the dangerous concessions made by the Spanish monarchs to towns and grandees as well as the ruinous consequences of their wars. The system obviously had its drawbacks and frailties. The revenues of the Crown were allowed to stagnate. Royal demands upon the shires were arousing strongly felt grievances by the end of the reign, while the involvement of the landowning classes in servicing the ends of the monarchy ensured that it could never deal with passive or indifferent subjects. But, given skilled councillors and firm but tactful handling, Tudor government could secure most of its principal objectives and survive immediate threats.

6. The Foreign Policy of Elizabeth I

G. D. RAMSAY

THREE months after the accession of Elizabeth Tudor, a memorandum on the relationship between England and its close neighbours was addressed to her secretaries of state by the elder statesman Lord Paget. He had served her father, brother and sister in high office but was now ailing and in retirement, unable to travel to Court without danger to his health. Perhaps he had been asked to put the fruits of his experience on paper. Paget had no doubt that there was a 'natural enmity' between England and France, and that this dictated more than ever 'the necessity of friendship with the House of Burgundy', which ruled over the seventeen provinces of the Netherlands. Two underlying assumptions he did not specifically mention: first, that between them the French and the Netherlanders controlled the north-west European littoral, from which an invasion of England might most easily be launched; and, second, that English foreign trade was most intimately bound up with the commodity traffic centred on the thriving commercial metropolis of Antwerp. It was here that most English textile products, comprising the bulk of the kingdom's exports, passed from the hands of members of the Company of Merchants Adventurers to those of their foreign buyers. From the export tax on English woollen cloths the Queen derived most of her assured revenue, so that on the security of the cloth trade there hung not merely a measure of social stability but the financial strength of the English Crown and the international prestige this engendered. There is no reason to doubt that these two premises were crystal clear in the mind of the new queen and her chief councillors.

I

For the first decade of her reign the new ruler followed the traditional pathway in her dealings with her neighbours, perhaps with incipient disillusion. The situation was complicated by the fact that at the moment of her accession the representative of the House of Burgundy as ruler of the Netherlands was Philip II of Habsburg, who was also King of Spain and lord of the New World beyond the Atlantic. He had been the husband of her deceased sister and predecessor, Mary Tudor; and only a little earlier his influence had been exerted to rescue the life of Elizabeth when it was threatened by sisterly suspicion and jealousy. Not long after the death of Mary he offered his hand to Elizabeth, whose rejection of the marriage was the first important decision she made in the field of international relations. Her personal opinion of this unflinchingly Catholic, high-principled, hard-working but intellectually dull man, she kept to herself; though she must have met him sufficiently often during his two visits to England as King consort to form a decided judgement, and she had learnt Spanish in order to be able to talk to him.[1] The fact that many years later she was to wage a bitter war against him should not blind us to the welcome and even deference which she extended, as far as possible, to his envoys; nor to the indubitable reliance she placed upon his friendship as her chief international buttress during the first ten years of her reign. Indeed, it would hardly have been prudent of her to reject it, since, apart from the traditional ties it personified, it provided a guarantee of commercial business for her subjects, particularly for the merchants of London. Her regret was genuine when less than a year after the death of his English wife Philip quitted the Netherlands and northern Europe. For the remaining nearly forty years of his life he chose to reside in Spain, to the detriment of Anglo-Burgundian relations.

Events in France and Scotland were soon to underline the fundamental importance of the ancient alliance with the House of Burgundy. When Elizabeth came to the throne, negotiations were in progress to end the Habsburg–Valois war, into which England, as a Burgundian satellite, had been dragged. The peace treaty agreed in April 1559 left the fortress of Calais, the last English foothold on the continent, provisionally in French hands. It was, in fact, lost for ever, though the hope of recovering Calais fluttered at the back of the new queen's thoughts down to the final decade of her reign. After three months, the scene grew more sombre when a new king ascended the French throne – Francis II, husband of Mary Stuart, Queen of Scotland and, as a granddaughter of Margaret Tudor, a plausible claimant to the English succession or even throne. Old rivalries were revived and new alarms sounded when Mary Stuart, with injudicious bravado, assumed the style of Queen of England. The presence of a French garrison at Edinburgh Castle heralded further trouble. Elizabeth acted with reluctance, building up an alliance with the Protestant noblemen of Scotland, who mistrusted their Frenchified queen, and going so far as to send an army that helped them to dislodge the Frenchmen. In the summer of 1560 Secretary Cecil himself travelled to Edinburgh, and a treaty was fashioned by which the Scots were left free to devise their own form of government and religious settlement. Throughout these events Philip II perforce remained on the sidelines. Whatever his antipathy to the establishment of a Protestant regime in any country, the presence of French military forces in Scotland was even more obnoxious to him. The Anglo-Burgundian alliance still stood.

French politics took a new turn in December 1560, with the death of the young Francis II, who was succeeded by his brother Charles IX. The dominating personality in the government of France was now the mother of the King, Catherine de Médicis, a realist politician. She had no interest in the promotion of her widowed daughter-in-law's schemes, and Mary Stuart sailed back to Scotland in the summer of 1561. Elizabeth had so far refrained from meddling in French affairs. But, when early in 1562 there occurred a massacre of Huguenots, followed by the outbreak of civil war, she ventured to side with the Protestants and even entered into a treaty with them. English troops were sent to France and the fortified port of Le Havre was handed over to an English garrison. She sought to allay any displeasure by Philip II at such moves in support of heresy by a disingenuous letter, in which she explained that her intervention was designed simply to rescue the French king from his presumptuous subjects and that she regarded Le Havre as a pledge for the restitution of Calais. There may have been some truth in both these excuses, the second of which could not be divulged to French Protestants. Before long, they were ready to reconcile themselves to the predominance of the Queen Mother; and the rival factions closed ranks against the intruding English. Elizabeth's garrison at Le Havre was mown down by an untimely visitation of the plague in the summer of 1563; the few survivors had no choice but to surrender the stronghold and go home. Anglo-French peace was restored by the Treaty of Troyes in April 1564, by which the irremediable loss of Calais was confirmed. The episode had been chastening for Elizabeth, who gained nothing from it but lost both materially and in credit.

Thus during the first few years of her reign Elizabeth had experienced the vicissitudes of international politics. She had achieved her purpose in Scotland but met with disaster in France. The political context of her actions would have been familiar to her forbears on the English throne, who would have comprehended her wish to keep in step with the representative of the House of Burgundy. But before long the range of her political contacts was to be transformed, and she was to be confronted by problems unfamiliar in their nature and more sweeping in their implications. In order to appreciate her approach to them, it is necessary to turn briefly aside and note the scaffolding of international diplomacy which the princes of Europe were gradually constructing, with the aim of sustaining continuous and peaceful communication among themselves; and at the resources in manpower available to the Queen of England for the maintenance of her diplomatic place among her neighbours.

II

The occasional dispatch of a herald or messenger no longer sufficed for the needs of international political intercourse. Henry VIII had personally cultivated the acquaintance of his contemporaries Charles V, the Holy Roman Emperor, and Francis I of France. Elizabeth during her reign did not meet other sovereigns, though she had, as we have seen, some previous acquaintance with Philip II, and doubtless met as members of his entourage some personages subsequently prominent in politics, notably the Duke of Alva and the counts of Egmont and Hoorn. From time to time, there were visits of German and Scandinavian princes or officials to England. French noblemen (especially those out of favour at home) were sometimes presented at her Court. But the exchange of ambassadors was by now a device normal throughout western Europe, and the rulers of England had been making use of it for more than a generation. During the 1560s there was usually a French and a Spanish diplomat in residence at the Court of Elizabeth, though the envoy of Emperor Ferdinand I was withdrawn in 1560 and not replaced, and the Republic of Venice, anxious to earn favour at Rome, neglected to maintain the embassy it had hitherto kept in England. But, tiny as the diplomatic corps at London generally was, it carried immense responsibility, as we shall see.

Reciprocally, agents from the English Crown were stationed on the continent. Elizabeth began by supporting an ambassador at the courts of her closest neighbours, the kings of France and Spain, as well as in Scotland. But her diplomatic organisation was makeshift. Its most striking defect was the failure to exchange envoys with the neighbouring country whose ties with England were most intimate – the Netherlands. Its ruler, the King of Spain, chose to be represented by one ambassador in England, always a Spaniard. Brussels from 1560 ceased to be a diplomatic centre, and English interests in the Netherlands were usually left to the Queen's financial agent Sir Thomas Gresham, who periodically slipped over to service her debts on the Bourse at Antwerp. This was a serious gap. A further problem lay in finding, in a country so small and relatively backward as England, the volunteers with the training and qualities need to fill an embassy abroad, where unfamiliarities of speech, climate, lodging, food, religion and other habits of life were to be expected. A great nobleman might consent to travel to a foreign country on a special mission, as did the Earl of Sussex to Vienna in 1567, but there was no question of his residing abroad for any length of time. For any humbler gentleman who could be persuaded to fill an embassy abroad, the rewards were vague. He could expect to be out of pocket; and the more successful he was, the more the Queen traded on his devotion. Perhaps worst of all, he had to suppress his personal likes and dislikes, if they conflicted with the fulfilment of his instructions.

The scarcity of men of suitable calibre to run an embassy provides good reason why Elizabeth had to make do with such a varied assortment of agents, from the former Jesuit Dr Christopher Parkins and George Gilpin, sometime secretary to the Merchants Adventurers at Antwerp, to Edward Stafford, the impecunious aristocrat compromised by his Plantagenet affinities, and the scholar Thomas Bodley, to name only four. Particularly during war time, the line separating diplomacy from espionage was unclear. Thus during the latter years of the reign an observation post was maintained at St Jean-de-Luz, on the Franco-Spanish frontier, partly to keep in touch with politics in Guyenne, but also to collect naval information from spies in Spanish ports, and occasionally to engage in high-level Anglo-Spanish conversations. The Queen relied above all on the mercantile connections of the City of London, especially those of the Merchants Adventurers and the other national trading companies: diplomatic activity followed where trade had led the way, and hence the merchants could be brought to shoulder much of the expense. Elizabeth also made use of the communications network of the world of commerce, where merchants' newsletters circulated from one centre to another: Gresham often forwarded copies home when he visited Antwerp. The merchants' postal arrangements were likewise used, if only because the dispatch of a courier was costly. Foreign as well as English merchants were roped into service, particularly the ubiquitous Italians, who were always ready to assist in the quiet resolution of political problems: hence the intervention of Guido Cavalcanti, the Florentine merchant, who sought to oil the Anglo-French marriage negotiations in 1571, and the even more remarkable achievements of the Genoese Horatio Palavicino, who began his career as agent for the distribution of papal alum in northern Europe, but changed his employer and served Elizabeth as a financial and even political agent on the continent.

Elizabeth controlled the actions of her scattered agents

abroad through one of her secretaries of state. Thus until 1572 the management of international relations passed through the hands of Secretary Cecil, later Lord Burghley, and from 1573 for seventeen years through those of Sir Francis Walsingham. Thereafter, Burghley resumed some charge over English diplomacy, but during the 1590s his son Robert Cecil increasingly took responsibility, though he was not formally appointed as Secretary until 1596. There were other secretaries of state at various times, though none is likely to have wielded an influence comparable to that of the Cecils and Walsingham – especially Burghley, a cool, learned and methodical person. Thanks to the survival of his papers in bulk, we know how he put the pros and cons of issues of the day before the Queen and sought to translate her wishes into detailed orders. He had some leaning towards moderate Protestant causes which she in no way shared; her political outlook was conservative, what in a later age might have been called legitimist. The views of the mercantile community reached Elizabeth through her secretaries, especially Walsingham, who, as the son of a City officer, son-in-law of a lord mayor of London and himself a customs farmer, was entirely at home in the City. The Queen also listened to what various courtiers and privy councillors, such as the Earl of Leicester or Sir James Croft, might have to urge about international affairs. She encouraged the foreign envoys at her Court to talk to her. Thus, information from a variety of sources helped her to make up her mind. It is beyond question that she was a highly intelligent woman, with a will very much of her own, and with an intense interest in the march of events outside her island kingdom. Her critics might grumble that she was indecisive, cheeseparing or even narrow-minded; but she firmly moulded relationship with her continental neighbours after her own fashion.

Letters to brother sovereigns, or to English envoys abroad, were normally drafted by a secretary of state, often in his own hand, and after he had ascertained the Queen's mind. Missives to German princes and cities had to be turned into Latin before they were sent off, and in all correspondence the more delicate and confidential passages were enciphered. Below the directing personages there was an establishment of clerks to make fair copies and keep the records; it grew in size

and gradually evolved into something like an informal secretariat whose leading figures, Hickes and Maynard, began to
acquire some influence in the later years of the reign. But a
foreign office as such did not exist. The Cecils and Walsingham
were responsible for internal as well as external business; and,
although they drove their clerks hard, there were sometimes
long delays in replying to the dispatches from Englishmen
stationed abroad in the service of the Queen. Envoys on
occasion grumbled, felt neglected and starved of news, and
even complained of shortage of funds.

III

The central issues in international politics for over half the
reign hung on the transformation of the Burgundian ally into a
reluctant enemy. The decisive moment came in December
1568, when all English merchants in the Netherlands were
arrested by order of the Duke of Alva, then serving as
governor-general on behalf of his distant sovereign in Castile,
and Anglo-Netherlands commerce was abruptly brought to a
halt. No doubt the first seeds of trouble had been sown when
Elizabeth, soon after her accession, refused the hand of Philip,
reformed the English Church in a moderately Protestant
direction, and lent help to the cause of heresy in Scotland and
France. But even in the face of such provocation Philip valued
the English alliance too much to be willing to endanger it. The
first steps to remind Elizabeth that she might by her behaviour
jeopardise his friendship were taken in 1563 by his regent, who
had preceded Alva in the government of the Netherlands. On
the flimsy excuse that the Netherlands must be shielded from
the plague infection carried to England by the troops evacuated
from Normandy, the Regent suspended commercial traffic
between the two countries, thus sundering the cloth merchants
of London from their vital Antwerp market. By this sudden
stroke, the Queen's finances were threatened with disaster and
the economic life of her kingdom with paralysis. Such an
outcome was averted only by the unexpected discovery of an
alternative market for cloths at Emden in the principality of
East Friesland, just beyond the Netherlands frontier, and by

the alarm of the Regent on the discovery that the embargo was harming Antwerp and the Netherlands more than London and England. Relations were mended after some negotiations, and trade was resumed in 1565. Elizabeth had been rapped over the knuckles not as an enemy so much as a cheeky junior partner, and the Anglo-Burgundian alliance survived.

But the realisation that perhaps the Antwerp market was not utterly essential for the cloth trade implied some weakening of the Anglo-Burgundian link. It lost some further strength as a result of the tactless behaviour of the English ambassador to Philip II, Dr John Man, who for some alleged misdemeanours was expelled. The Queen seems to have accepted that he had been maladroit, to judge by her frosty attitude to him on his return. His post remained unfilled, probably because of the difficulty in finding a suitable successor who would submit to exile in the fastnesses of central Castile, where Philip expected envoys accredited to him to reside. Anglo-Burgundian contacts at the highest level were thus restricted to those maintained by the tenant of the Spanish embassy at London, where in September 1568 a new incumbent took over his duty as representative of Philip II – Don Guerau de Spes. Few if any foreigners stationed at London in a diplomatic capacity in the sixteenth century enjoyed the experience, and it may be that Philip had to scrape the barrel to fill the appointment. De Spes arrived with a soldierly reputation; but he was unfamiliar with northern Europe and entirely unversed in the ways of the English. However, he made his way to London through the Netherlands, where he visited Antwerp and was informed by the viceroy Alva of the state of international relations and of the tight trade interdependence of London and Antwerp. Once in England, he speedily adopted a very jaundiced view of his environment, reporting to his master how Secretary Cecil and Lord Keeper Bacon were among the most bare-faced heretics, 'pernicious and enemies to Your Majesty'.[2] He also swallowed the false information that the Queen was in straits for money, and that a trade embargo would force her to return to the Catholic religion.

In little more than three months de Spes, through sheer bungling, managed to wreck the ancient Tudor–Habsburg alliance. The occasion of the disaster was the arrival of a flotilla of ships from Spain in English waters, in November 1568. They were on their way to the Netherlands, with bullion owned by some Genoese and Lucchese merchants: it was to be delivered on loan to Alva to pay his troops. In severe difficulty owing to the stormy autumn weather, and chased by privateers from the Huguenot base at La Rochelle, the ships made for harbours on the south-west coast of England. Here they were safe from the tempest, but not from the marauders lurking in darkness. De Spes in London, when consulted about measures to protect them, authorised the landing of the treasure, with a view possibly to forwarding it overland to some port further east, whence it might proceed under escort by short sea route to the Netherlands.[3] But there were many refugees in London and elsewhere from Alva's bloody regime, who held quite different ideas about what should be done; and there were some sympathetic English voices raised to urge the confiscation of the bullion. De Spes, seized by an attack of cold feet, and seeking to force the hand of the Queen, impulsively advised Alva to lay hands on all English merchants and their goods within his jurisdiction.[4] This action embodied a massive misjudgement. Alva could not ignore the request, but he obeyed it with the utmost misgiving. The fat was now indeed in the fire. When news of the arrest of all English merchants and their goods in the Netherlands reached Elizabeth, she ordered instant retaliation upon subjects of Philip II in England. There ensued a complete standstill of trade between England and the Netherlands, which from January 1569 endured for almost five years. When the Scheldt was once more open to the Merchants Adventurers, it had ceased to be a secure waterway; and the old days never returned.

While the events leading to the Tudor–Habsburg clash of 1568–9 have been clouded by controversy, one incontrovertible truth deserves to be recalled. The rupture did not come about because either of the chief protagonists had sought it. Philip was well aware that, owing to the disturbed state of French politics, in which Huguenots were playing a prominent part, a friendly England was more than ever important for him if effective communications were to be maintained between his dominions in Spain and the Netherlands. His instructions to de Spes at the outset of his mission were unambiguous: the envoy was being sent to oil the alliance, not to hamper it.[5] Alva, who knew Philip's mind well and had enough trouble already on his hands in his viceroyalty, was horrified by the whole episode. As for Elizabeth, she was undoubtedly taken aback by the sudden seizure of English persons and property in the Netherlands. Queen and Council too were thoroughly dismayed by the unexpected renewal of the threat to trade and finances inseparable from the closure of Antwerp, for which no measure of retaliation could compensate. In the City of London, consternation reigned. Elizabeth could hardly but lay her hands on the treasure now in English harbours, though it was not until 8 January 1569 that de Spes could confirm to his master that this had been done;[6] and, as if to demonstrate her lack of any need, the bullion was removed to the Tower of London, weighed and allowed quietly to gather dust for nearly three years, until in 1571 the Italians were paid off.[7]

IV

With this dramatic demise of the ancient Burgundian alliance, Elizabeth began to look around for alternative friends. Her first approach was to the north German princes, to whom she sent back her envoy to drum up support for a broad Protestant alliance; but the conversations in the summer of 1569 gradually ran into the sands, in part perhaps because tension subsided. Before Elizabeth and Philip actually went to war with each other, sixteen years were to elapse, during which there were moments when they seemed to be edging towards reconciliation. But this interval was also marked by a succession of incidents which were less and less weighed objectively and increasingly interpreted as signs of malevolence. The rebellion of the northern earls in England in the autumn of 1569 was followed in February 1570 by the issue of the papal bull *Regnans in Excelsis*, in which Elizabeth was denounced as a heretic and her subjects released from their allegiance. Just as Alva had unjustly been blamed for the Anglo-Netherlands rupture a year earlier, so behind this the hand of Philip was discerned – equally mistakenly, since in fact he did not accept the papal claims to depose sovereigns on which the bull rested. There was also the papally financed invasion of Ireland that materialised in 1579. On the other side, there were the unofficial English incursions into Philip's transatlantic preserves, which grew more provocative with the raids of Drake and others in the 1570s. Above all, there was an outbreak of rebellion in the Netherlands, commonly dated from 1566, whose full gravity became evident from 1572. From the outset, English involvement was overestimated abroad. Thus, although negotiations to bring the Tudor–Habsburg dispute to an end were pursued, and the river at Antwerp was once more opened to the Merchants Adventurers and their cargoes of cloth in the summer of 1573, it could hardly be said that relations had been mended. An envoy from Philip II was resident in England – another Spaniard – for a decade from 1574; but there was no English counterpart at either Madrid or Brussels.

Ripples from the incipient conflict were soon lapping on other shores. The French ambassador at the English Court was a shrewd observer of Anglo-Burgundian relations, and very interested in their evident deterioration. In the course of the 1560s the notion that Elizabeth might marry one of the younger sons of Catherine de Médicis had been floated in Huguenot circles without meeting much encouragement. Late in 1570 the suggestion was once again put forward. This time, it met with a startlingly favourable response. The ambassador had encouraging talks with both Secretary Cecil and the royal favourite Leicester, followed in December by an audience with the Queen, who exhibited both interest and pleasure.[8] Thus were initiated, seemingly in all seriousness, the Anglo-French marriage negotiations that with varying assiduity were pursued for nearly fourteen years, down to the death of the last available French prince in 1584. Neither the absurd disparity in years between the aging bride and the youthful bridegroom, nor the tough problems posed by differences in both religion and politics, need blind the historian to the significance of these conversations. Both parties at the bottom of their hearts were doubtless cynical, despite some nicely calculated signs of affection on either side. But, so long as the affair continued, the political weight of the Valois prince in his own country was increased by his eminence as the favoured suitor of the Queen of England, while Elizabeth acquired an influence in French politics that enabled her to interfere to best advantage with men and money in continental conflicts. The marriage negotiations were a personal contribution of the Queen's to the technique and substance of international relations. They marked her final departure from the guidelines drawn by old Paget at her accession, and provided the starting-point for a far-reaching *renversement des alliances* in Europe, which with some interruptions was to endure for a century.

In her dealings with the Valois princes and with the Queen Mother of France, Elizabeth was siding with the legitimate sovereign of the country, a stance she could maintain when during the 1580s the French conflicts broadened into a struggle for the succession to the crown. English aid, in the form of men and money, was forthcoming for Henry of Navarre, the legitimate and Protestant claimant, while Philip II backed the Catholic League. Even when in 1593 Henry turned back to the old faith and five years later made his peace with Philip, Elizabeth continued the new Anglo-French alignment. But the prop of legitimacy hardly sustained her other continental allies, the insurgents in the Netherlands, where the Estates of the northernmost provinces formally abjured the sovereignty of Philip II in 1581. She had connived at the passage of men and munitions to the rebel cause nine years earlier, and from 1576 she was lending money to the mutinous States-General of the Netherlands. The relationship was strengthened by the Treaty of Nonsuch in 1585, following which Elizabeth dispatched her personal favourite the Earl of Leicester as her special representative with the Dutch. When he overstepped the mark by accepting the title of Governor he was recalled in anger: Elizabeth had no intention of accepting sovereignty over the rebellious provinces, though she was careful to place garrisons in the 'cautionary towns' handed over as security for her loans. Military events in France and the Netherlands were closely linked. There was a single war zone stretching from Brittany to Holland, in which English soldiers and English money were deployed, though in quantity insufficient to enable the King of France to recover the fortified city of Rouen from his pro-Spanish subjects in 1592. Elizabeth's participation was always guarded in form and never generous in substance. She was no singleminded enthusiast for the Protestant cause, though alert to make tactical use of her credentials as an excommunicated heretic. Her objectives were limited: she sought to thwart any plans for an invasion of her kingdom, and she hoped for the restoration of a Burgundian state, dominated by neither France nor Spain, that retained its ancient liberties with a measure of ecclesiastical freedom.

v

The diplomatic realignment was only one of two major consequences of the Anglo-Netherlands breach of 1569–73. The other, no less significant, concerned the survival of the huge cloth traffic of the Merchants Adventurers, and thus affected intimately both the Queen and her subjects. The greater part by far of English exports had habitually been marketed at Antwerp, and now Antwerp was shut. The events of 1564 had shown that only at a disagreeable pinch could an alternative mart be found at Emden; but even Emden, only just beyond the Netherlands frontier, was not now secure from a strike by Alva's military force. Gresham, visiting Antwerp at the time of the iconoclastic riots in 1566, had been alarmed by the threat they seemed to present to social and political stability, and so with some foresight negotiations had been pursued for reaching the consumers of English products through Hamburg, sufficiently far to the east to be safe from Spanish intervention. Accordingly from 1569 onwards convoys of English merchantmen, freighted by the Merchants Adventurers and escorted by royal warships, sailed each year up the Elbe to Hamburg, where, as far as the sale of cloths was concerned, the market proved reasonably satisfactory. There were, however, certain disadvantages, the most serious of which was the lack of the southern wares normally available at Antwerp, the terminus of a well-organised transcontinental trade route. Antwerp had also been the staple for oriental spices and drugs carried by Portuguese ships around Africa and transhipped from Lisbon. Thus not only were the luxury textiles of Italian origin scarce at Hamburg, but wares from the Far East were also missing. And, as the ports of Spain and of the Spanish-ruled parts of Italy were included in the embargo, there was a dearth of Iberian and Mediterranean wines and fruits.

The switching of cloth shipments to Hamburg instead of Antwerp was therefore accompanied by a rise in the prices of southern products at London. This tempted some Italian merchants resident in the City to reopen the sea route past Gibraltar to their own country. Their enterprise was encouraged by customs privileges from the government; English merchants, expecting similar favours, soon followed them, and before long discovered how in the Mediterranean there were markets not only for English cloth but also for Newfoundland cod and Cornish tin. But the political welcome for English ships in the Mediterranean was mixed. A few rulers, notably the Grand Duke of Tuscany, gladly encouraged the northerners. Others found them a nuisance. Their ways were too irregular and opportunist. Some slipped into profitable business as tramps or carriers, not always stopping short of piracy. A dispute with the Republic of Venice was kindled by the attempts of some English ships to take over traffic between Crete and other Venetian possessions and Venice itself, hitherto jealously reserved for Venetian shipping. Even before 1580, the Spanish envoy at London was denouncing the sales of tin to the Turks, who needed it for casting their guns. The English intruders did not seem always to be on the side of the Christians, and in fact a *rapprochement* to link the English and the Turks duly developed. Its most notable achievement was the foundation of the Levant Company, chartered by the Queen in 1581. Like the Company of Merchants Adventurers, it was simply an association of merchants; but it helped to finance the presence of an English ambassador accredited to the Sultan at Constantinople. This envoy also had a political role to play in Eastern Europe. By the early 1590s he was able to claim that he was helping to deflect Turkish military attention from Poland towards the Habsburg lands, to frustrate Spanish diplomacy, and to give some advantage to that of the Protestant King of France. It was a far cry from the days of Lepanto, a mere twenty years earlier, when the Christian victory had been celebrated by a solemn thanksgiving in the cathedral of London, followed by bonfires and banquets in the City.

The trade agreement with Hamburg which came fully into operation from 1569 suffered from defects that were significant though not immediately dangerous: the privileges granted to the Merchants Adventurers were to be valid only for ten years; and they were not liked by the other member cities of the Hanseatic League. The significance of the time limit became evident when traffic with Antwerp was reopened in 1573, for the provinces of Zeeland and Holland were now in obstinate rebellion against Philip II; and the lower reaches of the Scheldt estuary (i.e. the shipping-lane to Antwerp) were no longer safe for merchantmen. They were controlled in the name of the Prince of Orange by the Sea Beggars, a ruffianly lot whose survival depended upon the booty in money or goods they could exact from the ships they waylaid. They were not much concerned about the ownership of their prizes, whether Spanish, English or local. The Queen lent her authority to remonstrances but to little avail; and ultimately in 1582 the Merchants Adventurers, despairing of the chronic insecurity prevailing on the Scheldt and with the concurrence of the English government, moved their Netherlands mart downstream to the port of Middelburg, on the island of Walcheren, where order was enforced by the rebel Estates of Zeeland and the English coast was at hand. They had never, during the intervening years, dared to risk more than a fraction of their total shipments to the Scheldt route, and thus from 1573 were maintaining two distribution points, or mart towns, for their cloth. One was in the Netherlands, the other and more important one in Germany. This was reflected in the heightened diplomatic activity of the English government inside the Empire during the latter half of Elizabeth's reign.

Most English textiles accordingly continued to find their foreign market at Hamburg until the ten-year grant expired in 1577. Renewal posed problems and brought into prominence the second defect of the agreement: the city of Hamburg was not a free agent. It owed allegiance to the German Emperor, whose authority was distant and lightly exercised. More vital was its membership of the Hanseatic League, a confederation of towns for the advancement of trade, whose directing body was the Hanse Congress that met periodically at Lübeck. In the past, much English foreign trade had passed through the hands of Hansards, citizens of the member towns resident in England, where they enjoyed far-reaching privileges granted by successive English kings. These had been withdrawn in 1552; and in reply to Hanse requests Elizabeth, in 1560, had merely consented that Hansards should be treated on the same basis as Englishmen in her kingdom as long as English merchants were reciprocally welcomed in Hanse towns. This concession did not satisfy the Hanse Congress, which continued to seek a restoration of the privileges forfeited in 1552. The senators of Hamburg, in boldly offering rights to the Merchants Adventurers in 1567, had neglected to gain the assent of their sister towns, where the prosperity brought by the English merchants to their new mart provoked envy and resentment. So, as a result of Hanse pressure, Hamburg in 1577 renewed the privileges of the Merchants Adventurers for one year only, and then allowed them to lapse, despite English protests. In the prolonged struggle that now followed, Elizabeth was drawn deeply into the complex politics of northern Germany. She at once withdrew the fiscal privileges that since 1560 had been extended to Hanse merchants in England, until the Merchants Adventurers should be reinstated at Hamburg. Hanse retaliation was brusque. Negotiations were reopened in earnest in 1583, and only by the narrowest of margins was the renewal of English trading-rights at Hamburg not agreed in 1587, by when the international situation had become more sensitive owing to the outbreak of open Anglo-Spanish war.[9]

The Merchants Adventurers always expected to enjoy some guarantee of freedom and security for their organisation at the continental mart town where they met the traders who delivered English textiles to their consumers in the interior. The political authority of the Queen was involved in negotiations for such assurances; she was always concerned about the selection of a site, and in playing off one German town against another she shared with her merchants the services of her ministers and diplomats. When the privileges at Hamburg expired in 1578, the Merchants Adventurers managed to surmount their immediate problems by returning to Emden, which remained their headquarters in Germany until 1586. Emden was not a member of the Hanseatic League; the effective patrons of the English there were the local territorial princes Edzard and John, counts of East Friesland, who were encouraged by a pension and other favours from Elizabeth. Then in 1587 the Merchants Adventurers were induced to move their mart to Stade, a mile or two from the left bank of the lower Elbe, where buyers from Hamburg and elsewhere might conveniently pursue their business. Apart from some short-lived reuse of Emden in 1599–1602, the English cloth mart in Germany remained at Stade until after the death of Elizabeth. There were parallel happenings in the Baltic, though on a much smaller scale; there, the English patronised the insignificant port of Elbing at the expense of the Hanse metropolis of Danzig. A helping hand was sometimes extended to the Merchants Adventurers by the territorial princes of north Germany, many of whom had Protestant sympathies, reinforced in some cases by an interest in the supply of mercenaries to fight the troops of Philip II in France and Netherlands. Thus the fortunes of the English cloth trade and of the fighting further west were unobtrusively but effectively bound together.

In 1582 the towns of the Hanseatic League sought to entangle the Merchants Adventurers in the cumbrous toils of the imperial constitution by persuading the Diet to pass a resolution denouncing and expelling them as monopolists. The resolution was not ratified by the Emperor, who was little moved by Hanse opinion and perhaps swayed by the adroit diplomacy of George Gilpin, English envoy to the assembly. But the Anglo-Spanish war soon completed the immersion of the English cloth trade in high German politics. The Hanse patricians were not all of one mind, and in their attitude to the traffic in English textiles they were very divided. Many, especially at Hamburg, sought as middlemen to profit by it, and would have welcomed the return of the Merchants Adventurers. But others, especially at Lübeck, were more involved in the transport of corn, shipbuilding materials and other Baltic products to Spain and Portugal, where cereals and naval stores were in seriously short supply. It was a traffic vital for Spanish sea power. As early as November 1585, Elizabeth delivered a formal caution to the senators of Hamburg, warning them that in the event of Anglo-Spanish hostilities this trade, as a matter of English security, could not be allowed to continue.[10] In effect, this was an announcement of the English intention to enforce what in a later age would have been called a blockade.

The warning was repeated more than once. But it collided with a widespread expectation that the King of Spain, with his troops on the offensive in the Netherlands and his Armada under construction, would soon strike a deadly blow to the Queen of England and her pretensions. Hence one reason for the failure of Hamburg to come to terms with the Merchants Adventurers in 1587. However, with the scattering of the Armada the next year the blow was seen to miscarry. Then, in 1589, Drake and Norris were sent to the Spanish coast to disrupt any preparations to refit and renew the attack. After the departure of their ships, news reached England that a Hanse merchant fleet of sixty-odd sail was north of Scotland, *en route* for the Peninsula, laden with the prohibited wares. So an urgent order in the name of the Queen was on 18 May sent to the English fleet, now in Spanish waters, to intercept them.[11] The Hanse ships were located off the mouth of the Tagus, outside Lisbon, seized and promptly taken to Portsmouth, so that permitted cargoes might be separated from those liable to confiscation. There was some theft and embezzlement at first, but subsequently the officials at Portsmouth, under Admiralty control, went ahead methodically to identify the contraband goods, whether because they were on the list of prohibited commodities or belonged to Netherlanders and other subjects of Philip II.[12] It was a slow business, continuing into 1590 and even later.

The shock, anger and distress at Lübeck and other Hanse towns at this violent stroke may be imagined. The seizures served notice on all who sought to evade passage through the Channel, where English privateers were lurking, that the blockade was indeed being enforced. There were severe repercussions throughout the Baltic region, where commercial prosperity was closely linked to the commodity trade to Spain and the Mediterranean. At an early moment, Elizabeth decided to put pressure on the impending Hanse Congress at Lübeck by announcing the detention of Hanse ships until it should appear whether a spirit of revenge animated the delegates or not.[13] She followed this up by sending Dr Christopher Parkins in 1590 on a diplomatic mission to the

Baltic, where he spent a year in visiting centres of trade and politics from Copenhagen to Warsaw. At Lübeck he delivered a sharp lecture in Latin to the Hanse representatives in justification of the English seizures, and warned his audience against affording aid to Spain; in the new year, he wrote to the Congress in similar vein from Copenhagen.[14] His homilies may not have improved tempers, but they underlined the significance of English naval strength: Anglo-Hanse relations stood henceforth on a somewhat different footing. In subsequent years the blockade continued to be enforced, and in time reports of the high price of corn in Spain, and of the scarcity of shipbuilding materials too, filtered into St Jean-de-Luz.[15] So, while Hanse trade southwards was subject to surveillance and restriction, the English merchants were able to continue their traffic without much actual interference at Stade – with the sympathy of the Protestant princes of north Germany, whose goodwill Elizabeth did not cease to cultivate. The Emperor contributed something towards a lessening of tension in 1591, by consenting to refer the problem of the presence of the Merchants Adventurers to the next meeting of the Diet, some years ahead.

The Diet duly foregathered in 1594, and proved a more conciliatory assembly than its predecessor of 1582. But the efforts to negotiate some Anglo-Hanse compromise fell through. The Emperor, who now had a full-scale Turkish war on his hands in the Danube valley, was offended by the information, not entirely untrue but perhaps exaggerated by Spanish trouble-making, that the English were supplying weapons and encouragement to his enemies. Hanse pressure on him was maintained. Accordingly, he issued a decree, dated 1 August 1597, by which the Merchants Adventurers were banished from the Empire on the ground, originally put foward in 1582, that they were illegally operating a monopoly. This order could never be effectively enforced because English diplomacy was sufficiently agile to raise influential allies among the Protestant electors and other German princes; but during the years 1598–1601 the English merchants had to resort to subterfuge and to use Middelburg and Emden as well as Stade for their imports of cloth into Germany. Ultimately, in September 1602, with trade in recovery, the Queen sent envoys to negotiate with representatives of the Emperor a comprehensive settlement of all Anglo-German issues. Their instructions were flexible, and they were told to carry out their mission with the advice and consent of nominees of the Company of Merchants Adventurers.[16] The negotiations ultimately started at Bremen in February 1603, and bade fair to prove fruitful; but they were cut short by news of the death of Elizabeth the following month. Anglo-Hanse reconciliation was thus postponed for a year or so.

VI

To sum up. To dignify the dealings of Elizabeth Tudor and her continental neighbours with the title of 'foreign policy' perhaps suggests more than her often hesitant groping could substantiate. The sound but old-fashioned principles laid down by Paget at the outset of her reign lost their relevance in little more than a decade. With the collapse of the Antwerp mart in 1569–73, the English cloth trade was released from its traditional dependence upon the House of Burgundy, and the Queen and her merchants were forced in their various ways to extemporise. Left to fend for herself, she struck up an entente with the Valois princes of France and reluctantly took up the cudgels on behalf of the rebels of the Netherlands, thereby preserving the nearby littoral of north-west Europe from complete domination by her enemies. As for the merchants, they had to risk their stock-in-trade and search out new mart towns all around the coast of the continent. In support of their solvency the Queen posed as a sincere Protestant and extended her skimpy network of diplomacy to both the Baltic and Mediterranean regions. She never forgot that the money she had to find to pay her soldiers or to finance her allies was derived principally from the taxes and loans supplied by the London cloth-exporters, nor that the prosperity of the City of London was the mainstay of her credit and so of her authority in international affairs. From the days of Secretary Walsingham onwards, she has been criticised for her dilatory, vaccillating and stingy habits when dealing with overseas problems, charges to which modern historians from Froude onwards have added ill-placed reproaches at her unwillingness to promote ideals, whether as the champion of

Protestantism or as the godmother of a reconstructed and liberated Netherlands. Her objectives were prosaic and local, but practicable. Her success is to be measured by the survival of the cloth-export traffic to central Europe and by the maintenance of the royal credit on bourses abroad, as well as by the defeat of the Armada in 1588 and the bold seizure of the Hanse merchant fleet a year later. Her policy, whatever its shortcomings in execution, had worked. By the time of her death, her kingdom had weathered the threat of invasion, and her merchants the crisis of commercial interdiction.

7. The Elizabethan Church and the New Religion

PATRICK COLLINSON

For this is a high brag they have ever made, how that all antiquity and a continual consent of all ages doth make on their side; and that all our cases be but new and yesterday's work and until these few last years never heard of. Questionless, there can nothing be more spitefully spoken against the religion of God than to accuse it of novelty, as a new-come-up matter: for, as there can be no change in God himself, so ought there to be no change in his religion.

John Jewel, *An Apology of the Church of England* (1562)

I

PHILIP Stubbes was a Londoner, a gentleman and that new phenomenon of the Elizabethan age, a nearly professional author. He was also a thoroughly professional complainer, whose most successful book, *An Anatomy of Abuses* (1583), castigated the many diversions of Merrie England. Not long after the defeat of the Spanish Armada, Stubbes escaped from an outbreak of plague by mounting his horse to undertake a three-month exploration of England, 'This our noble island, in the bowels whereof, as in the womb of my mother, I was both bred and born', a delectable country lacking nothing 'save only good people'.[1] This grand tour provided particular grounds for complaint, what Thomas Nashe called more muck for a melancholic imagination,[2] in Stubbes's inspection of sundry provincial amenities: the schools, almshouses, highways and bridges which were the accumulated social credit of earlier centuries. The most common of these public utilities were the parish churches, many of them beautified and extended in the last decades before the Reformation with soaring towers or spires, spacious and well-lit naves and aisles. Even an incorrigible Protestant such as Stubbes was impressed. 'And for good works, who seeth not that herein they went far beyond us. . . . What memorable and famous buildings, what stately edifices of sundry kinds. . . . What churches, chapels and other houses of prayer did they erect. . . .!'[3]

Thirty years after the Elizabethan religious settlement of 1559, what was the condition of these noble edifices? According to Stubbes, 'lamentable': in most places more like barns than habitations of prayer. The roofs, which were thatched with straw, reeds or other 'rubbish', let in the rain 'without measure'. The floors consisted of sand or choking dust, at best covered with grass, sedge 'or other such trash'. Structural damage was often extensive. 'And as for the pews and seats, they are such as would make a man too loth to come in them.'[4]

One is tempted to make of this remorseless catalogue of neglect a paradigm for the whole state of religion in the Elizabethan age. But the literature of complaint, like all forms of Elizabethan writing, was subject to rhetorical conventions, in this case the convention of hyperbolic indignation. Things are not likely to have been as bad as Stubbes made them out to be, not 'in most places, nay almost in all'. Nevertheless, modern tourists can use their own eyes to confirm that the later sixteenth century was better at pulling churches down than at putting them up. In Canterbury, the young Christopher Marlowe must have played around the steeple of the dissolved abbey of St Augustine, which lay awkwardly on the tilt, where it had fallen. Later this may have provided an image for *Tamburlaine*: that pillar of fair Babylon which made 'a bridge unto the battered walls'.[5] Even in London, there were many vacant lots where Shakespeare could have observed those 'bare ruin'd choirs where late the sweet birds sang'. On the architectural evidence and that of the inventories detailing their domestic possessions, Elizabethans of all classes invested in the building and furnishing of more comfortable houses for themselves, rather than in enriching the house of God. One might conclude that this was not a generation of faith or even of much serious interest in religion but an age as far gone in secularity and materialism as our own.

But, whereas it is proper to measure the strength of pre-Reformation religious sentiment by its material remains, it would be a mistake to gauge the quality of post-Reformation religion by the same criterion. For late medieval Catholics, the church itself was a sacred place, containing sacred objects charged with meaning, among them the symbol of the crucifix which stood aloft on a great beam, flanked with life-size images of the Virgin Mary and St John. In Catholic ritual, eyes were exercised rather than ears and were drawn beyond the 'rood' to the altar, where the clergy raised the elements of bread and wine at the moment when they became the body and blood of Christ in the mystery of the mass, a daily sacrifice atoning for the sins of those assisting at it. But Protestantism exposed the imagination to the invisible Word. It was a religion of plentiful prayers uttered in the name of a still and seated congregation and of readings from the English Bible: above all a religion of the sermon. At its heart, in the place of the elevated host, was a tale of bottomless human depravity from which the Christian man was lifted and redeemed without any merit or religious 'work' but by a God-given faith, that true and lively faith in Christ which was capable of sustaining a life of thankful and fruitful obedience to God's commandments. Those who found themselves in this way of salvation were taught that they had been chosen, 'elect' by God from the very foundation of the world. Consequently, these 'saints' had no need to fear for their ultimate redemption, although some anxious souls did. But the godless behaviour of others was nearly conclusive evidence of their exclusion from God's mercy. The sacraments of baptism and the Lord's Supper still held an important symbolic place in Protestantism, but for the purpose of such a religion the liturgical principles implicit in medieval church buildings were irrelevant and were disregarded in the common practice of filling every vacant space with high-walled box pews, 'convenient' seats which were allotted in order of rank and property to the heads of households and their families. Later programmes of restoration and adaptation have removed from all but a very few parish churches this not always unsightly evidence of the religious temper of the new age, which Stubbes disparaged when he complained that religion was now 'nothing else but plain talking'. A generation later, a Norfolk preacher spoke sarcastically of Christians who had turned all their organs into ears, 'for nothing else but hearing of sermons'.[6]

This was unfair. Protestants too saw themselves as builders, but the buildings they erected consisted of godly lives, their materials not bricks and mortar but hearts and minds literally 'edified' by the preaching of the Gospel. According to their beloved St Paul, such 'lively stones' were 'built upon the foundation of the apostles and prophets, Jesus Christ himself being the chief cornerstone, in whom all the building, fitly framed together, groweth unto an holy temple in the Lord'. 'Ye are God's building', St Paul told the unruly Corinthians: 'which thing you are not', continued the Protestant martyr John Bradford, 'but by the mason-work of God, hacking and hewing from you by the cross the knobs and crooked corners.' This scriptural metaphor, with its roots in the Old Testament, implied a task energetically undertaken, frustrated by opposition, and always far from completion. The Bishop of Durham, James Pilkington, himself a returned Marian exile, found much that applied to the Elizabethan Church in the prophet Nehemiah's account of the rebuilding of Jerusalem after the return of Israel from Babylon; 'As the building of this Jerusalem had many enemies, so the glorious Gospel of Christ Jesus hath many more.' So through the spectacles of this *topos* the historian gathers a dynamic but still pessimistic impression of the progress of the new religion.[7]

On the evidence of Elizabethan Lancashire, a frontier for the new religion and in its western parts Indian territory, Christopher Haigh has proposed that, as a missionary impulse, the English Reformation was mostly a failure. The causes were both systemic, a matter of inappropriate institutions and inadequate funding, and personal, the all-too-human weakness of clerics who were more interested in their own careers than in the conversion and cure of souls. But there was also a significant cultural reason for failure, in that Protestantism was an intellectually demanding and aggressive doctrine which threatened the traditional way of life, and especially the sporting-life enjoyed in Lancashire.[8] There is support for this critique in the analyses of the preachers themselves, which assure us that the truly religious were few and that churches often stood empty while pubs, betting-shops and theatres were full to bursting.[9] An Essex preacher reported that at country sermons it was a case of 'in at the one ear and out at the other'. A Lancashire minister complained that for every worshipper there were hundreds of dancers on the echoing green. But both made their observations in the course of expounding the Parable of the Sower, the point of which is that only a little of the seed falls on good ground. 'Of this great heap and rabblement of people that were so zealous and travelled so far to hear [Jesus], there were three parts which did not profit by his doctrine but continued still damned and forlorn creatures. Only one part of four are true scholars.' 'People hear much, learn little and practise less.'[10]

It remains likely that on Sunday mornings, if not in the afternoons or on holy days, most people with any stock in the local community took their places in church. Law, custom and convenience required it. What they made of the service and of the sermon we cannot say. We shall never know enough about the inmost thoughts of 'most people'. But a contemporary description of the Church of the Elizabethan Settlement as 'a constrained union' of papists and Protestants is very plausible, as is the claim of the Puritan divine Thomas Cartwright that there were 'heaps' of people who had cast aside the old religion without discovering the new. 'Why tell ye me of the pope?' asks an Essex villager in a fictitious but credible conversation from the middle years of the reign. 'I care not for him. I would both he and his dung were buried in the dunghill.' But the same man spurned the message of the preachers. According to George Gifford, the creator of this character, such men were not 'rank papists' but they retained 'still a smack and savour of popish principles'. In Kent, Josias Nichols made a practice, when he went into other parishes or when strangers came into his own, of finding out what people knew and believed. What he usually found was a kind of folk religion, expressing a Pelagian faith in the social virtues but not even an elementary understanding of the Protestant path to salvation.[11]

It was, said Cartwright, only a remnant 'of us' who had truly and faithfully believed. This was admittedly the opinion of a Puritan Calvinist who supposed that only the predestinate, a minority, could hope to be saved. But it was the sense of isolation in a sea of hostile indifference which encouraged Puritans such as Cartwright to consider themselves a religious remnant. Their ambition was still to convert or constrain the whole nation into at least the semblance of a godly people, an elect nation on the model of biblical Israel. It was beyond their imaginative powers to think of religion as it is with us, a sectional and voluntary undertaking. Yet the practical effect of their applied theology was to divide the nation against itself by calling into existence a converted, religiously serious subculture which contrasted starkly with the lax and nominal Christianity of the majority. Protestants in this complete sense used none of the traditional Catholic oaths which still punctuated everyday discourse. They thought it scandalous that the church should be used for ordinary social gatherings, buying and selling, drinking and fund-raising. But, when their hostility to 'good fellowship' drove people into the 'little hell' of the alehouse, they declined to follow. Within their own houses they maintained a daily routine of religious 'exercises', prayer, Bible-reading and catechising. Their robust singing of the Psalms of David in simple metre and to rousing tunes carried to the outside world through doors and windows and accompanied their demonstrative progresses to sermons, which they attended on working-days and in other parishes. In a society bound by custom, convention and conformity, this strange conduct was offensive. Men standing in the street denounced it and complained about 'Puritans'. According to a Suffolk writer, the sermon-goers were mobbed like owls in the daytime.[12]

And so the progressive internalisation of the Protestant Reformation was making a religious divide, or, as it were, a series of corrugations across the face of a country which in the past had been relatively homogeneous in its religious belief and practice. Deep in one furrow, almost invisible, lay that minority which chose to exclude itself by its principled, consistent practice of a modified version of the old religion. That is the subject of another chapter in this book. But, as Dr Haigh shows, the emergent community of Catholic recusants shades into a more amorphous and doubtless more numerous element of 'church papists', people whose religious outlook would have been more easily accommodated within a framework of

Catholic rites but who were not openly resistant to the law. In contemptuous Puritan perception, these were 'statute Protestants', 'injunction men', 'such as jump with the Queen's laws'.[13] Where do we draw the line of the next furrow, how indeed can any firm line be drawn, between such 'neuters' and those sincere but equally undemonstrative Protestants for whom the Prayer Book services were already settled habits of life and a source of comfort? No wonder so many historians have looked beyond to the next ridge, where the Puritans sit sunning themselves in open view!

The task of the religious historian of England between the Elizabethan Settlement and the Civil War is thus one of daunting complexity, if he is to confront the entire scene, with all these configurations. Somehow he must describe two almost antithetical processes: on the one hand, the emergence of a growing diversity in religious culture; on the other, the simultaneous adoption by a major section of the nation of a consensual Protestantism closely connected to a sense of national identity and to principles of civil obedience and deference, edged with a frank hostility for Catholic foreign powers and for the Pope himself. The late Victorian pioneer of social history, J. R. Green, sensed a moral and cultural revolution in the late sixteenth and early seventeenth centuries which he believed to have been national in scope: 'No greater moral change ever passed over a nation than passed over England during the years which parted the middle years of Elizabeth from the meeting of the Long Parliament. England became the people of a book, and that book was the Bible.'[14]

How can we be so sure about the mind of 'a nation', of 'England'? 'England' in the 1630s and 1640s seems to have repudiated by a large majority both 'popery' and the 'Arminian' tendency which was suspect as popery in thin disguise; only to reject in the 1640s and 1650s those more extreme forms of Puritanism which threatened the foundations of the established Church from the opposite direction. Evidently by the mid seventeenth century much of 'England' was well grounded in its Protestantism and its Anglicanism. But sizeable minorities of religious extremists existed outside the consensus, both in reality and even more in the enlarged and distorted perceptions of their opponents. Protestants who leant towards

Puritanism suspected a papist under every bed. Protestants whose views were in sober truth not very dissimilar but who inclined towards an 'Anglican' conformism were equally alarmed by the bogey of 'Anabaptists' and sectaries. These antipathies, real and imagined, did much to impel the nation into civil war, a war which, said Richard Baxter, was begun in our streets before the King and the Parliament had any armies.[15]

We have strayed beyond the legitimate scope of this essay and out of the period covered by the volume in order to indicate the destination to which this critical, Elizabethan chapter of the English Reformation was tending: a Protestant nation containing deep tension and potential confusion within an outward shell of consensus. But at what point in the reign of Elizabeth or in its sequel had such a nation recognisably emerged? On the eve of her coronation, London displayed itself to the youthful Queen as a Protestant city, greeting her as Deborah, 'the judge and restorer of Israel' (Judges 4–5), presenting her with an English Bible and confronting her with a dumb show in which Pure Religion trod Ignorance and Superstition underfoot. 'So that, on either side, there was nothing but gladness, nothing but prayer! nothing but comfort!'[16] But London was not England and the history of the reign is, from one aspect, the story of the incomplete imposition of London ways on the provinces, through cultural influences which included the English Bible and the Protestant sermon. Noting that Preston consistently escaped bubonic plague between the Black Death of 1348 and the year 1630, Dr Haigh suggests, 'West Lancashire was insulated from dangerously contagious radical ideas as it was insulated from dangerously contagious diseases.'[17]

Presently that immensely influential writer, the martyrologist John Foxe, in his ambitious work of history *Acts and Monuments of the Church*, would condition his readers to a Protestant understanding of their nation's past, its recent excoriating experience under Mary, and its future destiny. It seems unlikely that 'Foxe's Book of Martyrs' had many readers in Preston. But by 1603 the combined effects of Foxe, the growing army of preachers and the Bible, interacting as a living commentary with the dramatic and religiously coloured events of the reign, had made some difference in other places. J. R.

Green's moral revolution, though doubtless still in its earlier stages, was by then irreversible, unlike the abortive reformation of Edward's reign. How had this been achieved?

II

Historians of the English Reformation describe it as a double-process, part official, part unofficial, reformation from above and below. That is to say, a formal distinction is made between the imposition by the government of statutory religious forms and the capacity of the new faith to make its own headway, almost regardless of politics. The dichotomy is true to a fundamental ambiguity in the nature of Protestantism itself, on the one hand lending itself to the purposes of an interventionist and paternalistic Tudor state, on the other having the capacity to energise the intellectual and active capacities of private persons in insubordinate agitation.

This is a useful theoretical tool but in practice the distinction constantly breaks down. The influence of preachers and other Protestant agents depended much upon patronage and other forms of political support, or on the public offices they occupied, or simply on the general identification of Protestantism with the interest of the state. (Yet religion was a potent force even when deprived of these advantages, as witness the history of Protestants under Mary and of Catholics under Elizabeth.) Conversely, the protestantising policy of the Elizabethan government would have made less impression as mere coercion, without the willing co-operation of Protestant activists. As for those in positions of some ecclesiastical authority, and especially that first generation of Elizabethan bishops who had returned from the Marian exile, they were in this respect amphibians, partaking of both the official and unofficial reformations. By virtue of an authority inherent in their office but effectively delegated from the Crown, they promoted a religious policy which was more their own than the Crown's and which partly derived from the unofficial Reformation.

Given the theme of his book *The Tudor Régime*, it was proper for Penry Williams's account of 'The Establishment of Protestantism' to concentrate on the imposition of the new faith from above. And it is also understandable that the historian of *Religion and Society in Elizabethan Sussex*, a backward county, should call his book 'A Study of the Enforcement of the Religious Settlement'.[18] But in this account of the new religion the emphasis will lie on the informal reformation from below, on evangelism rather than enforcement.

As every schoolboy used to know, what was enforced in the Elizabethan Church was not very much. Contrary to what the schoolboy was taught, it was Francis Bacon and not the Queen herself who spoke of her reluctance to make windows in men's souls, but the famous aphorism accurately encapsulates the limited aims of Elizabethan Church policy, seeking outward submission to the legally established religion rather than a willing, knowledgeable and conscientious assent to its propositional content. That is not to suggest that this degree of compliance was easy to obtain. It took great resources of constraint and patronage to sap rather than destroy the political strength of Catholic resistance.

The Act of Uniformity of 1559 followed the pioneering example of an earlier statute of 1552 in securing attendance at church by the force and sanction of secular law. But the statute assumed that enforcement would primarily concern the ecclesiastical authorities, the churchwardens who were empowered to impose the fine, not inconsiderable for wage-earners, of a shilling for each absence, and the Church courts which were to be alerted in cases of persistent truancy. In fact the records of these courts show that a very small proportion of the cases brought to their attention concerned simple absence from church, so few prosecutions for this offence that they provide the historian with no indication of the true extent of absenteeism; while it seldom occurred to ecclesiastical official-dom that the reason for absence might lie in mental disagreement with the Church's doctrine. The articles of inquiry in episcopal visitations asked about the outward conduct indicative of religious deviance, but instituted no searching investigation into the nature of the deviance itself. Evidently the jurisdiction of the Church did not exist to discover what individuals believed, still less to enforce or change belief. That is to say, it was not a form of inquisition, 'never fitted', wrote a

Scottish critic, 'for the reclaiming of minds'.[19] The principal corrective function of those courts with which the generality of the population had dealings, the archdeacon's court and the episcopal or 'consistory' court, was the exercise of what social historians summarise as 'social control', enforcing the accepted norms of sexual and marital conduct and restraining other forms of behaviour which were as antisocial as they were irreligious.

An exception must be made for Catholic belief, which later Elizabethan legislation came close to defining as a crime in itself, for in principle, and from time to time in practice, this earned the most fearful penalties. But while many, and perhaps most, Catholics escaped punitive treatment altogether, Catholicism remained, in effect, almost the only 'heresy' in which any persistent interest was taken, and in the perception of the government 'popery' represented potential or actual treason rather than heresy. It is hardly an exaggeration to say that the historian of Elizabethan religion knows little about the true nature of popular belief, since such belief was only rarely and sporadically a matter of official concern and searching inquiry.

The titles of the *Homilies*, or prepared sermons prescribed for public reading in church, are indicative of a similar order of priorities. It is true that several homilies are theological in content, some of them the work of Archbishop Cranmer and nearly perfect, if cautious, expressions of Protestant belief concerning salvation, faith and good works. But these are more than balanced by a preponderance of addresses on themes of social morality and civil discipline: disobedience and wilful rebellion, contention and brawling, 'the right use of the church or temple of God and of the reverence due unto the same'. With harsh irony, the Puritan authors of the *Admonition to the Parliament* (1572) asked, 'Are not the people well modified [*sic*] think you, when the homily of sweeping the church is read unto them?'[20]

It would be foolish to deny to either the *Homilies* or the *Book of Common Prayer* the capacity to distil and drop into the mind, almost by an osmotic process, familiar forms of words which may have done more than anything else to form a Protestant consciousness: 'Because all men be sinners and offenders against God . . .'; 'We do not presume to come to this thy table

(O merciful Lord) trusting in our own righteousness but in thy manifold and great mercies . . .'; 'O God, forasmuch as without thee we are not able to please thee. . . .' These too were instruments of conversion to a moderate, balanced faith, part old part new. Yet the Elizabethan Church, on the evidence of its public documents, appears to have been less concerned with a converting mission than with the conservation of an ideal but in many ways traditional vision of Christian order, for which the principles of Protestantism provided a fresh rationale and foundation. This was not quite the same form of 'godliness' as 'the godly', the more enthusiastic and committed of Elizabethan Protestants, sought to promote.

III

Nevertheless, Protestantism was a new religion wheresoever and for whomsoever it represented a new and authentic discovery. Protestant controversialists themselves denied that it was in any sense new, but, as has been said of Martin Luther at the moment of his discovery of its doctrinal heart, the Gospel, 'it was new for him'. It was new for Thomas Bilney and Hugh Latimer in the 1520s, new for rural villagers as late as the 1620s. When, in about 1575, the minister of a Derbyshire mining community found himself in trouble with the bishops for nonconformity, two aged colliers appeared in court to testify that they had lived as 'ignorant and obstinate papists' until, with the arrival of a preacher in their midst, they had 'attained to a comfortable feeling of their salvation in Christ'. More than thirty years on, a Puritan divine of some note, Samuel Crook, was 'planted' in the village of Wrington, in a quarter of Somerset hitherto innocent of Protestant preaching. In the terms of a pious platitude which tells us little about the real response of the local peasantry, it was said that his sermons disclosed 'the Heavenly *Canaan*, which before was to most of them a *terra incognita*, as an unknown land'. Twenty years later, in the 1620s, preachers were distributed in Somerset in about the density which had been achieved in Suffolk in 1570. But in the Welsh-border counties, pockets of dereliction persisted, strings of parishes still served by elderly or otherwise incompetent clerics, unable or unwilling to preach and perhaps with nothing to say if they could.[21] As for the principality itself, it was considered (to use a twentieth-century French term) as *pays de mission* as late as the period of the Puritan Commonwealth.

The Act of Parliament of 1650 which set up commissioners and channelled funds 'for the better propagation and preaching of the Gospel' in Wales, is evidence in itself of the late persistence of the primary evangelical impulse of the English Reformation. It was also almost without precedent for Parliament or any other public agency to assume strategic responsibility for the 'advancement' of the Gospel. In Elizabeth's reign the provision of a 'godly preaching ministry' was a major preoccupation of many members of the House of Commons, but as parliamentarians the only steps they contemplated were defensive, to protect from episcopal interference those preachers already in place, whom they and their friends had 'planted' through piecemeal acts of patronage. As for the Queen herself, she shocked Archbishop Grindal by suggesting that three or four preachers were sufficient for a shire.[22] It was in the absence of any governmental programme for the establishment of a fully qualified, standardised preaching ministry, adequately financed, that maximum scope was allowed to a more informal and unauthorised evangelism. In view of its often voluntary and even irregular features, this enterprise has been classified by historians as an aspect of 'Puritanism', thus representing it as a secondary, reactive episode, separate from the primary thrust of the Protestant Reformation of which it was properly a part. So-called 'Puritan evangelism' was nothing less than the full internalisation, for elements of English society, of the implications of the religion founded by Luther, Calvin and the fathers of the English Reformation.

In this as in all ages there were more ways than one to 'get religion'. According to the testimony of the famous seventeenth-century divine Richard Baxter, his father, a Shropshire gentleman whose youthful taste for gambling had brought him down in the world, was 'changed' by what his son calls 'the bare reading of the Scriptures in private'. What deflected the elder Baxter from gaming to Bible study we cannot say, unless it was the shame of his own folly. Such inner motives would occupy the novelist in whole chapters but are hidden from the historian. But Baxter is insistent that his father's conversion owed nothing to 'either preaching, or godly company, or any other books but the Bible'.[23] Others, like John Bunyan in a later generation, were deflected towards religion by those 'other books'.[24] As early as King Edward's time Protestants were won over by 'little new-fangled two-penny books'.[25] By the late Elizabethan period, the book market was well supplied with a variety of those works of religious edification considered 'practical', some of them cheap enough to find a place in the packs of travelling chapmen. By then another item popular with the booksellers was the catechism, providing a basic religious education in a nutshell. Scores of little unauthorised catechisms competed in a free market, a few destined to run to thirty or forty editions. These were not so much books to be read as tools to be applied by householders who took their religious responsibilities towards their children and servants seriously, and perhaps occasionally with pedagogical sensitivity. 'Stay somewhat for an answer, but not too long', advised a professional catechist in giving advice not to be despised by the modern university or sixth-form teacher. 'If one know not, ask another: if any but stammer at it, help him and encourage him by commending his willingness.'[26]

In countless cases of which we have no record, 'godly company' was the key, what the separatist leader Robert Browne in about 1582 called 'talking, pleading and mutual edifying' among kindred and friends. His colleague Robert Harrison told a Norfolk clergyman that, while he might boast of the parenthood of his spiritual children, the truth was that these 'children' had begotten each other 'by fruitful edifying of gracious speech and godly conference'.[27] So it had been long before the official Reformation, in the conventicles and whispered secrets which communicated the Lollard heresy and sustained it for more than a century of intermittent persecution.

Yet even Robert Browne doubted the possibility of finding salvation without the help of a preacher. His friend Harrison suggested that sometimes faith could be wrought by the mere reading of the Scriptures. 'R. B. said, no. For though it might be nourished and increased by such reading, yet the first working thereof is by hearing the word preached.'[28] An up-to-date social historian might be tempted by such a text to speculate about the persistence of a form of 'oral culture' at the very moment when 'print culture' was ostensibly triumphant. What Browne said was certainly common orthodoxy, for St Paul had asked, 'How shall they hear without a preacher?' 'Public and continual preaching', Archbishop Grindal told the Queen, was 'the ordinary mean and instrument of the salvation of mankind'. 'God forbid, Madam, that you should . . . any way go about to diminish the preaching of Christ's Gospel.'[29]

With the Puritans it became a shibboleth that the 'bare reading' of 'lessons' in church, 'this seely reading', was a 'dead letter' – even worse, said that intemperate pamphlet the *Admonition to the Parliament*, than playing on a stage, since actors at least learned their parts by heart. 'Reading is not feeding.' In taking this hard line the Puritans were in odd company, for the Catholic controversialist Thomas Harding had accused the Protestant Church of England of encouraging 'spiritual dumbness' by its policy of reading the Bible to passive congregations, replacing 'holy thinking' with 'unprofitable hearkening'. The *Second Admonition* admitted that to read from the Bible was better than to read homilies which were 'popish and fond', but still insisted that 'the ministry of faith is the preaching of the same out of the Word of God by them that are sent of God'. Thomas Cartwright, defending what his opponent John Whitgift dismissed as an absurd position, boldly declared that 'the bare reading of the Scriptures without the preaching cannot deliver so much as one poor sheep from destruction and from the wolf'. For the preacher was much more than a communicator or instructor. He stood in the pulpit as the inspired impersonation of Christ: the very 'mouth of God', wrote Edward Dering, 'in whose person Christ himself is either refused or received'. It was in accordance with this convention that the preachers of Elizabethan Lancashire were called the 'planters or founders of religion in these parts'.[30]

This may be of some comfort to the historian of the Elizabethan Reformation who knows that, while preaching was not the only or even necessarily the most effective means by which the new religion was disseminated, it is the only one whose progress he can hope to map and tabulate.

IV

According to the dubious authority of the *Admonition*, in the 'old Church' of the half-mythical, apostolic age, 'the ministers were preachers: now bare readers'. 'Then, as God gave utterance, they preached the word only: now they read homilies, articles, injunctions etc.' Parliament was told: you must appoint to every congregation a learned and diligent preacher. This Cartwright defended as a 'moral law of God'.[31] Puritan extremists who rejected the ministry of non-preachers as no ministry at all, and their parishes as no churches, were pursuing this 'law' to a logical conclusion.

On the other side stood official ecclesiastical policy as defined in the Royal Injunctions of 1559 and subsequently elaborated by the bishops collectively in synod and individually in their visitation articles and injunctions. This was by no means silent on the subject of preaching. The Injunctions required a 'comely and honest pulpit' to be provided in every church and somewhat confusingly instructed the parish clergy ('all ecclesiastical persons having cure of souls') to provide four sermons a year 'at the least' and also sermons every month, again 'at the least', leading bishops in their visitations to inquire very frequently whether the parishes had received their 'quarter sermons' (and churchwardens to answer very often that they lacked them) and more rarely to ask after monthly sermons.[32] The matter was tidied up in the Canons of 1604, which required all beneficed clergy who were licensed preachers to preach one sermon every Sunday and others to procure one sermon a month to be made by a licensed preacher if, in the bishop's opinion, his living could stand the considerable expense of twelve sermons at half a mark each. The 1604 Canons speak of preaching, in terms acceptable to any Puritan, as soberly and sincerely dividing the word of truth to the glory of God and the best edification of the people.

But forty-five years earlier the Injunctions had understood by sermons setpiece 'collations' on prescribed subjects, not unlike the homilies which were to be read on other occasions in lieu of a sermon. The theme of the quarter sermons was to be papal usurpation (but surely not for ever and ever?); of the monthly sermons the works of faith, mercy and charity, contrasted with the superstitious 'fantasies' which were said to pass for good works in Catholicism. This was Protestant preaching of a kind, but not the 'lively' preaching, 'in season and out of season', 'as God gave utterance', envisaged by the Puritans: salutary instruction rather than 'edification' in the full Pauline sense.

Moreover, the Injunctions restricted the office of preaching to licensed preachers, who by implication would be university graduates holding at least the degree of Master of Arts. All other ministers were to content themselves with reading homilies and were to provide what Archbishop Parker's 'Advertisements' called 'a learned substitute' to preach the legal minimum of sermons. In the early Elizabethan Church graduate clergy of the rank of MA were everywhere scarce and in some dioceses almost non-existent. It was later recalled that men with these qualifications could set their sights above parish employment and hope for a deanery or something as good.[33] In the diocese of Worcester only 19 per cent of the beneficed clergy had any kind of degree in 1560, although the proportion was as high as 38 per cent in the diocese of Oxford, with its proximity to the university. But the majority of these would have been BAs. At first things got worse rather than better. At Chester only one graduate presented himself for ordination in ten years, one of 282 ordinands![34] There was such an absolute shortage of clergy in the early Elizabethan Church that the bishops were obliged to lay hands on large numbers of poorly qualified candidates, in many cases artisans or other 'men of occupation'. When even this failed to produce a sufficient supply of priests and deacons to fill the vacant parishes, it was necessary to resurrect the inferior order of 'lector' or 'reader' as an emergency measure.[35] Consequently, except in London and a few other favoured localities, the three or four preachers to a shire desired by Queen Elizabeth may have been the norm and even the legal minimum of quarter sermons was an impossible dream.

John Whitgift confronted the Admonitioners with stark reality. 'I wish that every minister were a preacher; but, that being unpossible as the state is now, I see not how you can condemn reading ministers, seeing reading is necessary in the Church, and faith cometh as well by reading the Scriptures in the book as by rehearsing of them without book.' That was sensible but also disingenuous, since for his opponents preaching meant much more than 'rehearsing' Scripture without book. Cartwright retorted, 'I hope you do not of purpose keep the Church in this estate.'[36] That was grossly unfair. As the leading figure in the affairs of Cambridge University, Whitgift was as concerned as anyone for the ecclesiastical promotion of graduates: and with such eventual success that in the course of the following decades the clergy began to assume the general aspect of a learned profession. Some bishops hand-picked outstanding recruits to the ministry, ordaining them on special and private occasions and placing them, so far as their limited powers of patronage permitted, in market towns and other strategic parishes. Edmund Grindal, for example, pursued this policy in London in the early 1560s, and later, as Archbishop of York, he 'procured' more than forty learned graduates and preachers to serve in his backward diocese. Some of these were the men who by 1620 had transformed the religious culture of the West Riding of Yorkshire.[37] Cartwright was also unfair to the system, in that the Royal Injunctions laid the foundations of a programme of in-service education for the underqualified clergy on which successive bishops and the Puritans themselves proceeded to build. To this we shall return. The bishops may not have agreed on all points with the more extreme Puritans as to the necessity and the objectives of the preaching-ministry, but they were equally concerned to bring into existence a learned ministry.

Nevertheless, the ever-realistic Whitgift, by then Archbishop of Canterbury, calculated in 1584 that a mere 7 per cent of parishes, scarcely 600 out of almost 9000, yielded an income capable of attracting and supporting a man with higher academic qualifications.[38] To establish a 'godly, learned, preaching ministry' it was necessary to do more than tell Parliament 'you must'. The intractable fact was that the Church was starved of resources, especially through the impropriation and diversion to other persons and uses of the revenues of thousands of parishes, an abuse which James I, unlike Elizabeth I, recognised but failed to remedy. Nevertheless, Whitgift was overpessimistic. Clerical incomes were capable of expansion or of supplementation. In the year Queen

Elizabeth died, more than half the beneficed clergy of the vast diocese of Lincoln were already graduates, 646 out of 1184, and not three or four but 712 were licensed preachers, while among the remainder were many 'well able to catechise and privately to exhort', if lacking the ability and 'audacity' to preach from the pulpit. By 1603 the standards of learning achieved in this diocese before the Reformation had been far exceeded.[39]

In practice Elizabethan Protestants of a Puritan outlook were obliged to be no less realistic than the authorities, cutting their coats according to the cloth and making use of such ability and audacity to preach as might be available. In the history of Elizabethan and Jacobean preaching we can distinguish four more or less distinct stages, not all reached in the same decade or even half-century in every diocese or county, and the fourth of these stages not necessarily attained at all in all places. The first of these was the 'apostolic' stage of occasional, itinerant preaching. The second saw preaching established and even concentrated in a number of centres, especially in the characteristic mid-Elizabethan institution of the 'prophesying', destined to remain a permanent feature of religious life for another century in the modified form of the 'combination lecture'. At the third stage, and partly as a result of the modest success of the prophesyings, a preaching-ministry was established in a great number of market towns and rural parishes, roughly in the same density as the grammar schools and often in the same places, so that it was no less feasible for those with the will and means to do so to 'gad' to sermons than for schoolboys to trudge to school. Finally the stage was reached when it could be said that sermons were 'common in this realm'.[40] In the more 'civil' counties and above all in London most parishioners could expect to hear a sermon Sunday by Sunday from the pulpit of their own parish church. Whether or not they found it acceptable was, of course, another question.

The Royal Injunctions themselves relied for the provision of a skeleton preaching-service on an itinerant, almost irregular ministry; recommending the reading of homilies 'unless some other preacher sufficiently licensed . . . chance to come to the parish for the same purpose of preaching', whereupon the officers of the parish were to receive him 'gladly', 'without any resistance or contradiction'. What Puritans themselves later came to regard with suspicion as a 'roving' apostolate, no part of the settled economy of a rightly reformed Church, seems to have been the principal means of propagating the new religion in the early years of the English Reformation. There are familiar examples in the preaching-tours made by Thomas Bilney in East Anglia and later by John Bland in east Kent, John Bradford in the Manchester area and, elsewhere in Lancashire, by George Marsh, the future Bishop Pilkington, Thomas Lever and Henry Pendleton; while such a giant as Hugh Latimer had ten-league boots which carried him on more extensive journeys.[41] In Yorkshire the avant-garde Sir Francis Bigod formed what the racing-fraternity might call a 'string' of preachers whom he conducted around the country, while nursing the ambition to climb up into the pulpit with them.[42]

In Edward's reign, itinerant preaching was intended to proceed by a kind of royal appointment. The young King noted in his diary that, of six especially appointed chaplains, only two were to be in attendance at any one time, while the remaining four were to be 'always absent in preaching', travelling circuits which were to begin with the most needy areas, Lancashire, Derbyshire and Wales. This scheme was abortive, although it was partly revived late in Elizabeth's reign in the appointment and public funding of four royal preachers in Lancashire.[43] Bishop Nicholas Ridley half complained, half boasted that he could not keep the preaching canons of St Paul's with him in London. John Bradford, John Rogers and Edmund Grindal were forever absent on preaching sorties into the country parts of his diocese.[44]

After the hiatus of Mary's reign, when preachers moved around the country more discreetly, the Edwardian itinerant tradition revived as a necessity and, perhaps, as an expedient for unorthodox and unconventional preachers who were otherwise unprovided for. The active, Bigod-like encouragement of influential patrons was now much in evidence and probably involved both financial and political sponsorship. In 1567 six prominent Suffolk gentlemen wrote to the Archbishop of Canterbury in support of John Laurence, a gentleman of independent means without any ecclesiastical standing and perhaps not even in orders, but the only preacher for twenty miles to the north and ten miles to the east of Ipswich, 'in the

which circuit he was wont to travel'. We hear of the aged
Henrician priest of one Suffolk parish who left the church when
Laurence preached but was enjoined by the Bishop to hear him
'at his next coming thither'.[45] In early Elizabethan Kent, the
records of the archdeacon's court allow fleeting, but from the
court's point of view wholly sympathetic, glimpses of a blind
preacher passing through the partly hostile villages of the
Weald, 'divers honest men' with him, another preacher at
Goudhurst competing valiantly with dancing at the market
cross, and a third being shouted down by the wife of the richest
clothier in Cranbrook.[46] In Herefordshire in the late 1570s, the
only sermons heard at Lyonshall were provided by a native of
the place, Walter Stephens, who was one of the first preaching
ministers in Shropshire. On his regular return visits to his
birthplace the ploughmen were said to unhitch their teams
crying 'Away to church! Mr Stephens is come!'[47] When Bishop
Richard Curteys arrived in the backward county of Sussex at
about the same time he brought from Cambridge as many as
twenty university men and besides helping to settle them into
parishes led them on preaching-tours through this county,
which was both physically and socially intractable. It was said
that he had 'gone three times through this whole diocese of
Chichester, . . . preaching himself at the greatest towns'. Since
in his predecessor's time, it had been 'a rare thing' to hear a
sermon in Sussex, we may confidently date the beginnings of
the real rather than nominal reformation of the county from
about 1570.[48]

Some of Bishop Curteys's preaching-engagements were
fulfilled in the course of the so-called 'exercise of prophesying',
which his arrival in Sussex helped to promote at both
Chichester and Lewes. An alternative to bringing the preacher
to the people was to bring the people to the preacher, especially
into market towns and if possible on market day, when they
were likely to be present on other business in great numbers.
This was part of the rationale of 'prophesying', a Pauline word
for preaching which, thanks to its slightly exotic associations,
has occasioned some confusion, among historians no less than
contemporaries. In the parish the preachers were supposed to
have a captive and perhaps unwilling audience. At a prophesying, in spite of the encouraging and even coercive presence of

local worthies and magnates, the attendance was of a more voluntary character, consisting of the converted and nearly converted, as well as the inevitable schoolboys. Was this the thin end of a wedge of Puritan sectarianism, or a new and superior strategy for bringing elements of the majority of 'the people' within the sound of the preacher's voice?

Whatever the answer, the prophesyings provide another example of the convergence of official policy with the more or less self-directed efforts of unofficial Protestantism. One of their prime functions was to advance the education and abilities of the academically incompetent clergy. They were called 'the universities of the poor ministers'. This was an objective outlined in the Royal Injunctions and elaborated in subsequent episcopal and synodal orders, which required non-graduate ministers to study the New Testament and other suitable books, making written notes which were to be shown to the bishops or their archdeacons or other deputies. With some local variations, the common feature of a prophesying was that it brought the clergy of a locality together at, as it might be, monthly or fortnightly meetings under the moderation of one or more of the local élite of preaching ministers. This provided an excellent opportunity to monitor the academic progress of the unlearned and (something not envisaged in the Injunctions) to encourage them to serve their apprenticeships as preachers in the public forum of the prophesying. This took the form of two or three sermons preached in turn on the same text in the presence of the other ministers and of a lay audience, followed by more private conference among the clergy in which the preachers were subjected to the 'censure' of the moderator and the whole company. This seems to have taken place over dinner. Certainly dinner with a cup or two of wine was an essential and agreeable amenity on these occasions, and an encouragement to a growing sense of collegiality among the preaching clergy.

The model was Swiss and foreign to the English Church, so that prophesying appeared with a certain spontaneity and not by order. But several bishops, deploying a power which the Queen later denied that they had, lent their support, published the orders of proceedings in their own names and delegated to the moderators the power to enforce attendance and exercise discipline. In the 1570s the institution flourished in many parts of the southern province of Canterbury, as, for example, in several towns in Lincolnshire, in most parts of Essex and East Anglia, in the Archbishop's own diocese and in the central Midlands. When their future was threatened, an enthusiastic Puritan supporter wrote that their suppression would be 'such a service to Satan as unless the whole religion should be overthrown a greater could not be done'.[49]

This proved a great exaggeration. In 1577 the Queen first suspended her Archbishop of Canterbury, Edmund Grindal, for refusing to use his own authority to suppress the prophesyings on her command, and then took the rare step of communicating directly with every bishop in his province in order to put them down herself. No episode did more to dramatise the distance between Elizabeth's attitude to religion and that of the growing and ebullient Protestant and Puritan movement.[50] But it was not long after this that a form of prophesying was launched for the first time in the northern province, spreading from Lancashire to the West Riding and building on earlier beginnings in Nottinghamshire. If the towns of early sixteenth-century Yorkshire were famous for their mystery plays, by the end of the century the 'exercises', sermons preached morning and afternoon and punctuated by dinner, were beginning to take their place as the most conspicuous cultural feature of the region, in Halifax and Leeds, Pudsey and Otley.[51]

In the south, the Queen's order made little difference to market day for devout Protestants. They could still perform their business while hearing a different preacher every week or fortnight. The ministers now dropped the unfortunate word 'prophesying', reduced the preaching-conference to a more conventional single sermon or 'lecture', but otherwise continued as before, gathering and dining together as a 'combination'. Some of the larger and more prestigious towns, such as Ipswich and Colchester, preferred to appoint a preacher or lecturer of their own on a substantial retainer. A commanding, even patriarchal, figure was looked for, to take charge of religion and morals. But many smaller places found it a great convenience to secure their sermons from the country clergy, for the price of a little wine and much goodwill. By the second and third decades of the seventeenth century, 'lectures by combination' had, it seems, been adopted almost universally.[52] For example, every little market town in Cheshire seems to have had one, and in East Anglia it was said sarcastically that there was hardly an eating-house or bowling-green which could survive without the assistance of a lecture. In Bury St Edmunds, the general emporium of west Suffolk, the country ministers came into town to preach on Monday, market day, from soon after the Elizabethan Settlement until the eve of the Long Parliament and perhaps for many years after that. A member of this combination remarked in 1590, 'Your townsmen of Bury are such diligent hearers of the Word on the Monday exercises that they may easily be singled out from other men.'[53]

It was true that sermon-tasters were well off in Bury. The ministers of the two parish churches offered further lectures on Wednesdays and Fridays. (The draconian discipline imposed by the Puritan magistracy ensured that townsmen with other tastes were less fortunate.[54]) But the very fact that the market towns of the eastern counties could rely on preachers from the country parishes suggests that the Word was by now very widely available. As early as 1577 the character of 'Youth' in a Puritan dialogue is made to say that sermons are not 'dainty' but 'very plenty'. 'And therefore no such great need or haste to run to hear sermons.'[55] The number of preaching incumbents was rising fast, and in many places various forms of initiative from within the community had established parish lectureships, such as the famous lectureship at Dedham, founded by a local clothier in 1578 to provide for his brother-in-law, a suspended Puritan divine of some distinction and subsequently occupied by the hellfire preacher John Rogers. In Ipswich people said, 'Let's go to Dedham to get a little fire!' The Dedham lectureship has lasted in one form or another into the last quarter of the twentieth century. These Elizabethan clothiers were builders for the future in a minor way which makes an odd kind of footnote to the heroic efforts of their great-grandfathers, who had completed those glorious churches of the Stour valley which later served as theatres for the Calvinist drama and later still formed a backcloth for Constable.[56]

Those who rode or 'gadded' to sermons now did so not so much to escape spiritual starvation as to enjoy a varied diet. In this way the father of John Winthrop, the first governor of Massachusetts, contrived to hear thirty-three preachers in a single year without leaving Suffolk and the neighbouring parts of Essex.[57] Members of this religious subculture, for that is what it was, carried in their heads a map which named in heavy type the parishes of the more 'edifying' preachers, and mental clocks and calendars to remind them of the regular days and times of 'exercise' at this place or that. In the major preaching-centres there were whole days of fasting and humiliation, to which the godly travelled considerable distances in order to suffer a marathon of sermons. This was a kind of super-prophesying, and a remote pointer to the camp meetings of nineteenth-century America, which derived from the Great Awakening which in its turn had revived the Puritan tradition in eighteenth-century New England. Some of the more heated symptoms of the revivalism of later centuries were already in evidence: at Bury St Edmunds 'the deep, passionate, trembling, singultive twang . . . the women's sighs and the men's hawkings'; at Dedham men hanging weeping on the necks of their horses after Mr Rogers's sermon had acted out a little scene in which God threatened to take away the Bible from the English people. Even the hints of rather too great a familiarity between the sexes would be repeated in future ages. 'Many of this gadding people came from far and went home late,' wrote a critical observer in late Elizabethan St Albans, 'both young men and young women together.'[58]

As late as 1628 a distinguished ecclesiastical lawyer defended in Parliament the legal rights of parishioners to go out of their own parish to hear the Word of God elsewhere when they had no preaching at home. The point was one of some importance for the likes of Richard Baxter's father, the thinly scattered godly folk of Shropshire and Herefordshire and Montgomeryshire. But in the same year a satirist poked fun at the 'she-Puritan' who would 'ride behind her husband five mile in pilgrimage to a coughing minister when there is a better sermon at her own parish'.[59] Long before that it had become a matter of concern, even in the more conservative of Puritan circles, to 'persuade the people to reverence and attend the ordinance of

God in the ministry of their [own] pastors'.[60] For by now, in more 'civil' counties, that ministry was as often as not acceptable, if not necessarily electrifying, upholding in weekly sermons a common stock of doctrines and values which characterised what Professor and Mrs George called in the title of their book 'the Protestant mind of the English Reformation'.[61] Soon this would be called 'orthodox Protestant religion', not so much the new religion as 'the ancient practice of the Church of England' – a practice about to be shaken profoundly by the Arminian *coup d'état* which was the curtain-raiser to the Puritan Revolution which followed.

This is an attempt to make an end, but in effect there is no end. In the history of English religion the passing of Elizabeth made very little difference, unlike her accession and quite unlike the deaths of her father, brother and sister. One sympathises with the Restoration author who wrote carelessly of 'the long reign of Queen Elizabeth and King James', as if they made a single epoch.[62] When James came south in April 1603 the almost endless drama of the English Reformation had not reached its final act any more than in 1559, where so many of its historians have been content to leave it. For some the new religion would still be new, as it was for that strange Leicestershire lad George Fox who in 1647 heard a voice which said, ' "There is one, even Christ Jesus, that can speak to thy condition" and when I heard it my heart did leap for joy. . . . And this I knew experimentally.' So began Quakerism, which in 1671 was called the 'fag-end of the Reformation', but which brought almost its first taste of religious excitement to the far and hitherto neglected north-west.[63] So of that almost irrelevant date 1603 we may say what Churchill said of 1942: 'It is not the end. It is not even the beginning of the end. But it is, perhaps, the end of the beginning.'

8. The Church of England, the Catholics and the People

CHRISTOPHER HAIGH

THE puny mind of the historian, grappling with the almost infinite detail and complexity of the past, seizes with relief upon such simplifications as are to hand. Periodisation, the division of the past into manageable blocks for the purpose of study, is an essential, but dangerous, simplification. Our understanding of politics and religion in the sixteenth century has been bedevilled by the assumption that the period of 'the English Reformation' was definitively completed by 'the Elizabethan Settlement', leaving only the residual problem of those papists who did not realise that the Reformation struggle was over and they had lost. 1558–9 is too often regarded as a decisive turning-point: students are expected to change their mentors (Elton gives way to Neale), their organising-concepts ('the Reformation' gives way to 'the origins of the Civil War'), and their categories – medieval obscurantism is dead, and we are in the exciting new world of 'the rise of Puritanism', 'the rise of the gentry', and 'the winning of the initiative by the House of Commons'.

But the ecclesiastical history of Elizabethan England is more profitably viewed not from the whiggish perspective of 'the causes of the Civil War', but as the second phase of a Reformation which was incomplete in two senses. First, though a political decision for Protestantism was taken in 1558–9, the form of that Protestantism remained uncertain and few believed that even the official, legal Reformation had come to a halt – while contemporaries were much less certain than some historians that the Reformation was irreversible and Protestantism safe. Second, although a *legislative* Reformation had taken place, there had, as yet, been only a very limited *popular* Reformation. Though there is a substantial body of opinion, led by Professors Dickens and Elton, which holds that Protestantism spread rapidly in early Tudor England, there is a growing 'slow Reformation' school, composed partly of historians who have conducted local studies of religious change. Protestantism *did* make early progress in towns such as Bristol, Colchester, Coventry, Ipswich and London, but elsewhere, and especially in the countryside, the reformist breakthrough came much later. In Cambridgeshire, Cornwall, Gloucestershire, Lancashire, Lincolnshire, Norfolk, Suffolk, Sussex and Yorkshire, the Protestant Reformation was an Elizabethan (and often mid-Elizabethan) event.[1] For much of the reign of Elizabeth, the Church of England was a prescribed, national Church with more-or-less Protestant liturgy and theology but an essentially non-Protestant (and in some respects anti-Protestant) laity. This essay explores some of the consequences of this discrepancy, and of the competing evangelistic campaigns of Catholic and Protestant missionary clergy.

I

After the fluctuating religious policies of Elizabeth's predecessors, it is not surprising that few expected the laws and injunctions of 1559 to constitute a permanent 'settlement'. A little before Queen Mary's death, a Lancashire JP had acknowledged 'that this new learning shall come again, but for how long? – even for three or four months and no longer'. The Bishop of Carlisle reported in 1562 that his people expected a change in religion and prepared for it, and there were stories in Lancashire in 1565 that altars and crucifixes were to be restored. There were persistent rumours of a change of religion about 1580 (which led one candidate to postpone his ordination, and a minister to shave off his beard in expectation of becoming a priest), and fears and hopes in the 1590s that the death of Elizabeth would bring the restoration of Catholicism.[2] Clergy and parishioners were therefore reluctant to remove altars and rood lofts and deface images and mass equipment.

Most parishes yielded to presure from the bishops: church-wardens' accounts suggest that in most places altars and images were displaced in 1559–60, and rood lofts taken down in 1561–2. But half the churches of Lincolnshire kept their altars beyond 1562, and a quarter kept their images, while there was local resistance to the removal of 'monuments of superstition' at Throwley and Elmstead in Kent, Writtle in Essex, and Leigh and Wigan in Lancashire. Seventeen east Yorkshire churches still had Catholic fittings in 1567, and in 1574 a score of Northamptonshire churches had the forbidden rood lofts. Even when the removal of proscribed items from prominent places in churches was secured, it was difficult to enforce their destruction or sale. Bishop Bentham complained in 1560 that most Shropshire churches 'hath not only their altars still standing, but also their images reserved and conveyed away, contrary to the Queen's Majesty's injunctions, hoping and looking for a new day', and in Sussex in 1569 there were 'images hidden up and other popish ornaments ready to set up the mass again'. The churchwardens of most parishes did not sell their mass equipment and vestments until 1570–2, and the wardens of Masham in Yorkshire finally disposed of their Catholic vestments and altercloths in 1595. Once in private hands, such items might be kept for years in the hope that the mass would be restored, and five parishioners of Kneesall in Nottinghamshire were in trouble for this in 1594.[3]

For a decade or more, the Church of England was a Protestant Church with many Catholic churches; for even longer, it was a Protestant Church with many Catholic, or at least conservative, clergy. In the diocese of Lincoln in 1576, 40 per cent of the ministers had been ordained before 1559, of the kind described by Anthony Gilby as 'old monks and friars and old popish priests, notorious idolators, openly perjured persons, halting hypocrites, manifest apostates'. Some conservatives conformed as cynically as Gilby claimed: the rector of Bilborough in Nottinghamshire acknowledged in 1577 'that he had given his faith unto the Church, and that faith that was lost he had given to his wife', and others made no secret of their hope that the mass would be restored. Several ministers provided the sacraments of the official Church in public and Catholic ones in private, and many more taught Catholic beliefs: some of those ordained under Elizabeth were also hostile to Protestantism, and in 1598 the parson of Barton-upon-Humber was teaching his people that there were seven sacraments and that the doctrines of Luther and Calvin were 'damnable, heretical and devilish'.[4] If the character of the clergy of the Church of England changed only slowly, as such conservatives died or were dismissed, the church services they provided conformed only gradually to the rubrics of the *Book of Common Prayer*. Throughout the 1560s and 1570s, the Church courts dealt with ministers who tried to 'counterfeit the mass', by muttering Latin prayers, facing east during the service, or raising the bread and wine in an 'elevation': in 1599, the vicar of Marston-upon-Dove in Derbyshire was still reading the service like a mass at an altar. The continuing use of communion wafers (prescribed by royal Injunctions), rather than ordinary bread (required by the Prayer Book!), was one way in which parishes maintained continuity with the mass. References to 'singing cakes' in churchwardens' accounts suggest that at least a quarter of parishes used wafers in the 1560s, and, though there were attempts to suppress their use in the 1580s, there were parishes in Berkshire in 1584 and Hampshire in 1607 where the congregations refused to communicate except with wafers. The ecclesiological and liturgical rules of 1559 were thus implemented reluctantly, and often over ten or twenty years. In 1578 the parishioners of Weaverham in Cheshire were unusual only in the comprehensiveness of their disobedience:

> They want [i.e. lack] a Communion Book, a Bible of the largest volume, the first tome of the Homilies. There is in the church an altar standing undefaced. There lacketh a linen cloth and a covering for the communion table, a chest for the poor and keeping of the register in. The parishioners refuse the perambulation. The people will not be stayed from ringing the bells on All Saints' Day. They frequent alehouses in service time. Great talking used in the church. No levying for the poor of the absents from the church. Morris dances and rushbearing used in the church. Jane, an old nun, is an evil woman and teacheth false doctrine. They refuse to communicate with usual bread. None cometh to the communion three times a year. They refuse to bring in their

youth to be catechised. Crosses are standing in the church-yard.[5]

Under the tutelage of conservative clergy, the beliefs of the laity may have changed very little in the reign of Elizabeth. Preaching at Oakham in 1583, Thomas Gibson complained that by the influence of the old priests 'the people are still in ignorance and blindness and kept still in their old and popish errors, received from their forefathers; they know not the use of the sacraments, or to what end they serve, they hold still their papistical transubstantiation: some say they receive their maker, other say 'they never heard what a sacrament meant'. When, nearly a decade later, William Perkins listed 'these your common opinions' in an address 'to all ignorant people', he described a pattern of belief which also differed little from pre-Reformation popular Catholicism – little wonder that a Nottinghamshire man, required to recite his catechism in 1579, retorted that 'it is nothing but the old Christ in the Pope's time'. But where the Elizabethan church services were enforced in their entirety, there was a strong consciousness of change and a marked hostility to it. Francis Trigge objected in 1589 to the

weeping and bewailing of the simple sort, and especially of women. Who, going into the churches and seeing the bare walls, and lacking their golden images, their costly copes, their pleasant organs, their sweet frankincense, their gilden chalices, their goodly streamers, they lament in themselves and fetch many deep sighs, and bewail this spoiling and laying waste of the Church, as they think.

With a resentment of novelty came a nostalgia for the old: 'It was a merry world when the service was used in the Latin tongue', claimed an Essex man in 1581, and it was widely held that 'it was a good world when the old religion was, because all things were cheap'. Protestantism was blamed for high prices, bad weather, disease and threats from abroad; 'now we are in an evil way and going to the devil, and have all nations in our necks'.[6]

II

There was thus a substantial survival of conservative belief and practice in parishes served by ex-priests, and of conservative belief among the alienated anti-Protestants in parishes served by godly preachers. Those whose opinions were little influenced by the Elizabethan Reformation formed a reservoir of potential recruits for a separated Catholic Church, and even some ministers of the Church of England kept loyalty to Rome alive. In 1575 the curate of Guisborough 'did say that the Pope was and is head of the Church', and the vicar of Whalley, Lancashire, dismissed the English Church as 'a defiled and spotted Church', encouraging his parishioners to pray 'according to the doctrine of the Pope of Rome'. The vicar of Bonnington in Lincolnshire told his people in 1580 that they must make confession to Catholic priests, since only then could they be saved from damnation. Other clergy, perhaps more strong-minded than these, accepted the logic of such views and withdrew from the official Church, offering Catholic sacraments to the laity as recusant priests. By 1564, recusant priests were already working in the dioceses of Lichfield, Hereford, Worcester and Peterborough, and by 1571 there were thirty-eight such priests in Lancashire and a dozen more in Richmondshire and Claro: we know of seventy-five recusant priests who served in Lancashire in the reign of Elizabeth, and as many as 150 who worked in Yorkshire. Some of these men established themselves as domestic chaplains to the gentry, celebrating masses for their households and exercising little outside influence, but others, especially in the less well-governed areas of upland England, served unofficial congregations among their erstwhile parishioners or became itinerant priests to moorland hamlets.

It is difficult to assess the effectiveness of such priests, or to establish how many of the laity followed them into recusancy – or practised an ambidexterous religious life as 'church papists'. Neither the Privy Council nor the bishops made sustained efforts to identify recusants until the late 1570s, and our evidence is very patchy. But, when rumour or crisis prompted more serious investigation, substantial numbers of recusants were often found. In 1567, when the Bishop of Chester was

pressed into action by the Council, he discovered an established circuit of gentry houses in south-west Lancashire
providing bases for at least seventeen mass priests, and a
special visitation in 1571 found forty recusants among the
gentry. When the fears which followed the papal bull of
deposition in 1570 prompted a visitation of the archdeaconry of
Norwich, Bishop Parkhurst found 180 recusants and non-
communicants, and the Winchester consistory court dealt with
116 recusants and 128 non-communicants from Hampshire in
1570. In 1577, a hastily conducted national survey, which
concentrated on gentlemen and known malcontents, listed
1500 recusants, and there were certainly many more, besides
church papists: the 1577 list for Lancashire gives only forty-five
names, but in 1578 304 Lancashire recusants were detected.[7]
Twenty years after the accession of Elizabeth, therefore, the
prospects for English Catholicism were good: within the
framework of the Church of England, conservative opinion
remained widespread and, apparently, intractable; outside,
recusant priests and laypeople had begun to organise an
underground Church. It is true that the loyalty of mere
conservatives to traditional belief and practice was conditional
and partial, but they were at least potential full Catholics who
might be won for recusancy by energetic proselytising. It is also
true that as the recusant priests died off their opposition
Catholic Church would collapse, unless they were replaced by
new recruits. But both needs could have been met by the
Catholic missionary enterprise mounted from the mid 1570s,
which sent trained young priests to England for 'the preservation and augmentation of the faith of the Catholics'.[8]

III

The missionary effort of seminary priests and Jesuits has been
regarded by most historians as a great success, which rescued
English Catholicism from decline and preserved it against the
persuasions of Protestant preachers and the persecutions of a
ruthless regime. But it has already been suggested that
conservative opinion had held up well in the first half of the
Elizabethan period, and it will later be argued that the efforts of

godly ministers created in the second half a small Protestant minority rather than a thoroughly Protestant nation. Protestant propaganda did little to limit the achievements of the missioners, and it may be that persecution was also less significant than has been supposed. Despite the horrific deaths and heavy fines inflicted upon some, the authorities of Church and state applied real coercive pressure only to a very few Catholics[9] – though the vicious Act of 1585 made the work of the priests more difficult and dangerous, at times of crisis and in better-governed districts. Although the mission was triumphant in the sense that it created the seigneurially structured form of Catholicism which was to survive in England, that form was not inevitable; in the sense that it failed to maximise the size and distribution of the potential Catholic community, the mission was a failure – albeit a heroic one.

The task of the missionary priests was to sustain and strengthen existing Catholic loyalties, but this they were unable to do, for two broad reasons.[10] First, from the earliest years of the mission there was a geographical maldistribution of clerical resources. After their training at Douai, Rheims or Rome, most priests came into England through ports such as Dover and Rye, and they tended to concentrate in the south-east, where Catholics were fewer and prospects less good. In 1580, half of the missioners were working in Essex, London and the Thames Valley, where only a fifth of detected recusants lived; the north, which had 40 per cent of detected recusants (and many more undetected) had attracted only a fifth of the priests. Robert Southwell complained in 1586 that 'the priests actually working in the harvest betake themselves in great numbers to one or two counties, leaving the others devoid of pastors'. By about 1590, there are signs of a glut of priests in Oxfordshire and acute shortages in the north. The Catholics of Malpas in Cheshire were able to attend only three masses in two years, a pair of lovers from Cleveland had to travel to Lincolnshire to find a priest to marry them, and Richard Danby of Masham had to baptise his six children himself. While Catholic gentlemen in the Home Counties, East Anglia and the Thames Valley might have resident chaplains, the people of the north and west were too often left to go to the devil – or the Church of England. Areas such as Cumbria and north Wales, where the prospects for Catholic survival and consolidation had seemed good until the 1580s, declined into gross superstition and conformism thereafter – probably because of insufficient priestly provision. Recusancy was expanding rapidly in the far north-west at least until 1589, but ten years later the Bishop of Carlisle reported that the recusant gentry were moving out of his diocese, and that the main problem he now faced was not Catholicism but the ignorance of the people owing to the deficiencies of his own clergy.[11]

The second reason for the relative failure of the Elizabethan Catholic mission was that scarce priestly resources were devoted disproportionately to the spiritual needs of the gentry. Since many of the Jesuits and seminary priests came from the gentry or were patronised by them, it is easy to see why this happened, while there were sound justifications for it in both practice and policy. The high risk of arrest in the well-governed parts of southern England and in scare periods such as the years following the Armada may have forced some priests to seek safety in the houses of prominent Catholics. Above all, the focus upon the gentry was quite deliberate, for both political and pastoral reasons: Catholic gentlemen would provide backing for any future restoration of the old religion, and it was hoped that the influence of Catholic landlords would keep their servants and tenants loyal to the Catholic faith. The leaders of the missionary effort, and especially the Jesuits, envisaged the construction of a separated recusant community in a seigneurial, rather than congregational, form. The clerical employment agency organised by William Weston in 1585–6 and supervised by Henry Garnet thereafter, sought to place incoming priests in the households of reliable Catholic gentry, where they often became family chaplains rather than district pastors.[12] Though some priests devoted themselves bravely and selflessly to the poor, there was an increasing emphasis upon work with the gentry. For four years William Anlaby worked on foot and in simple dress among the poor Catholics of Yorkshire, but in 1582, 'humbly yielding himself to the advice of his brethren', he bought a horse, improved his clothes, and turned his attention to the gentry of the south. When William Freeman arrived in England in 1587, he worked first, with 'weariness of body and sundry perils', among 'the meaner sort' in the west

Midlands, until a Catholic gentlewoman took him in and made him tutor to her son.[13]

The consequence of this attention to the needs of the upper ranks was an inadequate provision for those of the lower orders. About 1590, the Jesuit Thomas Stanney was based with a gentry family in Hampshire and went on a circuit of local villages once a month. When asked to go out again to minister to poor Catholics, he replied 'that I had not been long since in those parts, where I was much fatigued with preaching, hearing confessions and administering the sacraments, the more because I was obliged to watch whole nights and to celebrate mass twice in the day, so that I had not, as yet, been able to recover myself'. 'Well, but Master,' he was told by his guide, 'we still have a great many hungry souls that want bread, and there is no one to give it to them; we have many also that would be glad to shake off the yoke of bondage, heresy, and embrace the Catholic faith, and I can find none to help them and receive them into the Church. What then must I say to them?' This was a question to which the Catholic leadership had no answer: no doubt Stanney was doing his best, but he needed help, especially from priests without obligations to the gentry. In Suffolk in the 1620s a lay sister complained that there were too few priests, and that those available were too often prevented by their gentry hosts from working among the poor; she claimed it took six months to find a priest to receive three converts into the Church, and she had to travel twelve miles to get him. By then the disparity in provisions for gentry and the poor was clear and fixed: gentry families with chaplains had mass every day, but the poor had masses monthly.[14]

There was, therefore, a high risk of leakage from the Catholic community. In the Catholic heartlands of Monmouthshire, Herefordshire, Lancashire and the North Riding, social pressures might keep even neglected lay Catholics firm to their faith: in 1578 a man from Boroughbridge in north Yorkshire justified his recusancy on the grounds that 'he doth see that no such number now come to church as did in the time of Latin service', and in 1602 Lancashire Catholics explained their allegiance by saying, 'It is safest to do in religion as most do.'[15] But in most parts of England the inducement of social conformity worked in favour of attendance at the parish

church, and the disciplinary mechanisms of the official Church
pressed in the same direction: the hard core of recusants always
had a penumbra of church papists, who might be seduced into
abandoning their sometimes-tenuous Catholicism. Furthermore, there were parishes all over England and Wales which
never received the attentions of recusant clergy or missionary
priests, where conservative opinion survived, albeit in attenu-
ated form, within the framework of the Church of England –
with or without the support of like-minded ministers. The
remainder of this essay explores the place of such conservatives
and anti-Protestants within the Church of England. Could the
energetic evangelism of godly ministers turn those who had
been content to be Catholic under Mary (but would not
disobey anti-Catholic laws under her sister) into believing
Protestants? And, if not, how would such 'mere conformists' fit
into a Church whose ministers wanted an informed and activist
laity and had little time for those

> that love a pot of ale better than a pulpit and a corn-rick
> better than a church-door; who, coming to divine service
> more for fashion than devotion, are contented after a little
> capping and kneeling, coughing and spitting, to help me to
> sing out a Psalm, and sleep at the Second Lesson, or wake to
> stand up at the Gospel and say 'Amen' at 'The Peace of God';
> and stay till the banns of matrimony be asked, or till the clerk
> have cried a pied stray bullock, a black sheep or a grey mare,
> and then, for that some dwell far off, be glad to be gotten
> home to dinner.[16]

IV

Protestant ministers two generations after the accession of
Elizabeth were conscious of the justice of the Catholic charge

> that we may have churches full of people but empty of sound
> Protestants: they will tell us in their books that a great part
> that are on our sides have no other motives to hold them
> there but only because they have been so born and bred, and
> received their religion as they do their inheritance, by

descent and custom of the country, men whom decrees of
Parliament and fear of laws keep with us, rather than any
certain knowledge of the truth of our religion by the
Scripture.

Their answer in the 1620s, as it had been in the 1560s, was
preaching – preaching, and still more preaching. In a complementary essay in this volume, Professor Collinson demonstrates with force and elegance how the provision of preaching
improved over the reign of Elizabeth and after; but it is worth
reminding ourselves how acute was the shortage at the
beginning of the reign and how numerous were the gaps at its
end. In the probably typical diocese of Peterborough, there
were nine preachers for 285 parishes in 1560, and forty in 1576,
though after a last-minute increase there were 144 by 1603. A
series of surveys in 1586, admittedly compiled by critics of the
bishops, suggests that only a fifth of parishes had preachers: in
Surrey there were fifteen resident preachers, leaving 125
congregations 'altogether destitute of sufficient teachers'. In
1603 an investigation by the bishops showed that there were
4830 preachers in England for 9244 parishes, but in Staffordshire in the following year there remained '118 congregations
which have no preachers, neither have had (for the most) now
more than 40 years'.[17]
    There was, by the middle of Elizabeth's reign, a preacher
within reach of most villages, for the godly to go 'gadding' to his
sermons; but the 'ungodly' would not 'gad', and the preachers
must go to them. The system of quarterly sermons, by which
churches which did not have their own preachers were to
receive sermons from visitors every three months, seems to
have been ineffective in many areas. Fifty-eight parishes in west
Sussex had their quarterly sermons in 1579, but forty-six did
not, and twenty-three parishes had sermons once a year or less
frequently: at Barlavington and elsewhere, the churchwardens
reported that they had no sermons, 'our parish being very small
and not able to maintain the charge thereof'. In the diocese of
York in 1575, 150 ministers were not providing sermons for
their people, and the system was unsatisfactory in Oxfordshire
in 1586. But, even where quarterly preaching did take place,
the godly had little faith in its efficacy: 'Four sermons in the

year are as insufficient ordinarily to make us perfect men in
Christ Jesus . . . as four strokes with an axe are unable to fell
down a mighty oak', it was said in 1585, and George Gifford
thought even weekly sermons too few. In parishes without
frequent preaching, it was claimed in 1588, 'what a pitiful thing
it is to come into a congregation of one or two thousand souls
and not to find above four or five that are able to give an
account of their faith in any tolerable manner, whereby it might
be said probably "This is a Christian man, or he is a child of the
church."' 'Wherefore (good brethren),' cried John More of
Norwich, 'if ye will be saved, get you preachers into your
parishes.'[18]

But, though the godly pleaded with the Queen and the
bishops for more preaching, their less-committed neighbours
did not share their enthusiasm. A Northamptonshire woman
complained in 1590 that 'Mr Sharpe and Mr Barebone had
preached so long at Badby that they had brought all to nought,
and that Welton was almost as bad. And that it was a merry
world before there was so much preaching.' When John Bruen
supplied preachers for Tarvin in Cheshire, they were 'much
slighted by many, little regarded by the vulgar sort, much
opposed by the popish and profane and too much undervalued
by all'. Lengthy sermons were especially disliked: the people of
Minsterworth in Gloucestershire complained in 1563 that their
curate 'does weary the parish with overlong preaching', and the
spokesman for the common man in a 1581 dialogue was told
that 'if the preacher doth pass his hour but a little, your
buttocks begin to ache and ye wish in your heart that the pulpit
would fall'. We may sympathise with Henry Hasellwood, of
Coggeshall in Essex, called before the Church court in 1601 for
standing in the churchyard during a sermon and throwing
stones onto the church roof, 'to the great disturbance of the
whole congregation'; he explained that 'he was at Mr Stough-
ton's sermon two hours and a half, and being urged to
exonerate nature was compelled to go out of the church'.
Sermons on moral reform seem to have pleased the godly but
offended the rest: in 1592 an Essex man called his parson
'"prattling fool" for preaching against drunkenness, saying
moreover that he could, if he had authority, within a fortnight
space make as good a sermon as he', and preachers against

'good fellowship' were widely unpopular – especially among innkeepers. In 1606 the vicar of Long Bennington, Lincoln- shire, confessed that he had abandoned his attempts at moral reform because of the abuse he received from the parishion- ers.[19] Predestinarian preachers were also unpopular: 'they be over hot and severe, and preach damnation to the people . . ., they meddle with such matters as they need not, as election and predestination'.[20]

If hostility to their preaching was a problem for godly ministers, sheer uncomprehending boredom in congregations was another. We should not suppose that Elizabethan church- goers sat in attentive rows, listening patiently to their preachers: they chattered, scoffed, squabbled and fought, and if the tedium grew unbearable they walked out. In 1592 eight Manchester parishioners were reported for walking out of sermons, eleven for talking in the churchyard during services, six for walking in the fields, and five for allowing drinking in their houses at service and sermon times. Sleeping during sermons may also have been common (eighteen were in trouble at Ramsey in 1597): the minister of North Colingham in Nottinghamshire told his people in 1598 'that some came to church more for a sleep than for the service of God, and others had more mind of going home to dinner than to hear God's word'. The noted Lancashire preacher John Angier com- plained later of parishioners sleeping in his sermons: 'some sleep from the beginning to the end, as if they came for no other purpose but to sleep, as if the sabbath were made only to recover that sleep they have lost in the week'. But Angier knew the preachers would have the last laugh: 'Hell was made for sermon-sleepers.' Although godly ministers had supposed early in the reign of Elizabeth that if the number of preachers could be increased their evangelistic campaign would be successful, there was a growing recognition later that sermons often did not work. 'We hear say that many painful preachers, both in towns and cities, exercising the word three or four times a week, yet do complain of the small profitting of the flock', lamented a petition to Parliament printed in 1585, and the position was much the same forty years later:

what excuse will they have who have been bred up in

parishes that have had preaching almost time out of mind? Here one would think, in regard of time and means, men might be teachers rather than learners, but it is nothing so. Here also shall you meet with hundreds that shall need to be taught their very ABC in matters of religion: it is no marvel to see children or young men ignorant, when you shall have old men, 50, 60, yea 80 years old, whose grey hairs show that they have had time enough to learn more wit, yet in case to be set to school again . . . ask them the meaning of the articles of faith, of the petitions in the Lord's Prayer, or of other common points in catechism, and mark their answers, you shall see them so shuffle and fumble, speak half words and half sentences, so hack and hew at it, that you may almost swear they speak they know not what, of matters out of their element: though they be the wisest and craftiest-headed men in a parish, take them in other matters, yet in these things you would think verily they were born stark naturals and idiots.[21]

v

It was clear to the ministers, as it must surely be to historians, that the preaching-campaign had produced only a small minority of godly Protestants, leaving the rest in ignorance, indifference or downright antipathy – 'Which cannot be imputed to the want of good preaching, but rather to the want of good hearing.' How could the people be brought to better hearing? After the first two decades of Elizabethan preaching, it was increasingly argued (especially by authors of catechisms) that the answer lay in regular catechising: 'The neglect of this duty in those ministers that be preachers is in very deed the cause why their preaching taketh so little effect amongst their parishioners', wrote a leading exponent of 'the profit and necessity of catechising, that is, of instructing the youth and ignorant persons in the principles and grounds of Christian religion'. The Royal Injunctions of 1559 required ministers to hold catechism classes in church for half an hour every holy day and every other Sunday, though the bishops soon increased the duty to an hour every Sunday, as well as holy days. But the task was widely neglected: of the west Sussex parishes which answered a question on catechising at the visitation of 1579, ten had classes, fifteen did not, and in four places the minister tried to hold classes but no one turned up. In Lancashire there was no catechising in seven churches in 1592, four in 1595, six in 1598, seven in 1601 and nine in 1604; in the diocese of Norwich in 1597 there was no catechising in seventy-eight parishes, and it was infrequent in fifteen more. The consquence in such parishes was, of course, ignorance: 'For the catechism', complained the parishioners of Eastergate in Sussex in 1579, 'we do think there be many cannot say it as it ought to be said, for lack of instructions.'[22]

The fault was not always the minister's: the churchwardens of Poling in Sussex reported in 1586, 'catechising given over in the default of parents and masters', who failed to send their young charges to classes. Though absence from classes was punishable, and though learning the catechism in the *Book of Common Prayer* was encouraged by excluding those who could not recite it from communion and refusing to allow them to marry or act as godparents, resistance was common: there were many more interesting things to do on Sunday afternoons. The minister of Woolavington in Sussex complained in 1579 that 'Graffham is a parish of great misrule upon sabbath days, dancing etc., whereto old and young of my parish go, so as I have seldom any at the catechism', and in 1590 a group of Lancashire ministers reported that because of Sunday games and dancing 'the youth will not by any means be brought to attend the exercise of catechising in the afternoon, neither the people to be present at the evening service'. At Cromwell in Nottinghamshire in 1594, two men got into trouble for 'dancing and keeping of evil rule so near to the church' that their noise drowned the minister's catechising, and at Sheringham in Norfolk in 1597 it was reported that a fiddler regularly enticed the young from catechism.[23] The whole process of compulsory catechism and examination seems to have been much resented. Two Nottinghamshire men scoffed during catechism in 1579, and at Bloxham in Oxfordshire in 1584 a man refused to learn the catechism by heart on the gounds that he was able to read it. At Coggleshall in 1586, three truculent youths refused to recite the Ten Commandments during a catechism class, and one 'sat unreverently with his hat on his head, to the evil example of all the rest of that sort'. Testing that communicants could say the catechism before they were allowed to receive often caused trouble: sometimes it was simply one woman who refused to be examined, as at Broadchalke in Wiltshire in 1584; sometimes almost a whole congregation, as at an Essex parish in 1588. The minister of Hatfield Peverel was presented to the Bishop of London for nonconformity by parishioners who objected to the rigour of his examinations in 1585, and in another Essex village, Inworth, a man protested in 1592 that his minister 'asked me frivolous questions, as what should become of their bodies when they were in the grave, and whether all the world should be saved'.[24]

Although it is clear that catechising provoked hostility, the small numbers rejected from communion on grounds of ignorance suggest that the exercise was usually effective – the Prayer Book catechism was, after all, only a thousand words long, and the recitation of the Creed, Ten Commandments and Lord's Prayer posed no difficulty for those willing to learn. But the official catechism taught nothing that was specifically Protestant, and the godly ministers expected much more than rote learning of short formularies. To this end, about a hundred more demanding catechisms were published in the reign of Elizabeth, many of them in the 1580s, and the best sellers, such as those by John More and Eusebius Pagit, went through more than a dozen editions each. The problems of teaching Protestant beliefs to ordinary people in simple form were recognised, and the authors of shorter catechisms criticised their rivals for using 'more words than can be carried in mind of the ignorant man'. Thomas Ratcliffe, minister at St Saviour's, Southwark, explained in 1592 that 'I have brought the question and the answer to as few words as I could, and that for the ease of children and common people, who cannot understand or gather the substance of a long question or a long answer confirmed with many reasons'. Some ministers found that 'they cannot bring the unlearned in letters unto this knowledge', but Eusebius Pagit claimed he was able to teach his catechism to a whole household, including servants (except 'three or four whose capacity was but mean and simple'), in four months. But Pagit's catechism was, together with the Creed, Commandments and Lord's Prayer, about 3000 words long, broken up into short answers for ease of learning: two-thirds of the catechisms published were over 4000 words long, and often posed daunting tasks. Alexander Nowell's semi-official *Catechism or First Institution of Christian Religion*, described as 'being of a middle sort' and 'to be learned of all youth next after the little catechism' (i.e. after the Prayer Book catechism), asked 246 questions, was 15,000 words long, and was 115 pages in the pocket-edition – but it was reprinted eight times in the reign, and tens of thousands of young people must have suffered it.[25]

Pagit's catechising triumph took place in a private household, not in church, and he succeeded in four months by daily, not weekly, classes. Robert Cawdrey thought a child could learn the basic essentials of Protestantism in six months, but he expected family catechising three times a week, as well as the minister's Sunday classes. It was, indeed, often argued that catechising by the minister was worthless unless backed by further teaching at home: 'let the minister never so diligently catechise in the church, unless there be also a furtherance of his travail in several families at home, ere the next assembly all or most of the seed by him sowen before is gone, trodden under foot, or choked'. But most families, of course, did *not* have home catechising: Thomas Sparke thought in 1588 that only one household in a hundred had catechising, and that those who had were 'mocked at and derided as precise and curious fools'.[26] Large numbers of catechisms were published, and presumably sold, and certainly catechising was a feature of the life of the godly household – but there, if not exactly preaching to the converted, catechising was preaching to the children of the converted, and in the homes of the unconverted majority such worthy devotion was lacking. So preaching did not make Protestants unless backed by clerical catechising; the ministers' catechising did not make Protestants unless backed by family catechism; and only the godly Protestant minority catechised at home. It was almost impossible to break the circle.

Richard Greenham, rector of Dry Drayton in Cambridgeshire from 1570 to 1591, was an exemplary Protestant pastor. At Dry Drayton he preached six sermons a week (about 6000 in all), and catechised twice a week; he composed his own thoughtful and well-organised (but impossibly long) catechism; and his commonplace book shows him to have been a diligent visitor of the sick and a sympathetic comforter of troubled souls. But after twenty-one years of exhausting effort he stumped off in disgust to London, because of 'the intractableness and unteachableness of that people among whom he had taken such exceeding great pains' – and an analysis of Dry Drayton wills suggests that his conclusion that he had, in all but a few families, failed, was just about right.[27] If Richard Greenham, of all men, in Cambridgeshire, of all counties, could not make committed Protestants of more than a tiny handful of his parishioners, then nobody could and the task was impossible. In Elizabethan conditions, with low levels of literacy and with the alehouse and the village green to distract the people from sermons and catechism, the English people *could not* be made Protestants – they could not be made to understand, accept and respond to the Protestant doctrines offered to them, justification by faith and predestination. A Kentish minister, Josias Nichols, told his readers in 1602 that

> I have been in a parish of 400 communicants, and marvelling that my preaching was so little regarded I took upon me to confer with every man and woman before they received the communion. And I asked them of Christ, what he was in his person; what his office; how sin came into the world; what punishment for sin; what becomes of our bodies being rotten in the graves; and, lastly whether it were possible for a man to live so uprightly that by well-doing he might win heaven. In all the former questions I scarce found ten in the hundred to have any knowledge, but in the last question scarce one, but did affirm that a man might be saved by his own well-doing, and that he trusted he did so live, and that by God's grace he should obtain everlasting life by serving of God and good prayers.

Nichols was testing if those parishioners were Protestants, and they were not. The sketches of 'the religion which is among the common sort of Christians, which may be termed the country divinity' provided by authors such as Cawdrey, Dent, Gifford and Perkins in the second half of Elizabeth's reign are impressively unanimous. 'Most men' believed in salvation by works, that they would earn places in heaven by charity and prayers: 'If a man say his Lord's Prayer, his Ten Command-ments and his Belief, and keep them, and say no body harm, nor do no body harm and do as he would be done to, have a good faith God-ward and be a man of God's belief, no doubt he shall be saved without all this running to sermons and prattling of the Scripture.'[28] Worthy sentiments these may be, but, at the end of Elizabeth's reign, they are not Protestantism – and the godly ministers were still trying to crush them.

VI

The failure of Protestant evangelism in some parishes and among some people is, of course, only one side of the story; the other side is dealt with in Professor Collinson's essay. But the consequence of the two sides, of the fact that godly preaching created an activist Protestant minority and left the majority unmoved at best, and infuriated at worst, was trouble. It was a common accusation against godly ministers that their preach-ing was divisive. In a 1588 dialogue, an innkeeper complains of a preacher that 'He setteth men together by the ears, the town was never at quiet since he came, he teacheth such doctrine as some do like and some not, so they fall at variance'; a critic of the preachers of Kent at about the same time asked, 'Hath not Minge brought Ashford from being the quietest town of Kent to be at deadly hatred and bitter division?', and claimed that other ministers had divided Chart, Tenterden, Cranbrook and elsewhere, while Nichols did 'offend all the congregations where he cometh'. In Essex, too, the ministers provoked clashes between 'the godly people' and 'the profane multitude' in about a dozen parishes between 1582 and 1591; the town of Maldon was riven, at least between 1584 and 1595, by disputes between the godly followers of George Gifford and a 'multitude of papists, heretics, and other enemies to God and her Royal Majesty'. At Rochdale in 1585 and Peasmarsh, Sussex, in 1588, communities were split into godly supporters of activist preachers with strong views on morals and sabbath obser-vance, and hostile parties led by local alehouse-keepers.[29] Such parochial conflicts often polarised between the church on the one hand and the alehouse and village green on the other: the godly of King's Langley, Hertfordshire, petitioned in 1593–4 for the suppression of Ellis Coggdell's alehouse, where there had been dancing and drinking during evening prayer. At Hayley in Oxfordshire in 1596, Simon Wickins was 'requested by the youth to brew some ale, and thereby he had resort into his house upon a sabbath day, and had a minstrel, so that the youth did not repair unto the church at evening prayer'; in the same year Nicholas Hargreaves, of Newchurch in Pendle, was presented 'for playing upon organs in the house and drawing people from evening prayer upon the sabbath'.[30]

Some of the fiercest conflicts took place in the 1580s, when godly ministers and town corporations tried to suppress maypoles and May Day dancing. At Lincoln in 1584–5 there was a struggle for power between the godly party, who sought to impose strict controls on alehouses and sabbath observance, and a rival group who espoused the cause of maypoles and May festivities. At Shrewsbury in 1588, the maypole was put down by the magistrates and resistance by the Shearmen's Guild led to a number of imprisonments. There was trouble at Banbury over maypoles in both 1588 and 1589, with street demonstrations and counter-demonstrations in 1589, and disputes continued over Whitsun ales and morris dancing: the Privy Council had to intervene to ensure order was restored. When the Mayor of Canterbury forbade the maypole in 1589, the disaffected organised a protest morris dance outside his house.[31] The attempts of the godly to control the behaviour of their fellows led to the accusation that they were 'busy controllers': 'I perceive you are one of those curious and precise fellows, which will allow no recreation. What would ye have men do? – we shall do nothing shortly.' The godly were 'Scripture men' and 'precise fools', 'no Protestants but pratlingstants, that use to tell lies'. 'A shame take all professors,' cried an Essex woman in 1591, 'for they are all dissemblers and liars'; in 1599 a Chipping Ongar man was reported as 'a railer of our minister and most of the inhabitants who profess religion, calling them all heretics, hypocrites, such as he hath ever and in every place detested, clowns, etc.'[32]

Committed Protestants and their ministers were often the butts of coarse jokes and abuse, which mocked their claim to be 'godly'. At Rayleigh in Essex in 1589, the customers at an alehouse acted out a scene in which they impersonated the vicar, churchwardens and 'honest men of the parish'; Eve Tilie, of Yatton Kennell in Wiltshire, was 'a maker of rhymes and lewd songs' in 1599, who mocked her honest neighbours 'to the grief and disquietness of some of the better sort of people within the same parish'. The parish clerk of Winwick in Lancashire was 'generally noted to gibe and mock the ministers of the word', and his favourite trick was to give the names of men and women who disliked each other to the curate to read out as marriage banns, to the confusion of the curate and the amusement of the congregation. Married ministers and their wives were especially likely to be attacked; abuse of married clergy at the beginning of Elizabeth's reign occasions no surprise, but it is striking how widespread this remained later. Richard Fox, a Nottinghamshire man, thought in 1584 that 'it was never a good world since priests were married, and called the vicar's wife of Gringley "painted stock". Also he said that priests' calves and bishops' calves would overrun the realm.' Two years later, a woman of Seamer in north Yorkshire agreed: 'it was never a good world since ministers must have wives'. In 1592 John Mous, of Little Stambridge, Essex, was in trouble for 'using bad speeches towards the minister, and for reporting in the presence of many persons of good credit that all priests wives are whores and their children bastards', and a Sussex woman claimed in the following year 'that all priests wives were counted trulls'.[33]

Such cases as these may be no more than examples of the perpetual conflict between the Church and the world, the godly and the reprobate. But sometimes issues of principle, and religious principle at that, were at stake: some communities were not just divided over maypoles and ale; they were divided over church services and beliefs. At East Hanningfield in Essex in the 1580s, there were two religious groups: the godly, called 'saints and scripture men' by their opponents, met in conventicles, and the rector refused to give communion to the rest of the parish, who trooped off to West Hanningfield to receive the sacrament there. At Kingston-upon-Thames in 1586, the minister and 'the children of God' formed an exclusive sect, and 'If any will not join with them, they will not cease to slander him in most spiteful and ungodly manner, reporting him either to be a papist, an atheist, of the Family of Love, or one that hath no religion, or raise some evil slander against him'; the rejected sought revenge by accusing the godly of unorthodox opinions. Divisions in religion may have been involved in the conflicts over the maypole at Banbury in 1589. Sir Francis Knollys claimed that John Danvers, who had led the defence of ales and maypoles, 'leaned passionately to the strict observance of the ceremonies of the *Book of Common Prayer*'; but Anthony Cope, a leader of the anti-maypole group, had presented the presbyterian 'bill and book' to Parliament in 1587. When Thomas Bracebridge, who had encouraged the attack on maypoles, was deprived of the vicarage of Banbury for nonconformity, ninety-five fellow-citizens petitioned Burghley in his defence in 1590, but there were significant absentees from the list of his supporters. Ten years later, the godly group, who had attacked maypoles and backed Bracebridge, threw down the market crosses in Banbury and nearly provoked a riot: their opponents claimed that the strict godly regime which had been imposed on the town had driven the country people to use other markets. At Preston Capes, in Northamptonshire, there were also long-lasting religious disputes. The struggles between the nonconformist vicar, John Elliston, and those whom he branded as 'blasphemers of God's name, profaners of the sabbath', in 1584–5 centred on the vicar's attempts to force even adults to attend catechism classes, and his opponents' attempts to force him to wear the surplice, baptise with a cross, and church women after childbirth. Through the 1590s, the next incumbent, Robert Smart, was regularly presented by parishioners for his nonconformity; in 1603 he was briefly suspended for flagrant disregard of the Prayer Book rubrics; and in 1604 he refused to give communion to those who insisted on kneeling for it. By 1604 there was a liturgical stalemate in Preston Capes and the neighbouring parish of Woodford Halse: in both the minister would give communion only to those who would stand, but some of the parishioners would receive only if they were permitted to kneel.[34]

A common theme in these conflicts is the demand for liturgical conformity, an insistence by some parishioners that their ministers should perform the Prayer Book ceremonies in full. In 1574 a group from Cirencester refused to receive communion because it was not administered according to the *Book of Common Prayer*, and in 1583 a gentleman from Dodding-hurst in Essex asked his minister to follow the Prayer Book; in return, he was abused in sermons. We have already noted the demand for surplice, cross and churching at Preston Capes in 1584–5, and there were similar troubles at Flixton in Suffolk in 1588–90: there some of the congregation followed the services in their Prayer Books to try to keep the vicar to the rubrics, but he retorted that 'they which would have service said according to the *Book of Common Prayer* are papists and atheists'. His-torians too frequently use presentments of ministers for non-conformity as evidence for widespread hostility to surplices and ceremonies; but many of them were rather pleas for conformity, efforts to force ministers to supply in full the restricted ceremonial endorsed in 1559, for omission of ceremonies was often unpopular and provocative. In 1597 the churchwardens of St Cuthbert, Thetford, complained that a woman had prevented their minister using the sign of the cross at a baptism, 'thereby giving great offence to many those inhabitants of Thetford then and there present'. In 1598 and 1601 it was complained that the vicar of Leyland in Lancashire did not use the cross in baptism, 'wherefore many of the parishioners do cause their children to be baptised at other churches'; the same was happening at Poulton in 1604, and at Kirkham in 1605, where sixty-one families were in trouble for having their children christened away from their parish church.[35] Perhaps we have heard too much of 'sermon-gadding' by the godly, and should be more sensitive to 'sacrament-gadding' by the rest!

VII

In some parishes the opponents of the godly were clearly the profane, but those who defended ceremonies against the godly can hardly be called 'the ungodly'. Despite the risk of anachronism, they may properly be spoken of as 'parish anglicans' – 'anglicans', because of their stress on the Prayer Book and insistence that 'there is as good edifying in those prayers and homilies as in any that the preacher can make'; and 'parish' because of their emphasis on the harmony and vitality of the village unit, at play and at worship. Their model minister was not the divisive godly preacher, but (to the fury of those who damned him as a 'dumb dog') the pastor who read services devoutly, reconciled quarrellers in his parish, and joined his people for 'good fellowship' on the ale bench.[36] These 'parish anglicans' and their favoured clergy had not been moved by the evangelistic fervour of the Protestant Reformation – indeed, in the sense that they knew little of doctrine and rejected justification by faith and predestination, they were not Protestants at all. But, despite some similarity between their views and those of their pre-Reformation forebears, they were no longer Catholics: they had been neglected by the missionary priests, and they attended the services of the Church of England and demanded obedience to its liturgy. Those (or the children of those) who had reluctantly surrendered Catholic ritual in the 1560s now expected from their ministers as much ceremony as the Church of England would sanction. Although theirs was a residual religion, and they were the spiritual leftovers of Elizabethan England, they should not be dismissed as 'mere conformists', for in their defence of ceremonies and festivities they formed a factor to be reckoned with. Indeed, it was their demand for some ritual in their services which made possible – even made necessary – the drive for liturgical uniformity carried out by Whitgift and Bancroft. Later, their kind would provide the parochial foundations upon which the Laudian Church was built, and a considerable body of support for Caroline ceremonialism and Arminian doctrine. But that is an unfashionable argument, and must be pursued elsewhere.

9. Poverty and Social Regulation in Elizabethan England

PAUL SLACK

AFTER the Anglican Church, the English poor-law was the most long-lasting of Elizabethan achievements. As finally codified in the legislation of 1601, it persisted without fundamental alteration until 1834. That is one reason why we should pay some attention to its origins. The poor-laws also played a major part in Elizabethan government. Any list of the 'stacks of statutes' which the Tudors imposed on the shoulders of justices of the peace will include the acts of 1563, 1572, 1576 and 1598 which were concerned with the relief of the destitute and the punishment of vagabonds, along with related legislation aiming to regulate the lives and behaviour of the 'commons', such as the Statute of Artificers of 1563. Social welfare and social regulation were matters of increasing public concern between 1558 and 1603.

So much is familiar historical ground. What is less clear is the reason for this development. Was it that poverty and the social disorders to which it was thought to be related were in fact increasing in the course of the reign? Most historians would think that they were, although they would disagree about the degree of change, some taking a much more optimistic view than others. On the other hand, it might be argued that a change in perceptions of social problems, rather than in the nature of the problems themselves, provoked new government initiatives. Again, most historians would probably agree that attitudes did change, to some extent independently of social and economic conditions. But there is as yet no consensus on whether these shifts of view were connected with other intellectual changes, in religion for example. This essay will explore these uncertain and controversial areas in order to try to throw some light on the relationship between social circumstances and people's reactions to them.

I

We ought to start by describing the developments which seem to require explanation. To begin with there was the poor-law itself, gradually shaped by successive statutes up to the great enactment of 1601. It had three essential features. The first, and ultimately the most important, was the poor-rate, the compulsory assessment in each parish which financed outdoor relief to deserving indigent households. In 1563 secular sanctions were threatened against those who refused to contribute to collections for the poor. In 1572 justices of the peace were empowered to determine the size of contributions, thus turning them into an imposed tax: they were to assess richer parishioners after surveys of the poor had been made to see what money was needed. Finally, in 1598, the ground was prepared for the widespread adoption of rates, when the main responsibility for levying them was transferred from overworked justices to the churchwardens and overseers of every parish.

The second feature of the poor-law, the *quid pro quo* in return for public taxation and outdoor relief, was a sustained but unsuccessful campaign against vagrants and beggars. Begging and casual almsgiving were prohibited unless licensed by authority, and successive poor-laws viciously attacked wandering paupers with a variety of penalties. In the end, under a second act of 1598, vagrants were to be summarily whipped and returned to their place of settlement by parish constables. Once again the execution of the law was made quicker and easier than before by placing it in the hands of parish authorities; it did not require the cumbersome intervention of justices in every case, as the Act of 1572 had done.

The third feature of the law was complementary to the others: an effort to provide work for the poor so that they would neither wander abroad nor needlessly claim relief. By an act of 1576 justices of the peace were authorised to provide any town which needed it with a stock of flax, hemp or other materials on which paupers could be employed, and to erect a house of correction in every county for the punishment of those who refused to work. In practice little was done before 1603. Although some of the larger towns had houses of correction, workhouses, or work stocks, they were always small, they rarely lasted long and they were often mismanaged. Nevertheless, the imposition of labour discipline was from the start as fundamental an ambition of legislators as the provision of public doles for the deserving poor and public whippings for vagrants.

It has long been recognised that these legislative prescriptions owed a good deal to earlier local initiatives which pointed in the same direction. Compulsory taxes for the poor had been instituted in London, Norwich, Ipswich and York in the later 1540s and 1550s. Tmporary expedients to begin with, they were well established there and in other towns such as Exeter, Cambridge and Chester before the Act of 1572.[1] That statute itself seems to have been influenced by experiments in poor relief begun in Norwich in 1570, which included a survey of the poor, an increase in rates, and fresh expedients to provide employment.[2] There were also local houses of correction before the Act of 1576, the first of them the London Bridewell, founded in 1553, which gave its name to many of its provincial imitators. Searches for vagrants and efforts to prevent begging had been common in many towns since the second decade of the century.

The importance of local precedents should not be allowed to obscure the large role placed by central government in framing social policy, however. Councillors knew the problems of the localities as well as MPs, and they also needed to demonstrate the paternalism of government, its concern for public order and the social harmony of the common weal. The government itself seems to have pushed for decisive legislation on poor relief in 1572, for example. Even at the local level, we often find national figures sponsoring new welfare experiments: the Earl of Huntingdon in Oxford, the Earl of Leicester in Warwick, Sir Francis Walsingham in Hampshire.[4] Moreover, historical attention has sometimes concentrated too much on statutes, on the poor-*law*. Conciliar action under the royal prerogative was equally innovative in the field of social welfare and imposed at least as many burdens on local authorities.

At first sight the concerns of the central government appear almost entirely negative, for the Council's most frequent declarations of social policy, in proclamations, concentrated on one simple target, rogues and vagabonds.[5] There was a more positive side to government policy, however, and that appeared in a major Elizabethan innovation: the printed Books of Orders circulated to all justices of the peace. There were two series of these, one describing actions to be taken during epidemics of plague, the other directing local responses to dearth and harvest failure. Each codified earlier practices and imposed a new uniformity on local authorities. According to the plague orders, published for the first time in 1578, infected houses were to be strictly quarantined; the sick and their families should be supported from special rates and guarded in order to prevent fresh contacts. The dearth orders, first published in 1586, kept justices and parish officers equally busy. They had to take local surveys of grain when the harvest failed, to arrange for surpluses to be brought regularly to market, and to see that they were sold there in small quantities to the poor. Both books were reprinted whenever plague or dearth recurred, and they were enforced, haphazardly but widely. Scores of towns were isolating and supporting large numbers of infected households in the plague epidemics of 1592–6 and 1603–9, and lists of grain stocks were drawn up in the hundreds and divisions of several counties in 1586–7 and 1597–8.[6]

Elaborate responses to poverty, dearth and disease were perhaps the most striking elements of Elizabethan social policy, but they were not the only symptoms of contemporary interest in social regulation and control. The Council tried to get at some of the roots of these problems in its prolonged battle against the growth of London: prohibiting new building and the subdivision of houses, at first through a proclamation of 1580 and then with the help of a statute passed in 1593. An act of 1589 against the erection of cottages on commons and wastes was directed against the same phenomenon in the countryside: rapid population growth which went hand in hand with impoverishment, disease and disorder. Statutes against enclosure and in favour of tillage in 1563 and 1598 exhibited a similar desire to prevent disruptive social and economic change. The Statute of Artificers of 1563 showed, among other things, that MPs wished the disciplines of apprenticeship to be widely enforced for the same purpose, in agriculture as well as in industry. Throughout the reign, proclamations enforcing sumptuary legislation were intended to perpetuate existing social distinctions in styles of dress.[7]

Much of this activity – apprenticeship restrictions, enclosure laws and sumptuary regulations in particular – had, of course, a long history behind it. But there was a change in emphasis in the course of the reign. Some old concerns fell into the background and others came to the fore. If we look at proclamations, for example, it is notable that six of the nine Elizabethan proclamations on apparel were issued before 1581, while ten out of thirteen proclamations concerning vagrants were issued after 1581. Parliamentary interest in the condition and conduct of the poor also increased in the last two decades of the reign. Sumptuary regulations were still debated, but government interference with the behaviour of the social élite now aroused opposition, and existing legislation on the subject was repealed in 1604. A warmer parliamentary welcome was given to proposals for stricter regulation of other matters: poverty, on which there were at least seventeen bills in the 1597–8 session alone: drunkenness, inns and alehouses, on which there were thirteen bills between 1576 and 1601; profanation of the sabbath, giving rise to six bills between 1584 and 1601; and bastardy and swearing, on which there were bills in 1597 and 1601 respectively.[8] The manners and behaviour of the lower orders rather than of their betters seemed urgently to require reformation at the end of the reign.

Similar anxieties can be found at the local level, in the by-laws passed by town councils and in the orders made by quarter sessions. By the turn of the century urban magistrates all over the country were trying to control lodgers and inmates, the subdivision of houses, the number of alehouses, and popular recreations, especially on the sabbath. Country justices were spending an increasing amount of time dealing with bastardy, alehouses, unlawful games, cottages, vagrants and the settlement of the poor.[9] Whether one looks at the records of the Council, of Parliament, or of local authorities, there can be no doubt that in the latter half of Elizabeth's reign people in authority felt threatened by rising populations, large numbers of vagrants and paupers, and the disorders they provoked. In the following section we must ask whether the realities were in fact as critical as contemporaries supposed.

II

The most obvious circumstantial explanation for some of the developments considered above lies not in general economic trends but in the temporary crises which occurred in Elizabeth's reign. The Rising in the North appears to have been a particularly formative event. Although there was no justification for the view that vagabonds caused rebellion, the myth was a potent force in the years immediately after 1569, as it had been after 1549. It stimulated searches for vagrants throughout the country, and probably led directly to the legislation of 1572. An associated political conspiracy in Norwich was followed by the remodelling of social welfare there in 1570, and fears for political stability may have inspired the revision of poor-relief machinery in Bristol in the same year. The 1570s were also a decade of considerable activity in London, with the Council prodding the corporation to produce new schemes for the relief and employment of the poor, for grain provision and plague control, especially after a sudden rise in food prices in 1573 and an epidemic in 1577–8.[10]

For the nation as a whole, the disasters of disease and dearth were much more serious in the last two decades of the reign. Plague spread to many towns after devastating outbreaks in London in 1593 and 1603, disrupting economic activity and throwing hundreds of victims onto parish relief. Harvest failures in 1586, and in 1595, 1596 and 1597, brought malnutrition, disease and further surges in mortality to the poorer suburbs of towns and to more isolated rural areas, such as the uplands of Cumbria, where cases of starvation were reported. Food prices rose everywhere, however, and the later 1590s in particular were years of social stress over much of the country. Widespread distress was accompanied by a peak in crimes against property, by a similar high point in illegitimacy rates, and by food and enclosure riots.[11] The comprehensive poor-relief legislation of 1598 was clearly prompted by critical circumstances.

It is much more difficult to judge the extent to which economic conditions were deteriorating in the longer term and producing a gradual increase in the number of the poor. There is no doubt that the standard of living of wage-earners and labourers declined. Population increased at a greater rate than productivity in the sixteenth century; prices rose faster than wages; and the purchasing-power of the latter dropped, to reach its nadir in the years around 1620. According to the available indices, the real value of wages fell by about a quarter in the course of Elizabeth's reign. However, there are serious problems in measuring how far (and how many) people were dependent on money wages, and hence in determining what this drop meant in actuality. All we can say is that it is unlikely that popular living-standards declined by as much as a quarter between 1558 and 1603. We should also beware the temptation to interpret the evidence of starvation and malnutrition in some parts of the country in the later 1590s as evidence that England as a whole was plunging into a 'Malthusian trap'. Even in these exceptional years, outright starvation was localised. By the middle of the seventeenth century the country was feeding a population twice that of 1500; and the growth in agricultural output which this implies had begun before 1600. As for industrial productivity, it has recently been shown that rural and urban industries were expanding by the early seventeenth century, and beginning to stimulate and to satisfy a mass market for all kinds of consumer goods. Again, this economic growth must have begun before 1600.

It would be a serious mistake to let recent revisionist trends in historiography distort our picture too far in the optimistic direction, however. If the traditional view of an unparalleled slump in Tudor living-standards needs some revision, as it certainly does, it retains more truth than an alternative which sees no decline at all. It is now clear that England was further away from a Malthusian situation in 1600 than it had been in 1300; and that prudential checks (notably late marriage and low fertility) rather than the stark positive checks of famine and disease stopped demographic growth in the end, in the mid seventeenth century.[12] But the prudential checks are themselves eloquent testimony to contemporary perceptions that economic conditions had been deteriorating and that per capita incomes had fallen sharply. Things were getting worse for the mass of the population.

Moreover, the gains in agricultural and industrial productivity which became evident after 1620 were achieved only by processes of adjustment which were painful and which seemed to promise little in the way of positive return before then. They required an increase in wage labour in agriculture, which reduced the status of the traditional English peasant, made more people dependent on the market and hence multiplied the potential victims of inflation. They depended partly on an expansion of rural industry, particularly in forest and pastoral areas where there were new squatter settlements formed by migrants from farming-regions where growing populations could not be sustained. Migration to towns, by the poor as well as by more well-to-do apprentices, similarly provided labour for urban industries and services. All these developments brought economic gains in the seventeenth century, but that could not be foreseen in 1603 when the country's labour resources were still demonstrably and grossly underemployed. To Elizabethans they seemed a threat rather than an opportunity.

It has been necessary briefly to sketch in this economic background because it explains many of the contemporary concerns which we noted earlier. We can see why Parliament legislated against squatters and cottagers and why the government was worried about the growth of London. The slow processes of adjustment to rising population also aggravated the two problems which the poor-law was designed to attack. Heavy migration made vagrancy seem an ever more serious threat. Cheap labour supplies meant the emergence in towns and villages of a large and vulnerable class of underemployed 'labouring poor' – a term which was coming into use in this period.[13] In neither case did contemporaries see the facts wholly as they were, but their anxieties produced documents which throw light on both phenomena and on the extent of contemporary misconceptions about them.

The local registers of vagrants punished after the Act of 1598 and the records of searches and examinations before that date are too partial to permit estimates of how many vagabonds there were on the roads of England; or even to prove – though they suggest – that the number was increasing towards the end of the reign. These documents tell us more about local concentrations, on main routes from the north and west to the south-east and in cities and market towns, and about short-term variations from year to year. The later 1590s were particularly bad, since dearth and high prices always pushed paupers onto the roads, moving to towns in search of charity. In Oxford, where a dozen or so vagrants were normally punished each year, there were sixty-seven in 1598; in Salisbury ninety-six vagrants were caught in the same year, compared with an average of less than twenty. One suggestive indication of trends over the longer term, however, comes from the records of Bridewell in London. The number of vagrants punished there rose from sixty-nine a year in 1560–1 to 209 in 1578–9 and to 555 in 1600–1. The city's population rose about threefold in the same period.[14]

Still more indicative of the mounting problem in the metropolis is the fact that vagrancy came to overshadow other categories of offences punished at Bridewell. Intended as it was to 'punish sin', Bridewell dealt with all kinds of petty crime, and especially with sexual misdemeanours. In the early 1560s therefore only 16 per cent of all offenders were vagrants. By 1600–1, however, they comprised 62 per cent of the total.[15] It would be difficult to argue that this change was caused by an autonomous shift in attitude on the part of magistrates or constables. The proportion of sexual offenders declined rapidly, not because of any increase in official tolerance, but because the crowds of rogues and vagabonds left little time for anything else. All the evidence suggests that from the 1570s until the end of the reign London's streets and those of many other towns were full of vagrants and beggars.

If contemporaries were right to regard vagrancy as a growing problem, they saw its character less accurately. William Fleetwood, the Recorder of London, went out himself into the streets one morning in 1582 and apprehended seventy-four rogues whom he sent to Bridewell. 'Some were blind', he wrote, 'and yet great usurers and very rich.'[16] His comment reflected the ineradicable commonplace prejudice that the mobile poor were a wilfully idle, deceitful and criminal class. Some of them certainly were, but they were not a majority. The records of assizes and quarter sessions show that a life on the roads often led vagrants to petty crime of one kind or another: there were thieves, pickpockets, and pedlars who doubled as receivers of stolen goods. But most of the vagrants dealt with summarily by constables after the Act of 1598 were not accused of crimes other than vagrancy: if they had been, they would have been brought before quarter sessions. Rather they were the unemployed, genuinely wandering in search of a living, at least at first. Many had once been apprentices or servants; sometimes they had trades after their names. But now, as one of them said, they 'lived poorly by the charity of good people' while they travelled.[17] The records of vagrants examined in Warwick and some of the Midland counties in the middle of the reign, in Salisbury and Oxford at the end, make it plain that the roots of the rising tide of pauper migration in the late sixteenth century lay in an economy which was unable to employ a growing population.

When local authorities turned to look at the other half of the problem of poverty, the needs of the domestic resident poor of each parish, they thought it could be reduced to manageable proportions by simple means. Once they had identified them, they could expel strangers and vagrants. They could apprehend the wilfully idle poor and discipline them to habits of work in houses of correction. That would leave only a rump of respectable paupers to be supported: in particular, the sick and disabled, widows and orphan children. In this way the disciplines of whip and workhouse could restrict poor-relief to the traditional categories of the deserving poor. This optimistic assumption inspired many of the censuses and listings of the poor which were taken in towns and villages in the later sixteenth century, and some of these valuable records survive.

Their contents scarcely justified optimism. Their authors often had different definitions of poverty in mind, and that makes comparison between them difficult. They were also prompted by diverse local circumstances: an industrial depression in the case of Norwich in 1570 the distress caused by dearth in Warwick in 1587, and in Ipswich, some parishes of

north Kent, and Crompton in Lancashire in the later 1590s.[18]
Nevertheless, they all revealed poverty to be a much larger and
more intractable phenomenon than their originators had
supposed. Roughly 10 per cent of the population of St Mary's
parish, Warwick, required relief in 1587. Nearly 12 per cent of
the inhabitants of three north Kent parishes were thought to
have a claim to public support in 1598. In nine of the twelve
parishes of Ipswich in 1597 13 per cent of the people were
unable to support themselves. No less than 22 per cent of the
English population in Norwich (foreign immigrants were
excluded) were classed as poor in 1570.

These figures are remarkable enough as indicators of the
perceived quantity of poverty in the later sixteenth century; but
the listings also tell us something about its quality. There is
little sign of the idle wastrels, sleeping in doorways and living
solely by begging, whom the Norwich citizens, for example,
expected to find.[31] Some disabled paupers and many small
children did go out to beg, but they were helping to support
small households whose other members, women and children
included, worked when they could, spinning or weaving,
making lace or stockings, nursing or doing domestic chores for
their betters. In Ipswich some of the poor had children 'at
school' learning trades. In Crompton they rented their own
houses. In Norwich a few of them even had mortgage debts.
They were trying to maintain, not flagrantly abandoning,
respectability.

In every listing of the poor, women and children in broken
families were particularly prominent: a reflection of the
burdens which old age, widowhood and the death of a parent
imposed on family budgets. Yet there were also plenty of
structurally 'normal' nuclear families, who were in poverty
simply because of low earnings. Married couples were at the
head of 38 per cent of the poor households in Warwick, of 51 per
cent in Ipswich and of 62 per cent in Norwich. These were the
labouring poor, not the poor by impotency or casualty, to use
contemporary terms. Their importance emerges most clearly in
the great Norwich census, which is full enough to permit an
estimate of the cause of poverty in each household. Old age,
illness or the death of a bread-winner accounts for the state of
35 per cent of the families; in 7 per cent of cases the family had

been deserted by the father; in 8 per cent poverty appears to have been the result of a large number of children; but in the remaining 50 per cent of cases it can only have resulted from irregular employment, unemployment or low wages. Here once more were the victims of an economy which was failing to employ an expanding population.

There was thus a whole spectrum of poverty, stretching from the marginal group of the impotent poor, who were generally acknowledged to be entitled to relief, to the labouring poor who would usually have been expected to support themselves and who could not readily be distinguished from ordinary society. It was not easy to draw strict dividing-lines across this spectrum, although contemporaries desperately tried. Only a small proportion of the people listed in the more comprehensive censuses was actually supported by the parish at the time: a quarter of the families listed in Norwich, and one third of the poor – 4 per cent of the population – in Ipswich. Yet in both towns other families were said to be equally 'deserving relief', and people slipped into abject poverty easily, especially in years of dearth. The Warwick census of 1587 included eleven families who had been well able to support themselves when an earlier listing was drawn up in 1582, and another thirteen who had then been 'ready to decay' but had not yet done so. We can conclude from the censuses that 4 or 5 per cent of the population of a town commonly received relief in the later sixteenth century, and that another 10 or 15 per cent was recognised to be 'poor' and liable at some time to claim it. But the line between the two was fluctuating and elastic. It was certainly never possible to restrict urban poor-relief to the impotent.

In the countryside the task of discrimination was easier, if only because the able-bodied poor often moved off to the towns. In the three north Kent parishes only 1.5 per cent of the population received public support, and they were the impotent. But by the end Elizabeth's reign even country parishes were finding that they had on occasion to help a labourer and his family, alongside the widows who were the familiar figures on relief-rolls.[19] As a result, outdoor relief and the poor-rates which paid for it became the essential elements in the poor-law. Whipping vagrants did nothing to reduce the burden of the domestic poor of towns; workhouses and work stocks employed no more than a tiny minority of them. Only the dole was left, and the number receiving it and the cost on the rates continued to increase, despite the desire of contemporaries to keep them down.

In this respect and more generally, therefore, circumstances help us to understand Elizabethan reactions to poverty. It is plausible to argue from the evidence that conditions were getting worse: there were more vagrants and more paupers with valid claim to public assistance, and both were the result, not just of frequent temporary crises such as dearth and plague, but of long-term economic trends which produced heavy mobility and underemployment. Whether one describes these realities as 'critical' is perhaps a question of semantics. We can readily appreciate why contemporaries thought them so. Even though they failed fully to appreciate its causes, 'the great plenty of poverty in all the cities, great towns and other inferior market towns in England and Wales' was obvious.[20] To understand the full nature of the contemporary response, however, why it was so energetic in some directions and so misconceived in others, we must turn from the circumstances which made it necessary to the attitudes which equally helped to shape it.

III

It might seem that the natural conservatism of any social élite is sufficient to explain Elizabethan reactions to the conditions described above. An instinctive desire to maintain degree, order and place would set all sixteenth-century authorities against mobility, idleness, urban growth and the disorderly consequences of poverty. That this is not the whole story, however, is suggested by the opposition which some of the measures taken aroused at the time. However conservative its inspiration, public action in the interests of social welfare and social discipline had radical implications.

Part of the opposition to the poor-laws was, of course, self-interested. Taxation for poor-relief was vehemently resisted, in Warwick and elsewhere, because it was taxation.[21]

Those who were the victims or beneficiaries of public action had equally good reason to object to its regulatory aspects, to abuse the magistrates who, in the words of a Thetford man in 1577, 'did more than they might do . . . dealing with the poor but not with the rich'.[22] But there were also issues of greater principle involved. In the parliamentary debates on the poor-law in 1571 and 1572, several members questioned whether the definition of a vagrant should be drawn so broadly that it encompassed such representatives of traditional wayfaring-life as minstrels. Miles Sandys thought the whole law 'oversharp and bloody': vagrancy could easily be eliminated if the justices worked to 'relieve every [poor] man at his own house'. On the other hand, Thomas Wilson urged harsh penalties because of the 'looseness and lewdness' of the times: 'he said it was no charity to give to such a one as we know not, being a stranger unto us'.[23]

Behind such controversy lay two related questions. The first was whether the relief of the poor was a matter for government intervention at all. Should it not be left to the old practices of neighbourly, and largely informal, charity? The parishioners of part of the West Riding adopted this view when they opposed the prohibition of begging and the introduction of rates in 1598 on the grounds that 'many are able to give relief which are not able to give money'; neighbours would support their neighbours with help in kind.[24] The second question was how much discrimination there should be in the giving of alms, whether public or private. Should minstrels or strangers be treated generously, as traditional ideals of hospitality might seem to simply?

These issues were never starkly articulated in this period, but they were tacitly present in much of the literature on charity and hospitality published in Elizabeth's reign. No English writers took as hard a line in favour of public intervention and discrimination as Martin Bucer and some continental reformers; still less did any of them openly oppose these innovations. While some stressed their necessity, however, others expressed reservations and insisted on qualifications. Robert Allen, for example, warned his readers against being too scrupulous in their giving: in the end it was better 'that alms should be cast away, than any creature should perish for want of relief'.[25] The

tension between old ideals of private hospitality and the newer
emphasis on public discrimination may even have been felt at
the village level. It has been argued that it helps to explain
many of the witchcraft accusations of the period, which had
their roots in the local antagonisms and feelings of guilt aroused
when neighbourly charity was denied.[26]

There was certainly a good deal of confusion in practice.
Informal and indiscriminate almsgiving continued, on an
unquantifiable but probably large scale. Vagrants went on
calling 'at many gentlemen's and honest men's houses to have
their charity'.[27] Although poor-rates became more common
after the Act of 1572, it was only in the generation after the 1598
statute that they spread to a majority of rural parishes. It is
unlikely that they raised anything like the sums given in alms in
the streets or in voluntary contributions in parish churches
before the end of the reign; just as they certainly did not match
the sums available for poor relief from privately endowed
charities.[28] The government itself was often forced to pay more
than lip-service to old ideals while advocating the new. In years
of dearth the Church was called upon to publicise the
traditional virtues of neighbourly hospitality, with scarcely a
hint of discrimination.

Yet the trend throughout the reign was plainly towards more
government intervention and direction of welfare activity. The
Books of Orders for dearth assumed that public regulation of
markets would replace neighbourly charity as a more efficient
and effective use of scarce resources when the harvest failed.
The Books of Orders for plague imposed on infected households quarantine restrictions which prevented the visiting of sick
neighbours, and thus, as some contemporaries complained,
flew in the face of traditional charitable obligations.[29] The
campaign against vagrants and beggars and against indiscriminate almsgiving grew in vigour. By 1603 some old ideals
were in retreat.

One reason for this was the commonplace assumption that
the old ideals had conspicuously failed in practice. Whether
enamoured of new developments or not, many contemporaries
bewailed the decline of charity. Thanks to W. K. Jordan's
studies of endowed charities, we can now see that they were
probably wrong. Though applying only to discriminating

forms of charitable endeavour, and though controversial, Jordan's figures show that the yield from private endowments for poor-relief had made good the loss of monastic almsgiving by the 1580s, and that it more or less kept pace with inflation throughout the reign.[30] Socially concerned observers had no inkling of that, however. They saw only the disappearance of the old religious charitable institutions, and the empty or absent poor-boxes in churches;[31] and some of them continued to think, as they had done since the 1540s, that the state must step in to make good the deficiency.

Continuous from before 1558, too, were the aspirations of governments anxious to prove their humanist credentials with a little social engineering in the interests of the common weal. William Cecil provides a link with the days of Thomas Cromwell in his encouragement of projects and projectors on economic and social matters; and the Books of Orders were one result of his interest in and correspondence about social problems, particularly in London. It seems clear also that the capacity for autonomous growth which infects most bureaucratic innovations was at work. The increasing use of divisional or petty sessions, for example, which allowed justices to regulate the affairs of their own neighbourhood, shows that once laws were on the statute book some local administrators were creative and energetic in implementing them.[32] Yet, in addition to all this, it may be argued that there was a new ideological input in Elizabeth's reign. It came from Protestant religious enthusiasm.

An older tradition of historical writing about Puritanism, associated particularly with R. H. Tawney, attributed to it a 'new medicine for poverty' which was characterised by punishment rather than relief and by harsh discrimination rather than real charity.[33] It is now clear, however, that that view is mistaken. More recent work has shown that the social attitudes and objectives of Puritans hardly differed from those of other members of the social, political and religious élite in Elizabethan England. They favoured discrimination in poor-relief, certainly, but then so did other people; and their support for the poor-law was not unqualified. Some of them shared contemporary doubts about aspects of it. Thomas Norton, for example, was one of the defenders of minstrels in 1571–2.[34]

Many of them wanted to increase generosity to the poor, to see new hospitals, almshouses and charitable doles, as well as to reinforce social discipline. The polarity between harsh repression and generous toleration assumed in the Tawney model is as misconceived as the contrast which has been assumed to exist between 'Puritan' and 'Anglican' social thought more generally.

Even so, there is considerable evidence that Puritans made a powerful contribution to the developments we have been seeking to explain. This lay first and foremost in what has been termed their 'social activism'.[35] Their determination to shape a godly commonwealth led them to undertake practical reforms in pursuit of what were fundamentally commonplace social ideals, while their less committed colleagues did nothing. Again and again we find godly ministers and magistrates, often in close alliance, initiating new regulations and new institutions. It was the presbyterian divine, Thomas Cartwright, acting, it has been said, like a Calvinist deacon, who inspired the listings of the poor in Warwick in the 1580s and who helped to reform poor-relief there. The result was certainly closer discrimination in the giving of relief, but also a large increase in the sums spent on poor households. The consequences were similar in Norwich a decade earlier, where new orders for the poor specifically provided for a deacon in every ward. The wholesale reform of social welfare there between 1570 and 1572 occurred under a mayor, John Aldrich, who had Puritan leanings, and on the eve of the city's greatest fame as a Puritan citadel guided by its 'apostle', John More. As an MP Aldrich may well have influenced the poor-relief legislation of the 1570s, just as later Puritans, such as Robert Wroth and George More, took a notable part on committees on the poor-law in the last parliaments of the reign.[36]

Energetic Calvinist paternalism had a further consequence. Directed as it was against a multitude of social and moral ills, it strengthened and multiplied the existing links between poor-relief and other forms of social regulation. In the 1570s some of the Norfolk justices had regular divisional meetings at the Acle Bridewell, where, after prayers, they punished rogues, bastard-bearers, drunkards and other unruly people. Walsingham reported to Cecil that it was work which was both 'necessary and . . . full of piety'.[37] In 1578 the Puritan justices of Bury St Edmunds similarly drew up a list of orders against offences from idleness and fornication to usury and witchcraft. In Parliament men such as Wroth and More were active on committees on a whole range of subjects concerning the conduct of the rude masses.[38] The relief and regulation of the poor was conceived as one part of a wider campaign for the reformation of popular manners.

The result could only be a hardening of established prejudices about the disorderly poor. Despite new generosity in the provision of outdoor relief, despite the facts which the censuses revealed about virtuous, inescapable poverty, the effect of much Puritan rhetoric was to associate the poor with social threats of all kinds. Puritan preachers and writers might admit the existence of the respectable pauper, but in their by-laws and orders Puritan magistrates spoke a different language, stressing the infectious vices which indigence bred. A proclamation in Norwich in 1571 pictured a society in which the lower orders slid inexorably 'from idleness to drunkenness to whoredom to shameful incest and abominable life, greatly to the dishonour of God and ruin of the commonwealth'. The overseers must therefore search the houses of the poor 'several times in every week' to identify men who broke down hedges for firewood, girls who wished 'to keep house by themselves', drunkards and those who absented 'themselves from their own houses at unseasonable times in the night'. Such orders display what Professor Collinson has called 'collective paranoia'; and it was a paranoia which prevented any cool appraisal of social and economic realities and which encouraged their misinterpretation.[39]

Not everyone took so committed or extreme a view, of course. Puritan magistrates and ministers were a distinct minority. But they were simply in the vanguard in the growing use of poor-relief as a means of social control, and their approach, in modified tone, was often widely adopted. While Puritans in Ipswich denied poor-relief to those who did not attend church, other local authorities refused it to those who broke hedges or 'unreverently abused any that is a contributor to the poor'. By the 1590s several towns had orders against the disorderly poor associating them, as in Colchester, with 'thefts, pilfering and

other lewd and ill vices'.[40] It was a less strident indictment than
that in Norwich in 1571, but its message was the same; and it
had the effect of branding as disorderly, with labels once
applied only to a small and marginal group, that larger class of
the poor which we have seen emerging in Elizabeth's reign.
That was a major and lasting achievement, contributing to the
closer definition of the respectable and unruly segments of
society and to the growing gap between them. ,

A final caveat should be entered here. Much of the reaction
to social problems described above was indeed rhetoric. Even
laws and proclamations were often not enforced: they too were
propaganda as much as prescriptions of viable solutions for real
problems. The most burdensome provisions of social legislation, those relating to apprenticeship or work stocks, for
example, were never fully implemented. Quarter sessions
dealt more readily with symptoms, attacking bastardy, alehouses, unlawful games and, of course, vagrants; and even this
campaign was only just beginning in the 1590s and was to
acquire greater momentum in the early decades of the seventeenth century.[41] We have seen that rhetoric and propaganda
influenced contemporary ways of thinking, but we must ask in
conclusion whether the efforts surveyed in this essay had any
more positive impact, in the alleviation of poverty or the
imposition of social control.

IV

As far as poverty is concerned, enough has perhaps been said
already to indicate that the effects of contemporary remedies
were probably marginal. The deliberate redistribution of wealth
from rich to poor by 1603 was minimal. For example, the total
yield of endowed charities for poor-relief amounted to less than
0.25 per cent of the national income;[42] and the amount raised
by poor-rates was much smaller than that. At the margin of
subsistence and in crisis years public measures probably had a
greater effect: control of markets, subsidised sales of grain, and
increases in outdoor relief must have done something to save
some people from starvation, especially in towns – though the
effects of these enterprises have never been quantified. But the

impact on poverty more generally was slight. It was to be economic growth not public welfare which alleviated social problems in the seventeenth century.

Much the same may be said about efforts to impose social control. Although the English welfare system might seem at first sight one reason why England had less internal disorder than some other countries at the time, it is difficult to substantiate the case. Against it we might point to the small numbers actually relieved, to the lack of effective police activity against vagrants, and above all, perhaps, to the fact that poor-relief was largely confined to social groups who would not have been major threats to public order anyway: orphans, widows, broken families and a few of the labouring poor. Again, the situation may have been different in crisis years. Grain policies, for example, were intended to prevent food riots and the threat or reality of disorder often prompted their use. They were implemented in Northampton in 1586–7 because 'our poor people are so hardly distressed that we stand in great doubt of some mutiny or unlawful attempt to arise amongst them'.[43] On the other hand, the frequency of food riots in the later 1590s hardly suggests that efforts to prevent them were wholly successful.

The issue is not quite as simple as that, however. Elizabethan social policies may have had a real effect, not through direct alleviation of poverty or disorder, but through their impact on attitudes. We return, in fact, to their role as propaganda. One function of the paternalism explicit in Elizabethan grain policies, for example, was to persuade poor consumers that the government shared their view of the social order and identified the same enemies of the common weal as they did: middlemen above all. The persuasion probably worked to some degree, and on this argument there would have been more disorder than there was in years of dearth if social policies had not existed. Even if scarcely successful in practice, welfare activities did something to encourage and to justify deference.[44]

Social policies also had a propaganda effect on those who were not their objects. One reason for the absence of popular rebellion and serious public disorder after 1569, it has been argued, was the reluctance of the 'middling sort' – prosperous farmers and artisans – to lead it as they had once done. There were economic reasons for that, as local communties were increasingly polarised between the relatively rich and the poor. But there was also an attitudinal shift as the middling ranks of society adopted the view of their superiors that popular behaviour was deviant, disorderly and dangerous. They became agents of social control themselves and, in some cases, enthusiasts for a reformation of manners.[45] Some of the policies we have described were an expression of that social distancing; but they also contributed to its formation.

The sticks as well as the carrots present in Elizabethan social policies thus helped to satisfy contemporary expectations and so to maintain social stability, even if the promise was greater than the performance in both cases. The ambivalent combination of charitable generosity and social discipline which we have seen in the vagrancy and poor-rate provisions of the law, in the ambitions of Puritan activists and in the efforts of local authorities, served a purpose. It was an uneasy combination, but regulation and relief, social control and provision for the poor, went hand in hand – as in social policies they always do.

Conclusion

CHRISTOPHER HAIGH

By 1960 Sir John Neale and Conyers Read had, it seemed, sewn up Elizabethan political history. Neale had contributed a warm-hearted and readable life of the Queen, three substantial books on the framework and events of parliamentary politics, and some imaginative essays on the working of the political system. Conyers Read had provided his selection of the essential detail, in a monumental three-volume biography of Sir Francis Walsingham and two volumes on William Cecil. The interpretative fortress they had built, out of four and a half thousand pages in books alone, seemed impregnable. Perhaps it was the apparent invulnerability of their work which brought advance in the political history of the reign to a virtual standstill for nearly twenty years – or perhaps, in the 1960s and after, historians were busy following Keith Thomas and Lawrence Stone into exciting new subjects: marriage, sex and witchcraft. There were some important new insights (most of them from Patrick Collinson) in ecclesiastical history, and some valuable county studies (especially Hassell Smith's of Norfolk), but few besides Wallace MacCaffrey soldiered on in central political history. Even the flood of biographies of Elizabeth abated in 1963 and became a trickle from 1974. The reign of Gloriana became – of all things – dull and predictable.

But, by the late 1970s, the revisionary ferment which had brought intellectual excitement to the study of the early Tudor and early Stuart periods had changed the context of Elizabethan history, and had begun to enliven the Queen's reign itself. The implications of county and ecclesiastical studies for the general history of the period began to be recognised, and historians came to see the reign from the standpoint of Neale's 'Elizabethan Political Scene' rather than his *Elizabeth I and her Parliaments*. 'Revisionism' has not taken over the reign of Elizabeth – any more than it has taken over interpretation of the reigns of her predecessors and successors – but it has made the period *lively* once again. Much new work is afoot, and some of the essays in this collection are exploratory forays and preliminary reports. Almost all the authors in the volume are now writing books on issues in Elizabethan history, and many others are engaged in work of equal (or greater) importance. It should be stressed that there is much that we do not yet know – and more that we will never know. It is to be hoped that (through the combined efforts of Sybil Jack, Christopher Coleman and James Alsop) the vexed and significant question of Elizabeth's finances will soon be sorted out – since all we know now is that the figures given in F. C. Dietz's *English Public Finance, 1558–1641* (1932) were derived from inappropriate records and are therefore wrong. The conclusion of the various studies of aspects of Court and aristocratic politics which are now in progress is also awaited, and perhaps some brave historian will take up the study of the career of Robert Cecil which was terminated by the untimely death of Joel Hurstfield. There is more to be done, but it is striking how much recently *has* been done. After years in which up-to-date general studies of the Elizabethan period could hardly be found, new volumes are appearing: David Palliser's social and economic history *The Age of Elizabeth* (1983) and Robert Ashton's *Reformation and Revolution, 1558–1660* (1984), with further surveys expected (at the time of writing) from Patrick Collinson and Penry Williams.

The authors in this volume are, therefore, conscious that they have written at an early stage in the revision of Elizabethan history, and they offer their conclusions with as much humility as they can muster. It is inevitable that the first phase of reconstruction should be in part critical and even destructive of what has gone before. A field which has been fallow for some years must be ploughed up before new planting can take place. Readers will certainly have noted the several explicit thrusts against the work of Sir John Neale, and probably detected covert criticism elsewhere. It is the fate of those who have dominated a subject to be attacked by those who come after – as it is the fate of those who stand on a giant's shoulders to be accused of trampling him down. The contributors to the volume were not recruited from any particular interpretative school: some had been taught by Neale, and all were influenced by his books. It is not claimed that the new work now reported upon will overthrow all that Neale and others wrote, still less that it will not itself be challenged. There is, indeed, a slight tension in the collection between those essays which stress cohesion and stability and those which reflect division and disruption in Elizabethan England. There are differences of emphasis (to say no more) over the definitiveness of the Elizabethan 'settlement', the extent to which Court disputes caused political difficulties, and the level and effectiveness of Protestant preaching. This volume does not present a party manifesto, rather an agenda for discussion of neglected issues. The academic 'controversy' is the historian's natural milieu, his equivalent of the scientist's laboratory and symposium. Only by debate can history be kept alive, and saved from reduction to inherited platitudes.

List of Abbreviations

AGR PEA	Brussels, Archives Générales du Royaume, Papiers d'Etat et de l'Audience
AMRE CPA	Paris, Archives du Ministère des Relations Extérieures, Correspondence Politique, Angleterre
APC	*Acts of the Privy Council*
BIHR	*Bulletin of the Institute of Historical Research*
BL	British Library
BL Add. MSS	British Library, Additional MSS
BL Lansd. MSS	British Library, Lansdowne MSS
Bod. Lib.	Bodleian Library, Oxford
CRO	County Record Office
CPSD	*Calendar of State Papers, Domestic*
CSPF	*Calendar of State Papers, Foreign*
CSPSc	*Calendar of State Papers, Scotland*
CSPSp	*Calendar of State Papers, Spanish*
Dudley MSS	Dudley Papers, Longleat House
EcHR	*Economic History Review*
EHR	*English Historical Review*
Haynes & Murdin	*Collection of State Papers . . . left by William Cecil, Lord Burghley*, ed. S. Haynes and W. Murdin (1740–59)
HJ	*Historical Journal*
HMC	Historical Manuscripts Commission
H of C, 1509–58	*The History of Parliament. The House of Commons, 1509–1558*, ed. S. T. Bindoff (1982)
H of C, 1558—1603	*The History of Parliament. The House of Commons, 1558–1603*, ed. P. W. Hasler (1981)
LASP	*List and Analysis of State Papers, Foreign*
P & P	*Past and Present*
PRO	Public Record Office
Rel. Pol.	*Relations Politiques des Pays-Bas et de l'Angleterre sous le Règne de Philippe II*, ed. J. M. B. C. Kervyn de Lettenhove (Brussels, 1882–1900)
RO	Record Office
STC	*Short Title Catalogue*, ed. A. W. Pollard and G. R. Redgrave (1926)
TRHS	*Transactions of the Royal Historical Society*

Bibliography

The place of publication of books is London, except where otherwise stated or for the publications of learned societies.

INTRODUCTION

There are no comprehensive, up-to-date general surveys of the reign: D. M. Palliser, *The Age of Elizabeth* (1983) is a thoughtful study of economic and social issues, but R. Ashton, *Reformation and Revolution, 1558–1660* (1984) has only about two hundred pages to spare for our period and is conservative in approach. Among older works, good sense is to be found in G. R. Elton, *England under the Tudors* (2nd edn, 1974), and energetic enthusiasm in A. L. Rowse, *The England of Elizabeth* (1950). There are lively, but very brief, essays in S. Adams (ed.), *Queen Elizabeth I: Most Politick Princess* (1984). The best biographies of Elizabeth are: M. Creighton, *Queen Elizabeth* (1896), J. E. Neale, *Queen Elizabeth* (1934), J. Hurstfield, *Elizabeth I and the Unity of England* (1960), and P. Johnson, *Elizabeth I: A Study in Power and Intellect* (1974); those who find the nationalism of the first and the romanticism of the rest unpalatable may prefer the more astringent tones of C. Erickson, *The First Elizabeth* (1983) – which is, however, weakened by an uncritical reliance on the suspect reports of Spanish ambassadors. The classic composite modern interpretation of Elizabethan politics will be found in the 4500 pages of: Neale's biography; J. E. Neale, *Essays in Elizabethan History* (1958); J. E. Neale, *The Elizabethan House of Commons* (1949); J. E. Neale, *Elizabeth I and her Parliaments* (2 vols, 1953, 1957); C. Read, *Mr Secretary Walsingham and the Policy of Queen Elizabeth* (3 vols, Oxford, 1925); C. Read, *Mr Secretary Cecil and Queen Elizabeth* (1955); and C. Read, *Lord Burghley and Queen Elizabeth* (1960). W. MacCaffrey's *The Shaping of the Elizabethan Regime* (1969) is a lively and innovative version of the years 1558–72, but his *Queen Elizabeth and the Making of Policy, 1572–1588* (Princeton, NJ, 1981) adds less to what was known and does not respond to the nuances of recent work. The constitutional and administrative structure of the kingdom is documented and discussed in G. R. Elton, *The Tudor Constitution* (2nd edn, Cambridge, 1982), and the realities of government and politics surveyed briefly in A. G. R. Smith, *The Government of Elizabethan England* (1967), and more extensively in P. Williams, *The Tudor Regime* (1979). Much new work is in process: in particular, the provision of good general studies of the period can be expected to improve soon with the appearance of Patrick Collinson's volume in the Arnold 'New History of England' series, and the Penry Williams contribution to the new Oxford histories. Further bibliographical guidance may be sought from C. Read, *Bibliography of British History: Tudor Period, 1485–1603* (2nd edn, Oxford, 1959) and M. Levine, *Tudor England, 1485–1603* (Cambridge, 1968).

1. ELIZABETH'S FIRST YEAR: THE CONCEPTION AND BIRTH
    OF THE ELIZABETHAN POLITICAL WORLD

Most of the historical debate about 1559 turns around Elizabeth's intentions toward the Church and the parliamentary action that resulted in the Elizabethan settlement. Since 1953 the standard account of the Parliament of 1559 has been provided by the first three chapters of J. E. Neale's *Elizabeth and her Parliaments*, I: *1559–1581* (1953). Neale's insistence that the religious settlement was shaped by a Puritan opposition in Parliament has recently been challenged by N. L. Jones, *Faith by Statute: Parliament and the Settlement of Religion, 1559*, Royal Historical Society Studies in History XXXII (1982). Jones demonstrates that the Queen was opposed by Catholics in the Lords who nearly wrecked her reform programme. W. S. Hudson, in his *Cambridge and the Elizabethan Settlement of 1559* (Durham, NC, 1980), has bolstered the rejection of Neale by arguing that the Elizabethan settlement was exactly what the leaders of the Elizabethan government desired. Further doubt has been cast on Neale's thesis by J. Loach, who showed that the resistance to the Crown by the Commons postulated by Neale is not in evidence between 1547 and 1559. In her 'Conservatism and Consent in Parliament, 1547–1559', in *The Mid-Tudor Polity c. 1540–1560*, ed. J. Loach and R. Tittler (1980) pp. 9–28, she finds dissent a characteristic more of the Lords than of the Commons. Lastly, K. Bartlett has shown that, contrary to Neale's assumptions, the Marian exiles did not make up a united party in the Commons in 1559: see 'The Role of the Marian Exiles', in *H of C, 1558–1603*, I, 102–10. Many of the speeches made in Parliament in 1559 are available in *Proceedings in the Parliaments of Queen Elizabeth I: 1559–1581*, ed. T. E. Hartley (Leicester, 1981) pp. 7–51.

Studies on various aspects of the religious settlement tend to cover more territory than this essay, but those interested in its immediate impact on the Church might consult some of the following. F. Heal's 'The Bishops and the Act of Exchange of 1559,' *HJ*, XVII (1974) 227–46, has been joined by N. L. Jones's 'Profiting from Religious Reform: The Land Rush of 1559', *HJ*, XXII (1979) 279–94, in exploring legislation that directly affected the Church's income. W. Haugaard's *Elizabeth and the English Reformation* (Cambridge, 1968) provides many insights into contemporary reactions to the settlement, and P. Collinson, in his *Archbishop Grindal 1519–1583: The Struggle for a Reformed Church* (1979), devotes a chapter to the role of his hero in the visitation of 1559. The most detailed study of the impact of the new settlement is H. Gee, *The Elizabethan Clergy and the Settlement of Religion 1558–1564* (Oxford, 1898).

In the realm of domestic politics and foreign policy W. T. MacCaffrey provides an excellent analysis of the beginning of the reign in *The Shaping of the Elizabethan Regime* (Princton, NJ, 1968). In order to understand the circumstances of Elizabeth's accession one needs to know the Marian background, a good summary of which is provided by D. M. Loades, *The Reign of Mary Tudor* (1979) pp. 458–74. R. B. Wernham provides a succinct account of the negotiations at Cateau Cambrésis in *Before the Armada: The Growth of English Foreign Policy 1485–1588* (1966) ch. 28. The only detailed study of the treaty of Cateau Cambrésis is A. Ruble, *Le Traité de Cateau Cambrésis* (Paris, 1889).

2. ELIZA ENTHRONED? THE COURT AND ITS POLITICS

It is impossible to do justice in a short survey to the voluminous literature relevant to a study of the Elizabethan Court. Some points of caution might be noted. Among the most difficult sources to employ are the seventeenth-century histories and collections of anecdotes, for the portrait of the Court they provide is of questionable veracity. In this category are William Camden, *Annales Rerum Anglicarum . . . Regnante Elizabetha* (1615; English edn 1688; modern abridged edn, ed. W. T. MacCaffrey, Chicago and London, 1970); Thomas Fuller, *The Worthies of England* (1662; modern edn 1952); John Aubrey, *Brief Lives* (1813; modern edn 1949); and, in particular, Sir Robert Naunton, *Fragmenta Regalia* (1641; modern edn 1895). More reliable, and valuable for the unconscious glimpses into the Court they provide, are the few contemporary memoirs: used in this essay were *The Memoirs of Robert Carey*, ed. F. H. Mares (Oxford, 1972); *The Private Diary of John Dee*, ed. J. O. Halliwell, Camden Society XIX (1842), and 'The Compendious Rehersal of John Dee . . . A° 1592, November 9', in *Johannis Confratis et Monachi Glastoniensis Chronica*, ed. T. Hearne (Oxford, 1726); *Elizabeth of England. Certain Observations concerning the Life and Reign of Queen Elizabeth by John Clapham*, ed. E. P. and C. Read (Philadelphia, 1951); Sir John Harington, *A Tract on the Succession to the Crown (AD1602)*, ed. C. R. Markham, Roxburghe Club (1880) and *The Letters and Epigrams of Sir John Harington*, ed. N. E. McClure (Philadelphia, 1930).

The basic modern study of the institutions of the Court is E. K. Chambers, *The Elizabethan Stage*, I (Oxford, 1923). For the Household, see also A. Woodward, 'Purveyance for the Royal Household in the Reign of Queen Elizabeth', *Transactions of the American Philosophical Society*, n.s., XXXV, no. 1 (Philadelphia, 1945), and R. C. Braddock, 'The Royal Household, 1540–1560: A Study in Office-Holding in Tudor England' (Northwestern University PhD thesis, 1971). A. Jeffries Collins, *The Jewels and Plate of Queen Elizabeth I: The Inventory of 1574* (1955), provides a useful account of the Jewel House and its Master, John Ashley; M. M. Reese, *The Royal Office of Master of the Horse* (1976), is more popular in style. G. E. Aylmer, *The King's Servants. The Civil Service of Charles I, 1625–1640* (1961), is the best introduction to the personnel of the early modern Court. Fundamental to any study of the Tudor Court is D. R. Starkey, 'The King's Privy Chamber, 1485–1547' (Cambridge University PhD thesis, 1974); the Elizabethan Privy Chamber is studied in a similar manner in the article by Pam Wright in *The English Court from the Wars of the Roses to the Civil War*, ed. D. R. Starkey (forthcoming, ?1984). (I am very grateful to the author for allowing me to see a draft of her article.)

There are several important surveys of Court politics: J. E. Neale, 'The Elizabethan Political Scene', British Academy Raleigh Lecture, 1948, repr. in *Essays in Elizabethan History* (1958); W. T. MacCaffrey, 'Place and Patronage in Elizabethan Politics', in *Elizabethan Government and Society. Essays presented to Sir John Neale*, ed. S. T. Bindoff, J. Hurstfield and C. H. Williams (1961); G. R. Elton, 'Tudor Government: The Points of Contact. III. The Court', *TRHS*, 5th ser., XXVI (1976); and P. Williams, 'Court and Polity under Elizabeth I', *Bulletin of the John Rylands University Library*, LXV (1973). In

'Faction, Clientage and Party. English Politics, 1550–1603', *History Today*, XXXII (1982), I have made some suggestions about the nature of Elizabethan factions.

The standard political histories and biographies of the reign all contain material of relevance, though not all their conclusions about Court politics should be accepted. The same applies to the studies of minor Court figures, which nevertheless provide useful information on personal relationships. In this category are E. K. Chambers, *Sir Henry Lee. An Elizabethan Portrait* Oxford, 1936); the two studies by C. A. Bradford, *Blanche Parry, Queen Elizabeth's Gentlewoman* (1935), and *Helena, Marchioness of Northampton* (1936); and L. C. John, 'Roger Manners, Elizabethan Courtier', *Hungtington Library Quarterly*, XII (1948). The publicaton of *H of C, 1509–1558*, and *H of C, 1558–1603* has, however, revolutionised the study of the Tudor political élite and will be fundamental for any future work on the membership of the Court.

3. PARLIAMENT

The history of the Elizabethan Parliament is most fully rehearsed in the work of J. E. Neale: *The Elizabethan House of Commons* (1949); *Elizabeth I and her Parliaments*, 2 vols (1953, 1957); 'The Commons' Privilege of Free Speech in Parliament', *Tudor Studies . . . Presented to A. F. Pollard*, ed. R. W. Seton-Watson (1924) pp. 231–57. For much of his interpretation he relied on W. Notestein, 'The Winning of the Initiative by the House of Commons', *Proceedings of the British Academy*, XI (1924) 125–75. Of late it has come to be recognised that these venerable works pretty thoroughly misinterpret what happened and leave important parts of the story untold, though the editorial contributions to *Proceedings in the Parliaments of Elizabeth I*, I: *1559–1581*, ed. T. E. Hartley (Leicester, 1981), still rely on Neale. Though the new approach has not so far produced a treatment as comprehensive as Neale's and able simply to replace him, enough has appeared to document the need to start again. On records and procedure, Sheila Lambert has cleared up many of the errors found in the old view: 'The Clerks and Records of the House of Commons, 1600–1640', *BIHR*, XLIII (1970) 215–31; and 'Procedure in the House of Commons in the Early Stuart Period', *EHR*, XCV (1980) 753–81. M. A. R. Graves, *The House of Lords in the Parliaments of Edward VI and Mary I: An Institutional Study* (Cambridge, 1981) at last, though not quite for the period in question, brings out the importance of the Upper House. Particular points of revision have been made by N. L. Jones, *Faith by Statute: Parliament and the Settlement of Religion*, Royal Historical Society Studies in History XXXII (1982); M. A. R. Graves, 'Thomas Norton the Parliament Man: An Elizabethan MP', *HJ*, XXIII (1980) 17–35; G. R. Elton, 'Arthur Hall, Lord Burghley, and the Antiquity of Parliament', *Studies in Tudor and Stuart Politics and Government* (Cambridge, 1983) III, 254–73. On the records of Parliament and their meaning see G. R. Elton, 'The Sessional Printing of Statutes, 1484–1547', ibid., pp. 92–109, and 'The Rolls of Parliament, 1449–1547', ibid., pp. 110–42, both of which document the transformational role of the reign of Henry VIII. Provisional attempts to provide a new interpretation for the

Elizabethan Parliament are found in three papers by G. R. Elton: 'Tudor Government – the Points of Contact: I. Parliament', ibid., pp. 3–21; 'Parliament in the Sixteenth Century: Functions and Fortunes', ibid., pp. 156–82; and 'The English Parliament in the Sixteenth Century: Estates and Statutes', in *Parliament and Community*, ed. A. Cosgrove and J. I. McGuire (Dublin, 1983) pp. 69–95. Since one of the apparent strong points of the Neale thesis lay in its supposed fit to pre and post-Elizabethan parliamentary history, attention is drawn to recent revisions in those surrounding periods: J. Loach, 'Conservatism and Consent in Parliament, 1547–59', in *The Mid-Tudor Polity c. 1540–1560*, ed. J. Loach and R. Tittler (1980) pp. 9–28; C. Russell, 'Parliament History in Perspective, 1604–1629', *History*, LXI (1976) 1–22, and *Parliament and English Politics, 1621–1629*, (Oxford, 1979); R. C. Munden, 'James I and "the Growth of Mutual Distrust": King, Commons and Reform, 1603–1604', in *Faction and Parliament*, ed. K. Sharpe (Oxford, 1978) pp. 43–72.

4. GOVERNMENT, FINANCE AND THE COMMUNITY OF THE EXCHEQUER

The essential introduction to Elizabethan government is P. Williams, *The Tudor Regime* (Oxford, 1979). The area of the central bureaucracy studied in greatest depth has been Chancery, most particularly in W. J. Jones, *The Elizabethan Court of Chancery* (Oxford, 1967). For financial administration the relevant portions of H. E. Bell, *An Introduction to the History and Records of the Court of Wards and Liveries* (Cambridge, 1953), J. Hurstfield, *The Queen's Wards: Wardship and Marriage under Elizabeth* (1958), and R. Somerville, *History of the Duchy of Lancaster, 1265–1603* (1953) are all valuable, as is C. E. Challis, *The Tudor Coinage* (Manchester, 1978).

Elizabethan Exchequer administration has been a neglected topic. The following are useful in their respective areas, although not always totally reliable in detail or perspective: W. H. Bryson, *The Equity Side of the Exchequer* (Cambridge, 1975); G. R. Elton, 'The Elizabethan Exchequer: War in the Receipt', available both in *Elizabethan Government and Society. Essays presented to Sir John Neale*. ed. S. T. Bindoff, J. Hurstfield and C. H. Williams (1961) pp. 213–48, and in Elton, *Studies in Tudor and Stuart Politics and Government* (Cambridge, 1974) I, 355–88; E. Green, 'The Management of Exchequer Records in the 1560s', *Journal of the Society of Archivists*, V (1974) 25–30; and J. C. Sainty, 'The Tenure of Offices in the Exchequer', *EHR*, LXXX (1965) 449–75. Other studies are of less weight apart from basic administrative routine, the chief work in this category being W. C. Richardson, *History of the Court of Augmentations 1536–1554* (Baton Rouge, La, 1961) ch. 13. For valuable insights drawn from a later period see G. E. Aylmer, 'The Officers of the Exchequer, 1625–1642', in *Essays in the Economic and Social History of Tudor and Stuart England*, ed. F. J. Fisher (Cambridge, 1961). In terms of individual administrators, most important is the formative (but optimistic) biography by S. E. Lehmberg, *Sir Walter Mildmay and Tudor Government* (Austin, Tex., 1964).

With respect to finance itself, no attempt has yet been made to supersede the pioneering surveys by F. C. Dietz, 'The Exchequer in Elizabeth's Reign', *Smith College Studies in History* (Northampton, Mass.), VIII, no. 2 (1923) 63–118, and *English Public Finance, 1558—1641* (New York and London, 1932). These works cannot be ignored and are of continuing value, but they have long since shown their age and must be used with caution. The most important specialist studies directly relevant to the Elizabethan period are: J. D. Alsop, 'The Theory and Practice of Tudor Taxation', *EHR*, XCVII (1982) 1–30; F. Heal, 'Clerical Tax Collection Under the Tudors: The Influence of the Reformation', in *Continuity and Change*, ed. R. O'Day and F. Heal (Leicester, 1976) pp. 97–122; J. Hurstfield, 'The Profits of Fiscal Feudalism, 1541–1602', *EcHR*, 2nd ser., VIII (1955–6) 53–61; C. J. Kitching, 'The Quest for Concealed Lands in the Reign of Elizabeth I', *TRHS*, 5th ser., XXIV (1974) 65–78; H. Miller, 'Subsidy Assessments of the Peerage in the Sixteenth Century', *BIHR*, XXVIII (1955) 15–34; R. B. Outhwaite, 'The Trials of Foreign Borrowing: The English Crown and the Antwerp Money Market in the Mid-Sixteenth Century', *EcHR*, 2nd ser., XIX (1966) 289–305; G. D. Ramsey, *The City of London in International Politics at the Accession of Elizabeth Tudor* (Manchester, 1975); and D. Thomas, 'Leases in Reversion on the Crown's Lands, 1558–1603', *EcHR*, 2nd ser., XXX (1977) 67–72.

5.   THE CROWN AND THE COUNTIES

Elizabethan government in general is described in G. R. Elton, *The Tudor Constitution*, 2nd edn (Cambridge, 1982), which contains documents and commentary; A. G. R. Smith, *The Government of Elizabethan England* (1967); and P. Williams, *The Tudor Regime* (Oxford, 1979). There is an admirable contemporary account in Sir Thomas Smith, *De Republica Anglorum*, ed. M. Dewar (Cambridge, 1982): the work is in English, despite its title, and this edition supersedes earlier ones. On the institutions of regional and local government there is a wide range of studies: R. R. Reid, *The King's Council in the North* (1921); P. Williams, *The Council in the Marches of Wales under Elizabeth I* (Cardiff, 1958); G. Scott Thomson, *Lords Lieutenant in the Sixteenth Century* (1923); L. O. J. Boynton, *The Elizabethan Militia* (1967); J. S. Cockburn, *A History of English Assizes, 1558–1714* (Cambridge, 1972); J. H. Gleason, *The Justices of the Peace in England, 1558–1640* (Oxford, 1969); P. Clark and P. Slack, *English Towns in Transition* (Oxford, 1976); L. O. J. Boynton, 'The Tudor Provost-Marshal', *EHR*, LXXVII (1962); J. Kent, 'The English Village Constable, 1580–1640', *Journal of British Studies*, XX (1981). There are two excellent contemporary accounts of the working of local government: William Lambarde, *Eirenarcha: or the Office of the Justice of the Peace* (1581, with many subsequent edns); and *William Lambarde and Local Government*, ed. C. Read (Ithaca, NY, 1962), an edition of Lambarde's working-notebook as a justice in Kent.

The early seventeenth century is at present better served than the sixteenth with county studies, largely because the local material becomes more abundant after 1600. A. Everitt, *Change in the Provinces* (Leicester, 1969), provides a stimulating introduction to the subject; it should be read in conjunction with C. Holmes, 'The County Community in Stuart Historiography', *Journal of British Studies*, XIX (1980); while both are more concerned with early Stuart England, their ideas are relevant to the Elizabethan era. The most valuable monographs on individual counties in the reign of Elizabeth are: A. Hassell Smith, *County and Court. Government and Politics in Norfolk, 1558–1603* (Oxford, 1974); P. Clark, *English Provincial Society from the Reformation to the Revolution: Religion, Politics and Society in Kent, 1500–1640* (Hassocks, Sussex, 1977); M. E. James, *Family, Lineage and Civil Society. A Study of Society, Politics and Mentality in the Durham Region, 1500—1640* (Oxford, 1974); S. J. Watts, *From Border to Middle Shire: Northumberland 1586–1625* (Leicester, 1975); C. Haigh, *Reformation and Resistance in Tudor Lancashire* (Cambridge, 1975); R. B. Manning, *Religion and Society in Elizabethan Sussex* (Leicester, 1969); A. L. Rowse, *Tudor Cornwall* (London, 1941); H. A. Lloyd, *The Gentry of South-West Wales, 1540–1640* (Cardiff, 1968); P. Williams, 'The Political and Administrative History of Glamorgan, 1536–1642', in *Glamorgan County History*, IV, ed. G. Williams (Cardiff, 1974).

There are two important but as yet unpublished doctoral theses: D. MacCulloch, 'Power, Privilege and the County Community: County Politics in Elizabethan Suffolk' (Cambridge University, PhD, 1977); and J. R. Dias, 'Politics and Administration in Nottinghamshire and Derbyshire, 1590–1640' (Oxford University, DPhil, 1973). I am grateful to both authors for allowing me to use their work.

Finally, anyone seeking to understand the ways in which early modern governments sought to enforce their commands upon localities should read I. A. A. Thompson, *War and Government in Habsburg Spain, 1560–1620* (1976).

6. THE FOREIGN POLICY OF ELIZABETH I

The basic sources of information about the foreign policy of Elizabeth I are the letters she and her ministers and envoys exchanged with their counterparts in foreign countries and also with each other. Many have perished, but what survives is of vast bulk. Much of it is comprised by the State Papers at the PRO; but there are important portions at the BL Department of Manuscripts, and at Hatfield House, Herts. Other archive centres in England and abroad also hold many documents of interest.

Selections from these original documents have been printed by a succession of editors since the seventeenth century, the most recent contribution being E. I. Kouri, 'Elizabethan England and Europe: Forty Unprinted Letters from Elizabeth I to Protestant Powers', *BIHR*, Special Supplement 12 (1982). During the last century and more, a methodical and pertinacious attempt has been made to calendar, list and index the State Papers Foreign for the reign of Elizabeth I at the PRO, and thus render them more readily serviceable for historians. The first volume, covering the years 1559–60, was published in 1863; the most recent, for 1591–2, in 1980. For the last ten years of the reign the State Papers Foreign remain uncalendared and unindexed, which helps to explain the comparative neglect of this decade by historians.

The study of Elizabethan policy from the documents was promoted by J. A.

Froude in his *History of England 1530–88*, 12 vols (1856–70) VII–XII. His diligence, honesty and literary skill, though not his judgement, have always attracted respect. The final years of the reign have been described in E. P. Cheyney, *A History of England from the Defeat of the Armada to the Death of Elizabeth*, 2 vols (1914). There are surveys of foreign policy in R. B. Wernham, *Before the Armada. The Growth of English Foreign Policy 1485–1588* (1966), and *After the Armada: Elizabethan England and the Struggle for Western Europe, 1588–1595* (Oxford, 1984), with which should be coupled his *The Making of Elizabethan Foreign Policy* (Berkeley, Calif., 1980) and his essay 'Elizabethan War Aims and Strategy', in *Elizabethan Government and Society. Essays presented to Sir John Neale*, eds S. T. Bindoff, J. Hurstfield and C. H. Williams (1961) 340–68.

Of the scores of specialised studies drawing on the original documents to elucidate one aspect or another of Elizabeth's foreign policy, only a tiny fraction may here be mentioned. The biographies by Conyers Read are storehouses of information: *Mr Secretary Walsingham and the policy of Queen Elizabeth*, 3 vols (Oxford, 1925); *Mr Secretary Cecil and Queen Elizabeth* (1955); *Lord Burghley and Queen Elizabeth* (1960). L. Stone, *An Elizabethan: Sir Horatio Palavicino* (Oxford, 1956), covers otherwise untrodden ground. For the administrative background, there is material in A. G. R. Smith, 'The Secretariats of the Cecils, *circa* 1580–1612', *EHR*, LXXXIII (1968) 481–504. Factions at Court have been investigated by W. T. MacCaffrey in *The Shaping of the Elizabethan Regime* (1969) and *Queen Elizabeth and the Making of Policy* (Princeton, NJ, 1981). Studies of relations with individual countries include E. I. Kouri, *England and the Attempts to Form a Protestant Alliance in the Late 1560s: A Case Study in European Diplomacy* (Helsinki, 1981), for Germany; N. M. Sutherland, 'Queen Elizabeth and the Conspiracy of Amboise, March 1560', *EHR*, LXXXI (1966) 474–89, and *The Massacre of St Bartholomew and the European Conflict, 1559–1572* (1973); H. A. Lloyd, *The Rouen Campaign 1590–1592* (Oxford, 1973); C. Wilson, *Queen Elizabeth and the Revolt of the Netherlands* (London, 1970). The contribution of the Merchants Adventurers and the City of London to the foreign policy of the Queen has been little explored: for the early years of the reign there is G. D. Ramsay, *The City of London in International Politics* (Manchester, 1975), while for the middle and later period it is necessary to consult R. Ehrenberg, *Hamburg und England im Zeitalter der Königin Elisabeth* (Jena, 1896), and L. Beutin, *Hanse und Reich im handelspolitischen Endkampf gegen England* (Berlin, 1929). Finally two influential articles deserve mention: C. Read, 'Queen Elizabeth's Seizure of the Duke of Alva's Pay-ships', *Journal of Modern History*, V (1933) 443–64; and R. B. Wernham, 'Queen Elizabeth and the Portugal Expedition of 1589', *EHR*, LXVI (1951) 3–26, 194–218.

It should be borne in mind that the scholars whose works are listed above are far from unanimity in their interpretation of motives and events. More than most topics of its age, the foreign policy of Elizabeth I is likely to remain a subject for debate.

7. THE ELIZABETHAN CHURCH AND THE NEW RELIGION

The most recent book claiming to be a *History of the English Church in the Reigns of Elizabeth and James I* was published by W. H. Frere as long ago as 1904. But helpful accounts will be found in II. G. Alexander, *Religion in England 1558–1662* (1968) and C. Cross, *Church and People 1450–1660* (1976). A number of themes relevant to this essay are investigated in P. Collinson, *The Religion of Protestants: The Church in English Society 1559–1625* (Oxford, 1982); and in a useful symposium in the 'Problems in Focus' series, *Church and Society in England: Henry VIII to James I*, ed. F. Heal and R. O'Day (1977).

More specialised studies of aspects and institutions of the Elizabethan Church abound. The affairs of the bishops are investigated in F. Heal, *Of Prelates and Princes: A Study of the Economic and Social Position of the Tudor Episcopate* (Cambridge, 1980), and the careers of the clergy at large in R. O'Day, *The English Clergy: the Emergence and Consolidation of a Profession 1558–1642* (Leicester, 1979). There is a detailed account of the provision of preaching by the institution of 'lecturing' in P. Seaver, *The Puritan Lectureships; The Politics of Religious Dissent, 1560–1662* (Stanford, Calif., 1970), but this should be supplemented by my article 'Lectures by Combination: Structures and Characteristics of Church Life in Seventeenth-Century England', which will be found, together with other relevant essays, in P. Collinson, *Godly People: Essays on English Protestantism and Puritanism* (1983). There are biographies of the three Elizabethan archbishops of Canterbury: Parker by V. J. K. Brook (Oxford, 1962), Grindal by P. Collinson (1979) and Whitgift by P. M. Dawley (1954).

The implications for England as a Church and people of the drastic proposition that the Pope is Antichrist are explored in W. Haller, *Foxe's Book of Martyrs and the Elect Nation* (1963), some aspects of which are corrected in R. Bauckham, *Tudor Apocalypse* (Appleford, Berks., 1978) and K. Firth, *The Apocalyptic Tradition in Reformation Britain 1530–1645* (Oxford, 1979).

The 'new religion' in its Elizabethan context has been defined by many historians as Puritanism, and of the making of many books on this subject there is no end in sight. M. M. Knappen's classic *Tudor Puritanism* (Chicago, 1939) holds its own, together with P. Collinson, *The Elizabethan Puritan Movement* (1967). There is a much briefer account of the matter in P. Collinson, *English Puritanism* (Historical Association pamphlet, G106, 1983). There are important corrections to earlier perspectives on the relation of Puritanism to 'mainstream' Elizabethan Protestantism in P. Lake, *Moderate Puritans and the Elizabethan Church* (Cambridge, 1982).

The impact of the new religion on English society is best measured by historians of the provinces and localities. See especially a number of essays in A. G. Dickens, *Reformation Studies* (1982); C. Haigh, *Reformation and Resistance in Tudor Lancashire* (Cambridge, 1975), and 'Puritan Evangelism in the Reign of Elizabeth I', *EHR*, xcii (1977) 30–58; R. C. Richardson, *Puritanism in North-West England: A Regional Study of the Diocese of Chester to 1642* (Manchester, 1972); W. J. Sheils, *The Puritans in the Diocese of Peterborough 1558–1610*, Northants Record Society xxx (1979); and R. B. Manning, *Religion and Society in Elizabethan Sussex* (Leicester, 1969). See also J. J. Goring, 'The Reformation of the Ministry in Elizabethan Sussex', *Journal of Ecclesiastical History*, XXXIV (1983) 345–66; and K. Wrightson and D. Levine, *Poverty and Piety in an English Village: Terling, 1525–1700* (1979).

The impact, or lack of impact, of the new religion on the mentalities of early modern England receives its fullest and most imaginative treatment in what is perhaps the only great book on English religion in this period to have been written in the twentieth century: K. Thomas, *Religion and the Decline of Magic* (1971).

8.   THE CHURCH OF ENGLAND, THE CATHOLICS AND THE PEOPLE

Historians of religion in Elizabethan England have generally found it easier to write about the well-recorded militants than about the indecisive or indifferent majority. There are therefore plenty of books about Catholic nonconformists and about Protestant nonconformists, and a few about both: there is useful material in E. Rose, *Cases of Conscience: Alternatives Open to Recusants and Puritans* (Cambridge, 1975), and the best survey of the two extremes is P. McGrath's *Papists and Puritans under Elizabeth I* (1967). But Professor McGrath's book is, not surprisingly, showing its age: both papists and Puritans have been the subjects of controversy and reinterpretation, and the conformists have been brought onto the historical stage. The Elizabethan Church is coming to look rather different, party because of shifts in our understanding of the English Reformation. When the Reformation (in both its legislative and its popular forms) was seen as fast and effective (as in A. G. Dickens's classic *The English Reformation*, 1964), it made sense to see the history of Catholicism in Elizabeth's reign in terms of early decline and later recovery. The monumental presentation of this version was A. O. Meyer, *England and the Catholic Church under Queen Elizabeth* (1915; but see the 1967 reprint, with a critical reassessment by J. Bossy), and Meyer's outline was refined and supported by A. G. Dickens in 'The First Stages of Romanist Recusancy in Yorkshire, 1560–1590', *Yorkshire Archaeological Journal*, XXXV (1943) 157–81, and by J. A. Bossy in 'The Character of Elizabethan Catholicism', *P & P*, XXI (1962) 39–59. The most exciting and sophisticated presentation of this view is in J. Bossy, *The English Catholic Community, 1570–1850* (1975) – but see the criticism in C. Haigh, 'The Fall of a Church or the Rise of a Sect? Post-Reformation Catholicism in England', *HJ*, XXI (1978) 181–6. The version of Reformation history presupposed by the present essay (that Reformation statutes were difficult to enforce and that Protestant beliefs were widely resisted) is sketched in C. Haigh, 'The Recent Historiography of the English Reformation', *HJ*, XXV (1982) 995–1007, and given more substance in J. J. Scarisbrick, *The Reformation and the English People* (Oxford, 1984). Some of the evidence for the survival of Catholic loyalties and conservative preferences into the reign of Elizabeth was collected in H. N. Birt, *The Elizabethan Religious Settlement* (1907), but local studies have produced much more: see especially the works of J. C. H. Aveling, of which the most accessible are *Northern Catholics* (1966) and *The Handle and the Axe: The Catholic Recusants in England from the Reformation to Emancipation* (1976); and also

C. Haigh, *Reformation and Resistance in Tudor Lancashire* (Cambridge, 1975), R. B. Manning, *Religion and Society in Elizabethan Sussex* (Leicester, 1969), K. R. Wark, *Elizabethan Recusancy in Cheshire*, Chetham Society (1971). An attempt has been made to construct a new framework for the history of Catholicism in this period, in C. Haigh, 'The Continuity of Catholicism in the English Reformation', *P & P*, xciii (1981) 37–69, and 'From Monopoly to Minority: Catholicism in Early Modern England', *TRHS*, 5th ser., xxxi (1981) 129–47. The second article is thought by some to have been unduly harsh to Jesuit and seminarist missioners; they are treated more sympathetically in P. Caraman, *Henry Garnet, 1555–1606, and the Gunpowder Plot* (1964); A. Morey, *The Catholic Subjects of Elizabeth I* (1978); and E. Waugh, *Edmund Campion* (1935). There are judicious surveys of recent controversies in A. Dures, *English Catholicism, 1558–1642* (Harlow, 1983).

Patrick Collinson's essay in this volume, and many of the works listed in his bibliographical essay, tackle those who responded enthusiastically to Protestantism. Those who were reluctant to throw themselves into the 'new religion' have been (unless they became Catholic recusants) much less frequently studied. Professor Collinson has some wise words on them in *Godly People: Essays on English Protestantism and Puritanism* (1983) ch. 1, and *The Religion of Protestants: The Church in English Society, 1559–1625* (Oxford, 1982) ch. 5; and Keith Thomas has ranged across many aspects of popular belief in his deservedly famous *Religion and the Decline of Magic* (1971). There are few general treatments of parish religion in post-Reformation England – and fewer still that can now be recommended: Keith Wrightson, *English Society, 1580–1680* (1982) ch. 7, is a sensitive starting-point. The conflicts between Protestant evangelists and resistant laypeople are best approached through local studies: P. Clark, *English Provincial Society from the Reformation to the Revolution: Religion, Politics and Society in Kent 1500–1640* (Hassocks, Sussex, 1975); W. Hunt, *The Puritan Moment: The Coming of Revolution in an English County* (Cambridge, Mass., 1983) (on Essex); R. B. Manning, *Religion and Society in Elizabethan Sussex* (Leicester, 1969); W. J. Sheils, *The Puritans in the Diocese of Peterborough*, Northants Record Society xxx (1979); C. Haigh, 'Puritan Evangelism in the Reign of Elizabeth I', *EHR*, xcii (1977) 30–58 (Cheshire and Lancs); R. A. Marchant, *The Puritans and the Church Courts in the Diocese of York* (1960); and R. C. Richardson, *Puritanism in North-West England: A Regional Study of the Diocese of Chester to 1642* (Manchester, 1972). Village studies are also proving illuminating: see M. Spufford, *Contrasting Communities: English Villagers in the Sixteenth and Seventeenth Centuries* (Cambridge, 1974); and K. Wrightson and D. Levine, *Poverty and Piety in an English Village: Terling, 1525–1700* (1979). Christopher Haigh is writing a book on the Church of England and its people between 1559 and 1642, but the most suggestive exploration of this theme was published in 1581: George Gifforde's *A Briefe Discourse of Certaine Points of the Religion which is among the Common Sort of Christians which may bee Termed the Countrie Divinitie*.

9. POVERTY AND SOCIAL REGULATION IN ELIZABETHAN ENGLAND

On the poor-law and its enforcement, the best guide remains E. M. Leonard, *The Early History of English Poor Relief* (Cambridge, 1900; repr. London, 1965). More recent, but shorter, summaries are John Pound, *Poverty and Vagrancy in Tudor England* (1971); and A. L. Beier, *The Problem of the Poor in Tudor and Early Stuart England*, Lancaster Pamphlets (1983). W. K. Jordan, *Philanthropy in England 1480–1660* (1959) contains material on the law and attitudes towards charity, as well as summarising the author's major work on philanthropic endowments. His statistical conclusions about the latter have been subjected to criticism in W. G. Bittle and R. Todd Lane, 'Inflation and Philanthropy in England: A Re-assessment of W. K. Jordan's Data', *EcHR*, 2nd ser., xxix (1976) 203–10; and, much more constructively, in J. F. Hadwin, 'Deflating Philanthropy', *EcHR*, 2nd ser., xxxi (1978) 105–17.

Of other social policies, those relating to apprenticeship have been most studied. S. T. Bindoff, 'The Making of the Statute of Artificers', in *Elizabethan Government and Society. Essays presented to Sir John Neale*, ed. S. T. Bindoff, J. Hurstfield and C. H. Williams (1961) pp. 56–94, is an exemplary demonstration of how a statute was shaped. Its enforcement is discussed in M. G. Davies, *The Enforcement of English Apprenticeship 1563–1642* (Cambridge, Mass., 1956). Among other social problems, crime is attracting increasing attention: a useful introduction is *Crime in England 1550–1800*, ed. J. S. Cockburn (1977). On witchcraft and its relationship to charity, see K. Thomas, *Religion and the Decline of Magic* (1971) ch. 17. Besides Bindoff, J. R. Kent, 'Attitudes of Members of the House of Commons to the Regulation of "Personal Conduct" in Late Elizabethan and Early Stuart England', *BIHR*, xlvi (1973) 41–71, usefully discusses the parliamentary background to social legislation. The government's concerns are illuminated in P. Slack, 'Books of Orders: The Making of English Social Policy, 1577–1631', *TRHS*, 5th ser., xxx (1980) 1–22, and more generally in P. Williams, *The Tudor Regime* (Oxford, 1979) pt ii, and F. A. Youngs, *The Proclamations of the Tudor Queens* (Cambridge, 1976) pt iii.

A good modern survey of the economic and social background is D. M. Palliser, *The Age of Elizabeth. England under the Later Tudors 1547–1603* (1983). This book, developing the same author's 'Tawney's Century: Brave New World or Malthusian Trap?', *EcHR*, 2nd ser., xxxv (1982) 339–53, presents a more optimistic view than that contained in the present essay. For an emphasis closer to that provided here, and for a forceful argument about social development, see K. Wrightson, *English Society 1580–1680* (1982). There is much relevant information on agrarian change and industrial growth in *The Agrarian History of England and Wales*, iv: *1500–1640*, ed. J. Thirsk (Cambridge, 1967); and J. Thirsk, *Economic Policy and Projects: The Development of a Consumer Society in Early Modern England* (Oxford, 1978). On temporary crises, see P. Slack, 'Mortality Crises and Epidemic Disease in England 1485–1610', in *Health, Medicine and Mortality in the Sixteenth Century*, ed. C. Webster (Cambridge, 1979) pp. 9–59; and, for long-term demographic trends, E. A. Wrigley and R. S. Schofield, *The Population History of England 1541–1871: A Reconstruction* (1981) esp. chs 10 and 11.

Both social problems and social policies are best illustrated, however, by local studies. Local records on vagrancy are discussed in A. L. Beier, 'Vagrants and the Social Order in Elizabethan England', *P & P*, LXIV (1974), 3–29; and P. A. Slack, 'Vagrants and Vagrancy in England, 1598–1664', *EcHR*, 2nd ser., XXVII (1974) 360–79. The problems of particular towns are described in A. L. Beier, 'Social Problems in Elizabethan London', *Journal of Interdisciplinary History*, IX (1978) 203–21; A. L. Beier, 'The Social Problems of an Elizabethan Country Town: Warwick, 1580–90', in *Country Towns in Pre-industrial England*, ed. P. Clark (Leicester, 1981) pp. 45–85; and in the editors' contributions (on Kent and Salisbury) in *Crisis and Order in English Towns 1500–1700*, ed. P. Clark and P. Slack (1972). *The Norwich Census of the Poor 1570*, ed. J. F. Pound, Norfolk Record Society XL (1971), throws a spotlight on local poverty, and has a good introduction. There is also relevant material in most modern local histories; for example: W. T. MacCaffrey, *Exeter 1540–1640* (Cambridge, Mass., 1958); K. Wrightson and D. Levine, *Poverty and Piety in an English Village: Terling, 1525–1700* (1979); and P. Clark, *English Provincial Society from the Reformation to the Revolution* (Hassocks, Sussex, 1977) chs 7 and 8. Finally, for a brilliant account of the reactions of Puritan ministers and magistrates to social instability, see P. Collinson, *The Religion of Protestants. The Church in English Society 1559–1625* (Oxford, 1982) ch. 4.

Notes and References

INTRODUCTION   *Christopher Haigh*

1. W. Camden, *Annales: The True and Royall History of the famous Empresse Elizabeth, Queen of England* (1625) sig. C; W. Camden, *The History of the most Renowned and Victorious Princess Elizabeth* (1675) p. 661. Further quotations are from the 1675 edition.

2. A. L. Rowse, 'Queen Elizabeth and Historians', *History Today* (1953) 630–41; J. P. Kenyon, 'Queen Elizabeth and the Historians', in *Queen Elizabeth I: Most Politick Princess*, ed. S. Adams (History Today Publications, 1984) pp. 52–5; J. R. Green, *A Short History of the English People* (1895 edn) pp. 369–420; M. Creighton, *Queen Elizabeth* (1906 edn) pp. 304–6; A. F. Pollard, *History of England from the Accession of Edward VI to the Death of Elizabeth* (1919 edn) pp. 184, 190, 192, 236, 277–8, 456–8.

3. BL and Bod. Lib. catalogues; A. L. Rowse, *The England of Elizabeth* (1981 edn) pp. v, vii, 266; J. E. Neale, *Queen Elizabeth I* (1979 edn) p. 218; J. Hurstfield, 'John Ernest Neale, 1890–1975', *Proceedings of the British Academy*, LXIII (1977) 409.

4. W. Haller, *Foxe's Book of Martyrs and the Elect Nation* (1963) pp. 124–7; E. C. Wilson, *England's Eliza* (Cambridge, Mass., 1939) pp. 6, 13, 36; J. Nichols, *The Progresses and Public Processions of Queen Elizabeth*, 3 vols (1823 edn) I, 311–15, 545–8.

5. R. Strong, *The Cult of Elizabeth: Elizabethan Portraiture and Pageantry* (1977) pp. 46–7, 114–28, 131–9; R. Strong, 'Icons of Power and Prophecy', in *Queen Elizabeth I*, ed. Adams, pp. 13–15; F. A. Yates, *Astraea: The Imperial Theme in the Sixteenth Century* (1975) pp. 59–61.

6. F. G. Emmison, *Elizabethan Life: Disorder* (Chelmsford, 1970) pp. 41, 42, 48, 55, 57, 58; C. Erickson, *The First Elizabeth* (1983) pp. 266–9; P. Clark, *English Provincial Society from the Reformation to the Revolution* (Hassocks, Sussex, 1977) pp. 249–50.

7. Wilson, *England's Eliza*, pp. 47, 52; Strong, *Cult of Elizabeth*, p. 15; T. Dekker, *Works* (1873 edn) I, 83; Yates, *Astraea*, pp. 78–9.

8. Camden, *History*, sig., a2, pp. 373, 393–4; H. Trevor-Roper, *Queen Elizabeth's First Historian: William Camden and the Beginning of English 'Civil History'* (1971) pp. 9–17; K. Sharpe, *Sir Robert Cotton, 1586–1631* (Oxford, 1979) pp. 89–94.

9. J. E. Neale, *Essays in Elizabethan History* (1958) pp. 14–15; A. Barton, 'Harking Back to Elizabeth: Ben Jonson and Caroline Nostalgia', *English Literary History*, XLVIII (1981) 712–29; Sharpe, *Cotton*, pp. 226–34; C. V. Wedgwood, *Oliver Cromwell and the Elizabethan Inheritance* (1970) pp. 7–8, 12–13.

10. Camden, *History*, pp. 31–2, 56–7, 439, 440, 441.

11. Wedgwood, *Cromwell*, pp. 7–8, 12–13; Trevor-Roper, *Queen Elizabeth's First Historian*, pp. 11, 27–8.

12. See, for example, Pollard, *History of England*, p. 236; R. Ashton, *Reformation and Revolution, 1558–1660* (1984) p. xvi.

13. Camden, *History* pp. 13, 31, 107, 191–2, 288–9. For a good, brief summary of recent views, see P. Lake, 'The Elizabethan Settlement: the Queen and her Church', in *Queen Elizabeth I*, ed. Adams, pp. 16–19; for more substantial statements, see the works by Collinson and Lake listed in the bibliography to ch. 7.

14. Camden, *History*, pp. 79, 122–3, 127, 217, 535, 551, 558; S. Adams, 'Faction, Clientage and Party: English Politics, 1550–1603', *History Today* (Dec. 1982) 33–9; W. T. MacCaffrey, *Queen Elizabeth and the Making of Policy, 1572–1588* (Princeton, NJ, 1981) pp. 17–20, 444–5, 502–3. See ch. 2.

15. R. E. Schreiber, *The Political Career of Sir Robert Naunton, 1589–1635* (1981) esp. pp. 125, 132–3; R. Naunton, *Fragmenta Regalia, or Observations on the late Queen Elizabeth, her Times and Favorits* (1641) esp. pp. 5, 6, 10, 15–16; Rowse, *England of Elizabeth*, pp. 281–4; C. Read, 'Walsingham and Burghley in Queen Elizabeth's Privy Council', *EHR*, xxviii (1913) 34–58; Neale, *Essays*, pp. 59–84.

16. Naunton, *Fragmenta Regalia*, pp. 8–9; J. Forster, *Sir John Eliot*, 2 vols (1872 edn) ii, 81–3, 191, 448.

17. Kenyon, 'Queen Elizabeth and the Historians', 54–5; Neale, *Essays*, p. 19; J. W. Burrow, *A Liberal Descent* (Cambridge, 1981) pp. 233, 248–9, 275, 295.

18. Neale, *Essays*, esp. pp. 13–14, 37, 124; J. E. Neale, *The Elizabethan House of Commons* (1976 edn) pp. 13, 415; Rowse, *England of Elizabeth*, pp. 1–2.

19. Hurstfield, 'John Ernest Neale', 410–12; Neale, *Essays*, pp. 113–24: J. E. Neale, *Elizabeth I and her Parliaments, 1559–1581* (1953) pp. 417–19.

20. Ibid., p. 419; Neale, *Essays*, pp. 21–44, esp. pp. 21–2,

21. Camden, *History*, pp. 5, 10, 14, 31–2, 56–7; J. Hurstfield, *Elizabeth I and the Unity of England* (1971 edn) p. 133; W. MacCaffrey, *The Shaping of the Elizabethan Regime* (1969) pp. 15–26, 308–17; MacCaffrey, *Queen Elizabeth*, pp. 3–20.

22. M. L. Bush, *The Government Policy of Protector Somerset* (1975); J. Loach and R. Tittler (eds), *The Mid-Tudor Polity, c.1540–1560* (1980) esp. the introduction and essays by Loach, Hoak and Weikel; J. Wormald, 'James VI and I: Two Kings or One?', *History*, lxviii (1983) 187–209.

23. I have tried to provide a short 'revisionist' version of the history of the period 1450–1625 in C. Haigh (ed), *The Cambridge Historical Encyclopedia of Great Britain and Ireland* (Cambridge, forthcoming) ch. 4(1).

24. Neale, *Essays*, pp. 29–44.

25. J. J. Scarisbrick, *The Reformation and the English People* (Oxford, 1984); C. Haigh, 'The Recent Historiography of the English Reformation', *HJ*, xxv (1982) 995–1007.

26. Compare Haller, *Foxe's Book*, esp. pp. 224–50, with C. Z. Wiener, 'The Beleaguered Isle. A Study of Elizabethan and Jacobean Anti-Catholicism', *P & P*, li (1971) 27–62.

27. The Association has been rather neglected by historians, but there is a short discussion in D. Cressy, 'Binding the Nation: the Bonds of Association, 1584 and 1696', in *Tudor Rule and Revolution*, ed. D. J. Guth and J. W. McKenna (Cambridge, 1982) pp. 217–26.

28. P. Williams, *The Tudor Regime* (Oxford, 1979) p. 129; L. Stone, *The Crisis of the Aristocracy* (Oxford, 1965) chs 5, 8; B. Coward, *The Stanleys, Lords Stanley and Earls of Derby, 1385–1672* (Manchester, 1983); G. R. Elton in *Times Literary Supplement* (1983) 991. A number of studies of Tudor nobles are in progress: Dr G. Bernard (Southampton) and S. Kershaw (Oxford) are looking at earls of Shrewsbury.

29. C. Russell, 'Parliamentary History in Perspective, 1604–1629', *History*, LXI (1976) 1–27; P. Collinson, *The Religion of Protestants* (Oxford, 1982); N. Tyacke, 'Puritanism, Arminianism and Counter-Revolution', in *The Origins of the English Civil War*, ed. C. Russell (1973) pp. 119–43; J. Morrill, 'Introduction', in *Reactions to the English Civil War*, ed. J. Morrill (1982) pp. 2–4; K. Sharpe, 'The Personal Rule of Charles I', in *Before the English Civil War*, ed. H. Tomlinson (1983) pp. 53–78; A. Fletcher, *The Outbreak of the English Civil War* (1981).

30. See particularly T. K. Rabb and D. Hirst, 'Revisionism Revised: Two Perspectives on Early Stuart Parliamentary History', *P & P*, XCII (1981) 55–99; L. Stone, 'The Revival of Narrative: Reflections on a New Old History', *P & P*, LXXXV (1979) 20–1; K. Thomas in *Times Literary Supplement* (1982) 479.

31. P. Collinson, 'A Comment: Concerning the Name Puritan', *Journal of Ecclesiastical History*, XXI (1980) 487; P. Collinson, *Godly People* (1983) chs 1, 13, 18, 20; P. Lake, *Moderate Puritans and the Elizabethan Church* (Cambridge, 1982) chs 1, 12.

32. M. A. R. Graves, 'Thomas Norton the Parliament Man', *HJ*, XXIII (1980) 17–35; G. R. Elton, *Studies in Tudor and Stuart Politics and Government*, II (Cambridge, 1974) ch. 28; III (Cambridge, 1983) ch. 35.

33. C. Read, *Mr Secretary Cecil and Queen Elizabeth* (1955); C. Read, *Lord Burghley and Queen Elizabeth* (1960); R. B. Wernham, *After the Armada* (Oxford, 1984) p. vi.

34. Clark, *English Provincial Society*, ch. 8; A. Hassell Smith, *County and Court: Government and Politics in Norfolk, 1558–1603* (Oxford, 1974) chs 11–13.

35. The best summary of recent issues in Elizabethan social and economic history is D. M. Palliser, *The Age of Elizabeth* (1983), whose argument is briefly stated in his conclusion.

36. C. Haigh, 'The Governance of the Realm: Bureaucracy and Aristocracy', in *Queen Elizabeth I*, ed. Adams, pp. 9–12, crudely summarising what I take to be the implications of Neale, *Essays*, pp. 59–84, and Stone, *Crisis*, ch. 8.

37. Some of the problems of these years are discussed in MacCaffrey, *Shaping*, chs 12–15. The danger of the position in 1569 is brought out in the only thorough study of the Revolt of the Earls, Susan Taylor's Manchester University PhD thesis (1981).

38. D. M. Loades, *The Reign of Mary Tudor* (1979) chs 11–12; C. Russell, *Parliaments and English Politics, 1621–29* (Oxford, 1979) chs 4–8; B. Sharp, *In Contempt of all Authority* (Berkeley, Calif., 1980), chs 2–4; J. Thirsk (ed.), *The*

Agrarian History of England and Wales, 1500–1640 (Cambridge, 1967) pp. 818–21.

39. Erickson, *First Elizabeth*, p. 388; Wedgwood, *Cromwell*, p. 10; D. H. Willson, *King James VI and I* (1956) p. 161.

1. ELIZABETH'S FIRST YEAR: THE CONCEPTION AND BIRTH OF THE ELIZABETHAN POLITICAL WORLD   *Norman L. Jones*

1. 'The Count of Feria's Dispatch to Philip II of 14 November 1558', ed. M. J. Rodriguez-Salgado and S. Adams, *Camden Miscellany*, XXVIII (1984) 329.

2. W. T. MacCaffrey, *The Shaping of the Elizabethan Regime* (1969) pp. 30–2.

3. J. E. Neale, 'Sir Nicholas Throckmorton's Advice to Queen Elizabeth', *EHR*, LXV (1950) 98.

4. PRO SP 12/1, fos 156–8.

5. BL Cotton MS, Julius F. VI, fos 167–9.

6. *Tudor Royal Proclamations*, ed. P. L. Hughes and J. F. Larkin (New Haven, Conn., 1969) II, 99–100.

7. PRO SP 12/1, fo. 3.

8. N. L. Jones, *Faith by Statute: Parliament and the Settlement of Religion, 1559*, Royal Historical Society Studies in History XXXII (1982) pp. 36–40.

9. *CSP Venetian*, VII, 2.

10. *Tudor Royal Proclamations*, II, 102–3.

11. *APC*, VII, 50.

12. M. F. Alvarez, *Politica mundial de Carlos V y Felipe II* (Madrid, 1966) p. 257; Jones, *Faith*, pp. 50–4.

13. 'Feria's Dispatch', 333.

14. Jones, *Faith by Statute*, pp. 54–6.

15. *CSP Venetian*, VII, 22.

16. *Proceedings in the Parliaments of Queen Elizabeth, I: 1559–1581*, ed. T. E. Hartley (1981) pp. 34–5.

17. Jones, *Faith by Statute*, pp. 83–103, rehearses the parliamentary action in detail.

18. *Tudor Royal Proclamations*, II, 109–11; Jones, *Faith*, pp. 120–2.

19. Jones, *Faith by Statute*, pp. 50–6.

20. PRO SP 70/2, fos 137v–8.

21. *CSPSp*, 1558–67, p. 32.

22. *The Zurich Letters*, ed. Hastings Robinson (Cambridge, 1842) I, 10, 27.

23. J. Foxe, *The Acts and Monuments*, ed. G. Townshend (1849) VIII, 691.

24. Jones, *Faith by Statute*, pp. 123–9.

25. *Zurich Letters*, I, 33.

26. 1 Eliz. I, c. 1 20; J. Strype, *Annals of the Reformation* (Oxford, 1824) I, ii, 400; Jones, *Faith by Statute*, pp. 130–4, 139–44.

27. 1 Eliz. I, c. 2; Jones, *Faith by Statute*, pp. 135–9, 145–52.

28. 1 Eliz. I, c. 4.

29. 1 Eliz. I, c. 24.

30. *Zurich Letters*, I, 23.

31. *Proceedings*, ed. Hartley, p. 51. See P. Collinson, 'Sir Nicholas Bacon and the Elizabethan *Via Media*', *HJ*, xxiii (1980) esp. 255–7, 266–73.

2.   ELIZA ENTHRONED? THE COURT AND ITS POLITICS
Simon Adams

The research on which this essay is based was made possible by generous grants from the University of Strathclyde, the British Academy and the Carnegie Trust for the Universities of Scotland. I should like to thank the Marquess of Bath for permission to employ the Dudley MSS at Longleat House. I am extremely grateful to the editor of this volume, Patrick Collinson, Geoffrey Elton, David Loades, Geoffrey Parker, Mia Rodriguez-Salgado, David Starkey and Penry Williams for their invaluable comments and criticisms.

1. See the bibliography for full references to the works mentioned.

2. BL Lansd. MS 34, fo. 95. The best surviving Household subsidy rolls are those for 1559 (BL Lansd. MS 3, fos 193–200), 1567 (PRO E 179/69/82) and 1576 (PRO E 179/69/93).

3. BL Egerton MS 2723, fos 32v, 33v.

4. 5 Eliz. I, c. 32 (An Act of Assignment of Certain Sums of Money to Defray the Charges of the Queen's Majesty's Household). The Cofferer's accounts are PRO E 351/1795–6.

5. PRO E 351/541–3. During the first years of the reign the Treasurer's ordinary annual expenditure lay in the region of £11,500; see E 351/541, and BL Vespasian C xiv (1), fos 68–75.

6. In 1576 Burghley computed Stables expenses at £4148 (BL Harleian MS 709, fos 19v, 22). In 1590 the wages bill alone came to an annual £2100; see M. M. Reese, *The Royal Office of Master of the Horse* (1976) p. 163. Total expenditure on 'incidents' for both Household and Stables was £15,188 in 1573 (BL Lansd. MS 21, fo. 127).

7. The Wardrobe account for 1559, for example, records an expenditure of £14,439, exclusive of the £17,662 the department spent on Mary's funeral (see PRO LC 5/32, p. 59). Tamworth's Privy Purse account for 1559–1569 (BL Harleian Roll 609) is printed in J. Nichols, *The Progresses and Public Processions of Queen Elizabeth*, iii (1805) B–C, 1–9.

8. PRO LS 13/280/82, see also fo. 134. For the latest discussion of the impact of inflation on foodstuffs see D. M. Palliser, *The Age of Elizabeth. England under the Later Tudors, 1547–1603* (1983) pp. 140–2.

9. The 1576 survey is now BL Harleian MS 609, largely printed in Nichols, *Progresses*, i (1788) A–F, 1–37. For other documents relating to the 1576 reforms see below, nn. 10 and 14. For the problem of staff wages, see BL Lansd. MSS 34, fos 95–6 (1583) and 86, fo. 108 (1598).

10. For Hall food, see BL Lansd. MS 21 fos 133, 139r–v. For Burghley's proposed reforms, BL Lansd. MSS 86, fos 107–8, 34, fo. 91r–v, 45, fo. 49.

11. BL Lansd. MS 21, fos 124, 129, 139. See also R. C. Braddock, 'The

Royal Household, 1540–1560: A Study in Office-Holding in Tudor England'
(Northwestern University PhD thesis, 1971) p. 35.

12. There are numerous references to Elizabeth's appeal to popularity: see
'The Count of Feria's Dispatch to Philip II of 14 November 1558', ed.
M. J. Rodriguez-Salgado and S. Adams, *Camden Miscellany*, xxviii (1984) 315 n.
1; BL Add. MS 34,563 fo. 11; *The Letters and Epigrams of Sir John Harington*, ed.
N. E. McClure (Philadelphia, 1930) p. 122; *Elizabeth of England. Certain
Observations concerning the Life and Reign of Queen Elizabeth by John Clapham*, ed.
E. P. and C. Read (Philadelphia, 1951) p. 69. For Elizabeth's urban receptions,
see the comments of Palliser, *Age of Elizabeth*, pp. 235–6, and, for Worcester,
Nichols, *Progresses*, I, I–O, 94 n.4.

13. BL Lansd. MSS 21, fos 130, 139v, 34, fo. 95. For the proposed 1574
progress, see AGR PEA 361, fo. 78v, printed in *Rel. Pol.*, vii, 122; and, for the
1575, BL Lansd. MS 20, fo. 128, printed in T. Wright, *Queen Elizabeth and Her
Times* (1838) ii, 11.

14. The surviving order book of the Compting House (PRO LS 13/168)
begins in 1598. See on this question, A. P. Newton, 'Tudor Reforms in the
Royal Household', in *Tudor Studies presented . . . to Albert Frederick Pollard*, ed.
R. W. Seton-Watson (1924) p. 249. For Burghley's comments, BL Lansd.
MS 21, fo. 130; cf. fo. 139v, and MS 34, fo. 95.

15. The Coronation roll is now PRO LC 2 4/3, see pp. 104–5; a garbled
list of the Privy Chamber in 1559 can be found in Bod. Lib. MS English Hist.
C 272, fo. 95. For the waged members of the Privy Chamber, see the Cofferer
of the Household's accounts, PRO E 351/1795 *passim*. BL Lansd. MS 3, fo. 192,
is a copy of the first warrant of January 1559; MS 59, fo. 43, gives the state of
the Privy Chamber on 22 May 1589.

16. For discussion of the structural stability of the post-Henrician Court,
see G. R. Elton, *The Tudor Revolution in Government* (Cambridge, 1953) p. 370;
D. R. Starkey, 'The King's Privy Chamber, 1485–1547' (Cambridge
University PhD thesis, 1974) pp. 415, 419; and Braddock, 'Royal Household', p. 35.

17. The book of fees of 1576–8 is printed in *A Collection of Ordinances and
Regulations for the Government of the Royal Household* (1790) 250–74; see also D. E.
Hoak, 'The King's Privy Chamber, 1547–1553', in *Tudor Rule and Revolution:
Essays for G. R. Elton from his American Friends*, ed. D. J. Guth and J. W.
McKenna (Cambridge, 1983) p. 89 n. 7.

18. On Household promotions, see Newton, 'Tudor Reform', pp. 254–5,
and the qualifications by Braddock, 'Royal Household', p. 213. On Manners,
see L. C. John, 'Roger Manners, Elizabethan Courtier', *Huntington Library
Quarterly*, xii (1948) 57–84.

19. *H of C, 1509–58*, ii, 103 (on Sir Francis Englefield) and 354 (Sir Richard
Southwell). For a comment on the purge, see AMRE CPA, xiii, fo. 256, A. de
Noailles to Montmorency, 7 June 1559.

20. BL Lansd. MS 20, fo. 164. For Croft's defence of sale of office, Royal
MS 18 A xlvi, fos 3v–4.

21. A. Woodward, 'Purveyance for the Royal Household in the Reign of
Queen Elizabeth', *Transactions of the American Philosophical Society*, n. s., xxxv,
no. 1 (Philadelphia, 1945) pp. 8, 14, 58.

22. See *inter alia*, G. D. Duncan, 'Monopolies under Elizabeth I, 1558–1585' (Cambridge University PhD thesis, 1976) p. 116; C. J. Kitching, 'The Quest for Concealed Lands in the Reign of Elizabeth I', *TRHS*, 5th ser., XXIV (1974) 66.

23. PRO SP 52/10/120; Haynes & Murdin, II, 764; D. Digges, *The Compleat Ambassador* (1655) p. 322.

24. BL Lansd. MS 7, fos 123–4; cf. PRO SP 12/126/13.

25. BL Lansd. MSS 21, fo. 75, and 102, fo. 230r–v; HMC, *Salisbury MSS*, II, 610; PRO SP 12/125/151–2.

26. For Buckhurst, see *Harington Letters*, pp. 90–1; for Nottingham, *The Memoirs of Robert Carey*, ed. F. H. Mares (Oxford, 1972) p. 59.

27. D. MacCulloch, 'Anglican and Puritan in Elizabethan Suffolk', *Archiv für Reformationsgeschichte*, LXII (1981) 280–1; P. Williams, 'Court and Polity under Elizabeth I', *Bulletin of the John Rylands University Library*, LXV (1983) 265, 267; G. R. Elton, 'Tudor Government: the Points of Contact. III. The Court', *TRHS*, 5th ser., XXVI (1976) 219, 224–7.

28. See, *inter alia*, *Sir John Harington's 'A New Discourse of a Stale Subject called the Metamorphosis of Ajax'*, ed. E. S. Donno (1962) p. 252; P. Collinson, *The Elizabethan Puritan Movement* (1967) p. 134; PRO PCC 11 Daughtry; and Dudley MS I, fo. 46.

29. For Mason, see 'Feria Dispatch', p. 319 n. 3; for an interesting general reflection on this apsect of the Court of 1559, see AMRE CPA, XIII, fo. 258v, memoirs of M. de Gondran, 15 June 1559 (transcribed in PRO 31 3/24/51).

30. N. L. Jones, *Faith by Statute. Parliament and the Settlement of Religion, 1559*, Royal Historical Society Studies in History XXXII (1982) p. 72 n. 50; PRO SP 12/7/190. See also A. Teulet, *Papiers d'état . . . relatifs a l'histoire d'Ecosse au 16ᵉ siècle*, I (Paris, 1852) 361. For Protestant discontent see PRO SP 12/12/1 and HMC, *Salisbury MSS* I, 679; cf. Dudley MS I, fo. 90.

31. The best account of this process to date is N. Canny, *The Elizabethan Conquest of Ireland: A Pattern Established, 1565–76* (Hassocks, Sussex, 1976) pp. 70–1. I have taken up aspects of the question in an unpublished paper, 'The Dudley Clientage, 1553–1563'.

32. BL Titus MS B II, fo. 31; PRO SP 12/31/23; AGR PEA 360/207, printed in *Rel. Pol.*, III, 153.

33. For reliable information on these clashes, see Haynes & Murdin, II, 760–1.

34. For Sussex's views on foreign policy, see *Illustrations of British History*, ed. E. Lodge (1791) II, 161–2, 177–86. For an eyewitness account of a clash with Leicester on 12 July 1581, see *The Private Diary of John Dee*, ed. J. O. Halliwell, Camden Society XIX (1842) p. 11. For Leicester's support for Protestant interventionism see S. L. Adams, 'The Protestant Cause: Religious Alliance with the West European Calvinist Communities, 1585–1630' (Oxford University DPhil thesis, 1973) pp. 37–9, 46–7. Conyers Read's portrait of a Council factionalised by the debate ('Walsingham and Burghley in Queen Elizabeth's Privy Council', *EHR*, XXVIII (1913) 34–58) is overdrawn.

35. Adams, 'Protestant Cause', p. 61; *The Correspondence of Robert Dudley, Earl of Leycester*, ed. J. Bruce, Camden Society XXVII (1844) esp. pp. 142–5.

36. Williams, 'Court and Polity', 263; cf. *Carey Memoirs*, pp. 42–3.

37. For evidence of good relations between Leicester and Sussex in the mid-1570s see BL Lansd. MS 21, fo. 75; BL Harleian MS 6991, fo. 27; and PRO SP 12/126/20. See also Susan Doron, 'The Political Career of Thomas Radcliffe, 3rd Earl of Sussex (1526–1583)' (London University PhD thesis, 1977) pp. 153, 334–5, 393, 396, 403; M. B. Pulman, *The Elizabethan Privy Council in the Fifteen-Seventies* (Berkeley, Calif., 1971) p. 49. On the other hand, Leicester did refer to Sussex posthumously as a liar (*CSPF*, xxi (3) 233).

38. See John, 'Manners', 69–75, esp. 71 n. 71. For Croft's comments on Pembroke see BL Royal MS 18 A xlvi, fos 6–8v.

39. PRO SP 12/126/20–1.

40. E. StJ. Brooks, *Sir Christopher Hatton. Queen Elizabeth's Favourite* (1946) p. 19.

41. See, *inter alia*, the comments of Clapham, *Observations*, pp. 92–3. For Ralegh's rise, see W. R. Wallace, *Sir Walter Raleigh* (Princeton, NJ, 1959) pp. 25–30.

42. PRO LS 13/168/24. For Elizabeth's attitude, see J. E. Neale, *Elizabeth I and her Parliaments*, i: *1559—1581* (1953) pp. 191–3.

43. See Archbishop Parker's comments to Burghley, 11 April 1575, BL Lansd. MS 20, fo. 149.

44. For examples of Elizabeth's treatment of her women, see *Harington Letters*, pp. 124–5, and C. A. Bradford, *Helena, Marchioness of Northampton* (1936) pp. 65–7.

45. For Essex's attempt to exploit his popularity after the Cadiz voyage and its effects, see Adams, 'Protestant Cause', pp. 138–9.

46. See for example AGR PEA 361/26, printed in *Rel. Pol.*, v, 505; and 362/145.

47. For Elizabeth's studies, see L. V. Ryan, *Roger Ascham* (Stanford, Calif., 1963) p. 223 (I owe this reference to Gail Stedard); *Harington Letters*, p. 123; and Nichols, *Progresses*, i, xi.

48. R. Strong, *The Cult of Elizabeth. Elizabethan Portraiture and Pageantry* (1977) pp. 30–1, 130–3; F. A. Yates, 'Elizabethan Chivalry: The Romance of the Accession Day Tilts', in *Astrea. The Imperial Theme in the Sixteenth Century* (Harmondsworth, Middx, 1977) pp. 88–111; AGR PEA 362/145, 150.

49. Starkey, 'Privy Chamber', pp. 51, 63; Williams, 'Court and Polity', 270–1; Braddock, 'Royal Household', p. 36; PRO LS 13/280/82.

50. National Library of Scotland, Advocates Library, MS 1.2.2., art. 39.

51. *CSPSc*, iv (1905) 36.

52. *Rowland Vaughan, his Book, Published 1610: The Most Approved and Long-Experienced Waterworks*, ed. E. B. Wood (1897) p. 57; 'The Compendious Rehersal of John Dee . . . A°. 1592, November 9', printed in *Johannis Confratis et Monachi Glastoniensis Chronica*, ed. T. Hearne (Oxford, 1726) ii, 499; *Carey Memoirs*, pp. 42–3.

53. PRO SP 70/39/110; see also BL Add. MS 48,023, fos 352, 353v, 366.

54. H. A. Lloyd, 'Camden, Carmarden and the Customs', *EHR*, lxxxv (1970) 781.

55. AGR PEA 360/273.

56. *Harington Letters*, pp. 123–4; for evidence of delegation to the Council, see PRO SP 12/103/97, and *CSPSc*, v (1907) 266.

57. *Correspondentie van Robert Dudley, Graaf van Leycester . . . 1585–1588*, ed. H. Brugmans, Werken van het Historisch Genootschap, 3rd ser., LVI–LVIII (Utrecht, 1931) II, 230, 310.

58. PRO SP 63/16/197v.

59. Geneva, Archives d'Etat, Pièces Historiques, 2066, report of Jean Maillet, Oct 1582–Oct 1583. I hope to publish an edition of this document in due course.

60. PRO SP 12/140/46–7; cf. Bod. Lib., Perrot MS 1, fos 163v–166v, and *Correspondentie van Leycester*, II, 227.

61. *CSPF*, XXI (3), 233.

62. *Sir John Harington. A Tract on the Succession to the Crown (AD 1602)*, ed. C. R. Markham, Roxburghe Club (1880) p. 51; *Harington Letters*, pp. 118–26.

3. PARLIAMENT G. R. Elton

1. The present state of the question prohibits much detailed citing of the evidence.

2. J. S. Roskell, 'Perspectives in English Parliamentary History', *Bulletin of the John Rylands Library*, XLVI (1964) 448–75.

3. See J. Loach, 'Conservatism and Consent in Parliament, 1547–59', *The Mid-Tudor Polity c. 1540–1560*, ed. J. Loach and R. Tittler (1980) pp. 9–28; C. Russell, 'Parliament History in Perspective, 1604–1629', *History*, LXI (1976) 1–22.

4. N. L. Jones, *Faith by Statute: Parliament and the Settlement of Religion*, Royal Historical Society Studies in History XXXII (1982) esp. pp. 99–103, 140–50. See above, ch. 1.

5. G. R. Elton, 'Arthur Hall, Lord Burghley, and the Antiquity of Parliament', *Studies in Tudor and Stuart Politics and Government* (Cambridge, 1983) III, 177–8.

6. Ibid., pp. 164 7.

7. S. Lambert, 'Procedure in the House of Commons in the Early Stuart Period', *EHR*, XCV (1980) 753–81.

8. M. A. R. Graves, 'Thomas Norton the Parliament Man: An Elizabethan MP', *HJ*, XXIII (1980) 17–35.

9. Jones, *Faith by Statute*, esp. pp. 63–9.

10. Cf. Elton, *Studies*, III, 176.

11. J. E. Neale, *Elizabeth and her Parliaments*, I: *1559–1581* (1953) pp. 167–8.

12. Elton, *Studies*, II, 34, 54–5, and III, 58–92, 122–33.

13. Ibid., III, 268–9.

14. Sir Thomas Smith, *De Republica Anglorum*, ed. M. Dewar (Cambridge, 1982) pp. 8, 78–9.

15. Simonds D'Ewes, *The Journals of All the Parliaments during the Reign of Queen Elizabeth* (1682) p. 350.

16. This is what happened to Peter Wentworth in 1576: *Proceedings in the*

Parliaments of Elizabeth I, I. *1559–1581*, ed. T. E. Hartley (Leicester, 1981) pp. 476, 491.

17. Bacon on management, in *Letters and Life of Francis Bacon*, ed. J. Spedding (1869) v, 176–91, offers some very revealing Elizabethan comments on Stuart neglect.

18. These calculations are based on *Lords Journal*, I, 667–702.

19. *Commons Journal*, I, 86 (26 Apr), 88 (7 May), 90 (16 and 18 May).

20. Ibid., pp. 78 (30 Nov), 79 (4 and 9 Dec), 81 (24 Dec). Cf. Neale, *Elizabeth I and her Parliaments*, I, 168–9. In the Elizabethan system of voting (ayes went forth and noes sat still) abstention was not possible for anyone actually present.

21. Joseph Hume, a very regular attender early in the nineteenth century, held that 300 members present would begin to make the Chamber uncomfortably crowded – and by his time it had been enlarged with galleries (P. G. D. Thomas, *The House of Commons in the Eighteenth Century* (Oxford, 1971) p. 127).

22. *Proceedings*, ed. Hartley. No record of debates exists before 1571. My argument is based on the index of persons. The long entry for Peter Wentworth misleads: it refers in the main to his troubles in 1576 and does not show him speaking often in debate.

23. Dr Graves is working on Fleetwood.

24. BL Harleian MS 253, fos 32–6. A later copy, it is falsely ascribed to Francis Tate, the antiquary, who was born in 1560 and did not sit until 1601. The date of 1572 and the identification of Hatton as the addressee rest on strong internal evidence; Norton was a close client of Hatton's.

25. *Parliamentary Papers*, HC (520) 1828, IV, 64.

26. Cited by C. Russell, in *The English Commonwealth 1547–1640*, ed. P. Clark *et al.* (Leicester, 1979) p. 150.

27. Lambert, in 'Procedure in the House of Commons', 759–60, draws attention to the error about 1571; for the correct story as summed up here I must refer to my so-far unpublished researches.

28. In the seven sessions between 1559 and 1581, Elizabeth vetoed thirty-four bills, of which at most four seem to concern the prerogative (Elton, *Studies*, III, 180).

29. For instance, in 1571 a bill concerning cloth manufacture in Shrewsbury, passed by both Houses, was vetoed; since a bill for the same purpose passed in the next session (14 Eliz. I, c. 12), it is plain that a conflict of interests was in the meantime resolved in the town.

30. Neale, *Elizabeth I and her Parliaments*, I, 152, 318–24.

31. P. Collinson, *The Elizabethan Puritan Movement* (1967) pp. 118–21, 307–15. Influenced by Neale, Professor Collinson rather overstates the brief success of Cope's move in 1587, but even so its real futility comes across.

32. D'Ewes, *Journals*, p. 158.

33. Cecil's difficulties appeared quite clearly even in the account of Conyers Read, *Mr Secretary Cecil and Queen Elizabeth* (1955) ch. 18, which tries to suggest that Cecil's support for the parliamentary agitation merely represented a hope that the Queen would marry. In fact, the Secretary helped to organise the pressure on her, as the evidence cited by Read reveals.

4. GOVERNMENT, FINANCE AND THE COMMUNITY OF THE
EXCHEQUER   *J. D. Alsop*

1. This and the following seven paragraphs are largely based upon the works cited in the bibliographical note and the following, more detailed, sources: T. Fanshawe, *The Practice of the Exchequer Court with its Several Officers* (1658), including reliance upon the important manuscript version in BL Lansd. MS 171, fos 410v–31v; L. Squibb, *A Book of All the Several Officers of the Court of Exchequer . . .*, ed. W. H. Bryson, Camden Society, 4th ser., xiv (1975) 77–136; PRO E 36/266, E 101/336/25–6, E 369/118, E 404/87/1/118, E 405/116–48, 489, 496–9, 507, 515, 527, 529, E 407/52–5, 68, 71–3; SP 11/3 fo. 23, SP 46/27–35; BL Lansd. MSS 106, 168, 171, *passim*; BL Add. MSS 6176, 34,215 fo. 75; BL Stowe MS 571, fos 6–7; Trinity College, Cambridge, MS 0.2.7; University of London MS 9; F. S. Thomas, *The Ancient Exchequer of England* (1848); H. Hall, *The Antiquities and Curiosities of the Exchequer* (1898) pp. 71–104; J. D. Alsop, 'The Exchequer of Receipt in the Reign of Edward VI' (University of Cambridge PhD thesis, 1978); C. H. D. Coleman, 'Arthur Agard and the Chamberlainship of the Exchequer, 1570–1615', *Derbyshire Archaeological Journal*, c (1980) 64–8; *The Report of the Royal Commission of 1552*, ed. W. C. Richardson (Morgantown, W. Va, 1974).

2. Hall, *Antiquities*, pp. 96–104.

3. *Report of the Royal Commission*, p. 173; J. D. Alsop, 'The Revenue Commission of 1552', *HJ*, xxii (1979) 528; 7 Edward VI, c. 1 (*Statutes of the Realm*, iv, 161–4).

4. Squibb, *Court of Exchequer*, *passim*; Trinity College, Cambridge, MS 0.2.20, p. 19. The oaths are in PRO E 36/266, E 164/2, with copies in *Reports from the Select Committee Appointed to Inquire into the State of the Public Records of the Kingdom* (1800) pp. 232–5.

5. A. G. R. Smith, 'The Secretariats of the Cecils, *circa* 1580–1612', *EHR*, lxxxiii (1968) 481–504; R. C. Barnett, *Place, Profit, and Power: A Study of the Servants of William Cecil, Elizabethan Statesman* (Chapel Hill, NC, 1969); W. J. Jones, *The Elizabethan Court of Chancery* (1967) pp. 100–73; W. T. MacCaffrey, 'Place and Patronage in Elizabethan Politics', in *Elizabethan Government and Society: Essays presented to Sir John Neale*, ed. S. T. Bindoff, J. Hurstfield and C. H. Williams (1961) pp. 95–126.

6. *Report of the Royal Commission*, pp. 211–16; Alsop, 'Exchequer of Receipt', pp. 4–5, 26–7; PRO E 101/336/26, E 404/229; Liverpool University Library MS 5.2 (3).

7. PRO E 165/10 fo. 184v, E 165/11 fos 152–3, 222v, E 101/336/26 fos 5, 6v, 7, 8, 12v, E 404/229, E 407/68/1–4 (unfoliated); SP 1/18 fos 266–73, SP 12/8 fo. 62; Thomas, *Ancient Exchequer*, p. 21; HMC, *Report on the Records of the City of Exeter* (1916) p. 262; Alsop, 'Revenue Commission', 518; Barnett, *Place, Profit and Power*, pp. 127–32.

8. Indeed, it was fully in keeping with the prevailing attitude that this new position was accepted only in the context of reintroducing the medieval issue roll in 1567 and thus furthering the restoration of the 'ancient course': PRO E 405/130 m. 114, 527 (unfoliated).

9. Private relationships amongst the Elizabethan personnel are illumi-

nated in wide-ranging published and manuscript sources, most particularly in probate, judicial, and departmental records. The references for the cases cited here are: PRO PROB 11/30 fo. 46v, 42B fo. 420, 48 fos 353–5; E 40/5358, E 163/13/26 fo. 123, E 165/11 fo. 19.

10. J. D. Alsop, 'Thomas Argall, Administrator of Ecclesiastical Affairs in the Tudor Church and State', *Recusant History*, xv (1980) 227–38, and 'Sir Samuel Argall's Family, 1560–1620', *Virginia Magazine of History and Biography*, xc (1982) 472–84; BL Egerton MS 2599, fo. 229r–v and *passim*.

11. Among other sources: PRO E 13/228 m. 3v, 237 m. 1, 253 m. 3, E 407/61/2; J. D. Alsop, 'Richard Hodges and Stowe Manuscript 15', *British Library Journal*, v (1979) 200–1; Hall, *Antiquities*, pp. 92–3, 99–103. Over sixty departmental officials are included in *H of C, 1509–1558* and *H of C, 1558—1603*. Although severely limited with respect to their Exchequer activities, all these possess some biographical value.

12. PRO E 192/1/7, E 315/473–6 (*passim*); SP 46/60; J. D. Alsop, 'An Elizabethan Manuscript Transcription of Cicero's *De Officiis*', *Manuscripta*, xxiv (1980) 48–51.

13. PRO E 101/429/11 mm. 15v–16, E 407/38/111–380 (*passim*), E 407/68/2–6; BL Add. MS 12,504, fo. 190; Trinity College, Cambridge, MS 0.2.20, p. 21; E. Green, 'The Management of Exchequer Records in the 1560s', *Journal of the Society of Archivists*, v (1974) 28–9.

14. Squibb, *Court of Exchequer*, p. 131; Hall, *Antiquities*, pp. 96–104; BL Lansd. MS 168, fo. 177; PRO E 407/52; REQ 2/3/202.

15. *H of C, 1558–1603*, iii, 86–8.

16. BL Cotton Charters, iv.4.

17. PRO E 407/52–3 (unfoliated).

18. PRO E 407/71–3; SP 46/27–35; Liverpool University Library MS 5.2; Trinity College, Cambridge, MS 0.2.20, p. 20 and *passim*; R. B. Outhwaite, 'A Note on The Practice of the Exchequer Court, with its Several Offices and Officers, by Sir T. F.', *EHR*, lxxxi (1966) 337–9.

19. BL Lansd. MSS 106 fos 8–15v, 61–7, 165 fo. 92, 168, 171 (*passim*) BL Add. MS 12,504; Staffs RO MS D (W) 1721/1/1; PRO E 380/1, E 405/242, E 407/68/2.

20. PRO SP 46/27 fos 96, 153, and note also SP 46/33 fo. 267v; E 407/71/15; BL Egerton MS 806, fos 36–7.

21. BL Lansd. MS 106, fos 14–15v; PRO SP 11/9 fos 101–2v; E 13/241 m. 11, E 101/676/72, E 165/10, fos 16, 29; C 3/33/14; J. Strype, *Annals of the Reformation* (Oxford, 1824) iii, i, 88–9.

22. Corporation of London RO, Repertories 7 fo. 255, 10 fo. 175v, 12.i fos 155v, 177, 19 fo. 35v; Cambridge University Library MS Dd.13.8, fos 6v–16v, 37v.

23. BL Egerton MS 2599, fos 139–41, 143, 146, 202, 229.

24. R. H. Fritze, 'The Role of Family and Religion in the Local Politics of Early Elizabethan England: The Case of Hampshire in the 1560s', *HJ*, xxv (1982) 267–87; C. Read, *Mr Secretary Cecil and Queen Elizabeth* (1955) pp. 441–3, and *Mr Secretary Walsingham and the Policy of Queen Elizabeth* (Oxford, 1925) i, 432; Coleman, 'Agard', 66–8; T. Newton, 'Epistle Dedicatorie' to *The Worthye Booke of Old Age . . .* trs. Newton (1569).

25. A. G. R. Smith, *The Government of Elizabethan England* (1967) p. 99.

26. *Report of the Royal Commission*, p. 173; PRO C 54/500 m. 5; E 101/336/26, E 159/321 Michaelmas recorda mm. 70–1, Hilary m. 74; Liverpool University Library MS 5.2 (14); BL Lansd. MS 106, fos 61–7.

27. B. W. Quintrell, 'Government in Perspective: Lancashire and the Privy Council, 1570–1640', *Transactions of the Historic Society of Lancashire and Cheshire*, cxxxi (1982) 40–2; Read, *Walsingham*, i, 428–31; *Thirtieth Annual Report of the Deputy Keeper of the Public Records* (1869) Appendix, pp. 212–41; *APC, passim*.

28. The comment is derived from I. Roots, 'The Central Government and the Local Community', in *The English Revolution 1600–1660*, ed. E. W. Ives (1968) p. 35. For illustrations note PRO SP 12/157 fo. 74r–v, SP 46/33 fos 266–7; BL Lansd. MSS 106 fos 8–15v, 151 fo. 103, 165 fo. 92.

29. The dispute and its sources are introduced in G. R. Elton, 'The Elizabethan Exchequer: War in the Receipt', in his *Studies in Tudor and Stuart Politics and Government* (1974) i, 355–88. The initial stages and the earlier management of the bureau are discussed in Alsop, 'Exchequer of Receipt', *passim*.

30. PRO SP 12/22, fo. 95.

31. PRO E 36/266, fo. 80, E 403/858–64, E 407/68/5–7; Trinity College, Cambridge, MS 0.2.20, p. 21.

32. PRO E 405/527 (unfoliated), E 407/71 fos 141, 176; BL Lansd. MSS 3 fos 203–7, 28 fos 2–3, 168 fos 260, 274, 171 fos 241v–3.

5. THE CROWN AND THE COUNTIES *Penry Williams*

1. A. L. Rowse, *The England of Elizabeth* (1950) p. 341; P. Clark, *English Provincial Society from the Reformation to the Revolution: Religion, Politics and Society in Kent, 1500–1640* (Hassocks, Sussex, 1977) pp. 116, 132, 145–6.

2. A. Hassell Smith, *County and Court. Government and Politics in Norfolk, 1558–1603* (Oxford, 1974) pp. 124–33, and 'Militia Rates and Militia Statutes, 1558–1663', in *The English Commonwealth, 1547–1640*, ed. P. Clark *et al.* (Leicester, 1979) pp. 93–110.

3. *Tudor Economic Documents*, ed. R. H. Tawney and E. Power, 3 vols (1924) ii, 267; Hassell Smith, *County and Court*, pp. 123, 247–65; P. Williams, *The Tudor Regime* (Oxford, 1979) p. 419.

4. K. Wrightson, 'Two Concepts of Order', in *An Ungovernable People?*, ed. J. Brewer and J. Styles (1980) pp. 21–46, and *English Society 1580–1680* (1982) ch. 6; J. Kent, 'The English Village Constable, 1580–1642: The Nature and Dilemma of his Office', *Journal of British Studies*, xx (1981) 26–49.

5. C. G. Cruickshank, *Elizabeth's Army* (Oxford, 1966 edn) p. 290.

6. A. H. Lewis, *A Study of Elizabethan Ship-Money* (Philadelphia, 1928).

7. HMC, *Salisbury MSS*, v, 419, and vi, 137, 534–6; Lewis, *Ship-Money*, pp. 76–7; *APC*, xxviii, 400–2.

8. Ibid. xxvi, 553–4. See also ibid., xxv, 295–301, and xxvi, 143–8, 273–5, for difficulties in the West Country. Cf. Hassell Smith, *County and Court*, pp. 281–3.

9. HMC, *Salisbury MSS*, IX, 199, and XI, 442. See also ibid., XII, 164, 181–3, 346, 355, 372, 478.

10. Ibid., XI, 481–2, and XII, 169, 208–9.

11. *APC*, XXI, 201, 319, 325, 343; XXII, 312; XXIV, 32; and XXIX, 28, 275, 289, 343, 377, 394, 414.

12. Ibid., XXVIII, 625–7; cf. XXXII, 47–9.

13. Hassell Smith, *County and Court*, pp. 293–302; HMC, *Salisbury MSS*, XI, 258.

14. J. Hurstfield, 'The Profits of Fiscal Feudalism', *EcHR*, VIII (1955) 53–61; *Select Statutes and Constitutional Documents*, ed. G. W. Prothero, 4th edn (Oxford, 1913) p. 292.

15. Simonds D'Ewes, *The Journals of All the Parliaments during the Reign of Queen Elizabeth* (1682) pp. 554–5, 558, 570, 573; J. E. Neale, *Elizabeth I and her Parliaments*, II: *1584—1601* (1957) pp. 352–6; HMC, *Salisbury MSS*, XI, 324–5.

16. *Tudor Economic Documents*, II, 269–92; Neale, *Elizabeth I and her Parliaments*, II, 376–93; *Tudor Royal Proclamations*, ed. P. L. Hughes and J. F. Larkin, (New Haven, Conn., 1969) III, no. 812.

17. Neale, *Elizabeth I and her Parliaments*, II, 380, 337; G. R. Elton, 'Parliament in the Sixteenth Century', *HJ*, XXII (1979) 255–78; M. A. R. Graves, 'Thomas Norton the Parliament Man; An Elizabethan MP', *HJ*, XXIII (1980) 17–35. See above, ch. 3.

18. Neale, *Elizabeth I and her Parliaments*, II, 383; *Tudor Economic Documents*, II, 292.

19. A. Everitt, *Change in the Provinces* (Leicester, 1969); C. Holmes, 'The County Community in Stuart Historiography', *Journal of British Studies*, XIX (1980) 54–73; A. L. Hughes, 'Warwickshire on the Eve of the Civil War: A County Community?', *Midland History*, VII (1982) 42–72; D. J. MacCulloch, 'Power, Privilege and the County Community: County Politics in Elizabethan Suffolk' (University of Cambridge PhD thesis, 1977) esp. pt II. I am most grateful to Dr MacCulloch for allowing me to consult his invaluable thesis in typescript.

20. *CSPD*, 1598–1601, p. 502.

21. V. Morgan, 'The Cartographic Image of "The Country" in Early Modern England', *TRHS*, 5th ser., XXIX (1979) 129–54.

22. Hassell Smith, *County and Court*, pp. 277, 246, 338; Clark, *English Provincial Society*, p. 146.

23. A. Wall, 'Faction in Local Politics, 1580–1620. Struggles for Supremacy in Wiltshire', *Wiltshire Archaeological Magazine*, LXXII–LXXIII (1980) 119–34; *The Earl of Hertford's Lieutenancy Papers, 1603–1612*, ed. W. P. Murphy, Wilts Record Society (1969) 30–1, 33, 39, 102–4; *Northamptonshire Lieutenancy Papers, 1580–1614*, ed. Jeremy Goring and Joan Wake, Northants Record Society XXVII (1975) xx–xxxi and nos 42, 83–4, 88.

24. Hassell Smith, *County and Court*, ch. 10; D. MacCulloch, 'Catholic and Puritan in Elizabethan Suffolk', *Archiv für Reformationsgeschichte*, LXXII (1972) 232–89.

25. R. B. Manning, *Religion and Society in Elizabethan Sussex* (Leicester, 1969) pp. 80–90; R. H. Fritze, 'The Role of Family and Religion in the Local

Politics of Early Elizabethan England: The Case of Hampshire in the 1560s', *HJ*, xxv (1982) 267 ff.

26. See above, ch. 2; P. Williams, *The Council in the Marches of Wales under Elizabeth I* (Cardiff, 1958) ch. 12. I now believe that I there exaggerated the extent to which local factions in Wales and the Marches were offshoots of those at Court before 1590. I owe much to discussion about faction with Dr Simon Adams.

27. Williams, *Council in the Marches*, pp. 281–9; H. A. Lloyd, *The Gentry of South-West Wales, 1540–1640* (Cardiff, 1968) pp. 112–18; A. H. Dodd, 'North Wales and the Essex Revolt', *EHR*, lix (1944) 348–70. Cf. Hassell Smith, *County and Court*, pp. 303–4, 340–2, for the impact of the Essex–Cecil rivalry in Norfolk.

28. Clark, *English Provincial Society*, chs 7–8; Hassell Smith, *County and Court*, ch. 15; P. Williams, 'Court and Polity under Elizabeth I', *Bulletin of the John Rylands University Library*, lxv (1983) 259–86; A. Fletcher, *A County Community in Peace and War: Sussex 1600–1660* (1975) ch. 2.

29. See, for instance, *APC*, xxi, 201, 319, 325; xxii, 312, 482; xxiii, 318; xxiv, 44, 364. Cf. D. Hirst, 'The Privy Council and Problems of Enforcement in the 1620s', *Journal of British Studies*, xviii (1978) 46–66.

30. C. Russell, *Parliaments and English Politics, 1621–1629* (Oxford, 1979) pp. 70–84, 324.

31. For a rather different view of James's problems and policies from that offered here see J. Wormald, 'James VI and I: Two Kings or One?', *History*, lxviii (1983) 187–209, where the weaknesses of the Elizabethan system are stressed, unduly so in my opinion.

32. I. A. A. Thompson, *War and Government in Habsburg Spain, 1560–1620* (1976) *passim*.

33. J. Wormald, *Court, Kirk and Community. Scotland 1470—1625* (1981) chs 1, 2, 9, 10; T. I. Rae, *The Administration of the Scottish Frontier, 1513–1603* (Edinburgh, 1966) *passim*.

6. THE FOREIGN POLICY OF ELIZABETH I   G. D. Ramsay

1. *Correspondance de Philippe II*, ed. L. P. Gachard (5 vols, Brussels, 1848–79) iii, 188.

2. *CSPSp*, 1568–79, p. 79.

3. Ibid., p. 88.

4. Ibid., p. 90.

5. Ibid., p. 67.

6. Ibid., pp. 95–8. The substantial truth of the narrative of events set forth in the royal proclamation dated 6 Jan 1569 has been confirmed by the publication of the Spanish state papers. There is a recent study from the Spanish point of view by Julio Retamal Favereau, *Diplomacia Anglo-Española durante la Contrarreforma* (Santiago, 1981).

7. Letters of Gresham dated 28 Aug and 4 Sep 1571, *CSPF*, 1569–71, nos 1959 and 1981.

8. See in particular the letters of the French ambassador dated 9 Nov and 29 Dec 1570, *Correspondence de la Mothe-Fénélon*, ed. A. Teulet (Paris and London, 1940) III, 357–60, 414–20.

9. For a brief account of Anglo-Hanse relations, see 'Compendium Ansiaticum', Apr 1590, *LASP*, I, no. 729.

10. The letter has been printed in E. I. Kouri, *Elizabethan England and Europe*, *BIHR*, Special Supplement 12 (1982) no. 24.

11. *APC*, 1588–9, p. 192.

12. Ibid., 1589–90, p. 1.

13. Ibid., 1588–9, pp. 110–13.

14. Summaries in *LASP*, I, no. 746, and III, nos 848–9.

15. Ibid., III, no. 717.

16. The instructions are PRO SP 82/4, fos 144 ff.

7. THE ELIZABETHAN CHURCH AND THE NEW RELIGION
Patrick Collinson

1. P. Stubbes, *A Motive to Good Workes. Or Rather, to True Christianitie Indeede* (1593) Epistle. I am grateful to Mr Keith Thomas for drawing my attention to this very rare book (*STC* 23397) and to Dr Frank Stubbings of Emmanuel College, Cambridge, for enabling me to consult one of the three surviving copies, part of the Sancroft collection.

2. S. Clark, *The Elizabethan Pamphleteers: Popular Moralistic Pamphlets 1580–1640* (1983) pp. 190–1.

3. Stubbes, *A Motive to Good Workes*, pp. 44–5.

4. Ibid., pp. 79–82.

5. *Tamburlaine the Great*, pt 2, v.i.63–8. I owe this characteristically ingenious suggestion to the late Dr William Urry.

6. Stubbes, *A Motive to Good Workes*, Epistle; R. Tedder, *A Sermon Preached at Wimondham* (1637) p. 12.

7. Ephesians 2: 19–22; 1 Corinthians 3:9; *The Writings of John Bradford*, ed. A. Townsend, Parker Society (1853) p. 204; *The Works of James Pilkington*, ed. J. Scholefield Parker Society (1842) p. 335.

8. C. Haigh, 'Puritan Evangelism in the Reign of Elizabeth I', *EHR*, XCII (1977) 30–58. Cf. many passages in Dr Haigh's *Reformation and Resistance in Tudor Lancashire* (Cambridge, 1975), and ch. 8 below. Cf. Also K. Thomas, *Religion and the Decline of Magic* (1971), and, for a German parallel, G. Strauss, *Luther's House of Learning: Indoctrination of the Young in the German Reformation* (1978) pt 3.

9. See P. Collinson, *The Religion of Protestants: The Church in English Society 1559–1625* (Oxford, 1982) pp. 203–5, for a critical scrutiny of these complaints.

10. G. Gifford, *A Sermon on the Parable of the Sower* (1582) sig. Avii. W. Harrison, *The Difference of Hearers* (1613), quoted by Haigh, 'Puritan Evangelism', 52.

11. H. Ainsworth, *Counterpoyson* (?Amsterdam, 1608) p. 228; *Cartwright-iana*, ed. A. Peel and L. H. Carlson, Elizabethan Nonconformist Texts I

(1951) 144; G. Gifford, *A Briefe Discourse of Certaine Points of the Religion which is among the Common Sort of Christians which may bee Termed the Countrie Divinitie* (1581) fo. 22, and *Foure Sermons upon the Seven Chiefe Vertues as Principall Effects of Faith* (1582) sig. C3v; J. Nichols, *The Plea of the Innocent* (1602) pp. 212–14. See also ch. 8 below.

12. B. Andrewes, *Certaine Verie Worthie Godly and Profitable Sermons* (1583) pp. 185–6.

13. Phrases allegedly used by the Puritan preacher William Dyke at Little Leighs in Essex in 1580/81: Hunts RO MS M 32/8/13.

14. J. R. Green, *History of the English People* (1876 edn) p. 447.

15. R. Baxter, *A Holy Commonwealth* (1659) pp. 456–7.

16. *The Passage of our Most Dreaded Sovereign Lady, Queen Elizabeth, through the City of London to Westminster, the Day before her Coronation* (1558), repr. in *Tudor Tracts 1532–1588*, ed. A. F. Pollard (1903) pp. 365–95.

17. Haigh, *Reformation and Resistance*, p. 325.

18. P. Williams, *The Tudor Regime* (Oxford, 1979) pp. 253–92; R. B. Manning, *Religion and Society in Elizabethan Sussex* (Leicester, 1969).

19. R. Baillie, *A Dissuasive from the Errours of the Time* (1646) p. 7.

20. *Certain Sermons or Homilies as Appointed to be Read in Church in the Time of the Late Queen Elizabeth of Famous Memory* was given fresh authorisation by James I in 1623, and was still part of the living resources of the Church of England in the nineteenth century. I possess editions of 1811 and 1840. The pert comment of the *Admonition to the Parliament* occurred for the first time in the 2nd edn – *Puritan Manifestoes*, ed. W. H. Frere and C. E. Douglas (1954 edn) p. 23 n. 5.

21. *Letters of Thomas Wood, Puritan, 1566–1577*, ed. P. Collinson, *BIHR*, Special Supplement 5 (1960) pp. 20–1; S. Clarke, *A Collection of the Lives of Ten Eminent Divines* (1662) p. 30; Collinson, *Religion of Protestants*, pp. 133, 135–6, 93.

22. *The Remains of Edmund Grindal*, ed. W. Nicholson, Parker Society (1843) p. 379. The Queen had probably repeated a commonplace. Four years earlier the *Admonition to the Parliament* complained: 'Nay, some in the fullness of their blasphemy have said that much preaching bringeth the Word of God into contempt, and that four preachers are enough for all London' (*Puritan Manifestoes*, p. 23).

23. *The Autobiography of Richard Baxter*, ed. N. H. Keeble (1974) pp. 3–4.

24. R. L. Greaves, *John Bunyan*, Courtenay Studies in Reformation Theology II (Appleford, Berks., 1969) 16. The books were Arthur Dent's *Plaine-Mans Path-way to Heaven* (1601) and Bishop Lewis Bayly's *The Practise of Pietie* (1613), replacing an earlier taste for popular romances, the 'pap' of the seventeenth century.

25. J. Foxe, *Acts and Monuments*, ed. G. Townsend and S. R. Cattley (1839) VIII, 728.

26. Collinson, *Religion of Protestants*, pp. 232–4. Cf. Peter F. Jensen's account of the catechisms in his Oxford DPhil thesis 'The Life of Faith in the Teaching of Elizabethan Protestants' (1979); and ch. 8 below.

27. *The Writings of Robert Harrison and Robert Browne*, ed. A. Peel and L. H. Carlson, Elizabethan Nonconformist Texts II (1953) 174, 52–3.

28. Ibid., p. 408.

29. Romans 10:14; *Remains of Grindal*, pp. 379, 382.

30. *Puritan Manifestoes*, pp. 22, 102; opinion attributed to the Essex preacher Robert Wright, Hunts RO MS M 28/4/53; *The Works of John Jewel*, ed. J. Ayre, IV, Parker Society (1850) 475; P. Collinson, *A Mirror of Elizabethan Puritanism: The Life and Letters of 'Godly Master Dering'*, Friends of Dr Williams's Library (1964) p. 11; Haigh, *Reformation and Resistance*, p. 296.

31. *Puritan Manifestoes*, pp. 11–12; *The Works of John Whitgift*, ed. J. Ayre, Parker Society, I (1851) 541.

32. But Bishop Overton of Coventry and Lichfield asked in 1584 whether the parson was a preacher 'or at the least whether he doth procure quarterly or monthly sermons according to the Queen's Injunctions, especially upon such days as the Holy Communion shall be ministered for the better instruction and preparation towards the action?' Cotton of Exeter asked in 1595, 'Whether have you had monthly sermons in your parish church at the least, or no?' In *Elizabethan Episcopal Administration*, ed. W. P. M. Kennedy, 3 vols, Alcuin Club (1924–5) III, 162, 327.

33. *A Century of Sermons . . . Preached by John Hacket* (1675) p. xii.

34. Collinson, *Religion of Protestants*, pp. 94–5, following R. O'Day, *The English Clergy: The Emergence and Consolidation of a Profession 1558—1642* (Leicester, 1979).

35. P. Collinson, *Archbishop Grindal 1519–1583: The Struggle for a Reformed Church* (1979) pp. 112–13.

36. *Works of Whitgift*, I, 539.

37. Collinson, *Archbishop Grindal*, pp. 114–16, 207–10.

38. J. Strype, *Life of John Whitgift* (Oxford, 1822) I, 380–1.

39. *The State of the Church in the Reigns of Elizabeth and James I as Illustrated by Documents Relating to the Diocese of Lincoln*, ed. C. W. Foster, Lincoln Record Society XXIII (Horncastle, 1926) lii–lix. Cf. M. Bowker, *The Secular Clergy in the Diocese of Lincoln 1495–1520* (Cambridge, 1968), and *The Henrician Reformation: The Diocese of Lincoln Under John Longland 1521–1547* (Cambridge, 1981).

40. Said in 1593 and quoted by Haigh, 'Puritan Evangelism', p. 30.

41. On Bilney, see J. F. Davis, *Heresy and the Reformation in the South-East of England, 1520–1559* (1983), and his article 'The Trials of Thomas Bylney and the English Reformation', *HJ*, XXIV (1981) 775–90; on Bland, the telling record in the evidence collected by Archbishop Cranmer in connection with the 'Prebendaries' Plot' of 1543, fully calendared as 'Cranmer and the Heretics of Kent' in *Letters and Papers of the Reign of Henry VIII*, XVIII (ii), no. 546, pp. 291–387; on the Lancashire preachers, Haigh, *Reformation and Resistance*, chs 10, 11. As for Latimer, *si monumentum requiris, circumspice* among the vast literature of the early English Reformation.

42. A. G. Dickens, *Lollards and Protestants in the Diocese of York 1509–1558* (Oxford, 1959) pp. 53–113.

43. *Literary Remains of King Edward the Sixth*, ed. J. G. Nichols, Roxburghe Club (1857) II, 376–7; Haigh, *Reformation and Resistance*, pp. 145–6; E. Axon, 'The King's Preachers in Lancashire', *Transactions of the Lancashire and Cheshire Antiquarian Society*, LVI (1944) 67–70.

44. *Works of Nicholas Ridley*, ed. H. Christmas, Parker Society (1843), pp. 331–4, 336–7.

45. *Correspondence of Matthew Parker*, ed. J. Bruce, Parker Society (1853) pp. 306–7; *The Letter Book of John Parkhurst, Bishop of Norwich 1571–5*, ed. R. A. Houlbrooke, Norfolk Record Society XLIII (1975) 260. For more on Laurence, see D. MacCulloch, 'Power, Privilege and the County Community: County Politics in Elizabethan Suffolk', (University of Cambridge PhD. thesis, 1977) pp. 190–3.

46. Cathedral Archives and Library, Canterbury, MSS x.1.9 fo. 66, x.8.5 fo. 104, x.1.3 fo. 74v.

47. BL Harleian MS 7517, fo. 36.

48. R. Curteys, *An Exposition of Certayne Words of S. Paule to the Romaynes* (1577) Epistle. See Manning, *Religion and Society*, pp. 63–4.

49. *Letters of Thomas Wood*, p. 22.

50. Collinson, *Archbishop Grindal*, chs 13, 14.

51. P. Collinson, 'Lectures by Combination', *BIHR*, XLVIII (1975) 191, 200–2. For the last days of the old culture, see H. C. Gardiner, *Mysteries' End: An Investigation of the Last Days of the Medieval Religious Stage* (New Haven, Conn., 1967).

52. In 'Lectures by Combination' I appealed for more information on the location of the lectures. Through references supplied by correspondents and my own further researches I have lifted the tally from sixty-three to eighty-five. The details are given in a gazetteer appended to the article as it is reprinted in P. Collinson, *Godly People: Essays on English Protestantism and Puritanism* (1983).

53. Bod. Lib., Tanner MS 68, fo. 2; T. Rogers, *Miles Christianus* (1590) p. 17.

54. Collinson, 'Lectures by Combination', 192, and *Religion of Protestants*, pp. 158–9.

55. J. Northbrooke, *A Treatise Wherein Dicing, Dauncing, Vaine Playes or Enterludes . . . etc. . . . are Reproved* [?1577] p. 4.

56. *The Presbyterian Movement in the Reign of Queen Elizabeth as Illustrated by the Minute Book of the Dedham Classis 1582–1589*, ed. R. G. Usher, Camden Society, 3rd ser., VIII (1905); *Oliver Heywood's Life of John Angier of Denton*, ed. E. Axon, Chetham Society, n.s., XCVII (1937); G. H. Rendall, *Dedham in History* (Colchester, 1937); Collinson, *Elizabethan Puritan Movement*, pp. 222–39.

57. *Dictionary of National Biography*, sub Winthrop.

58. Collinson, 'Lectures by Combination', 208; Rendall, *Dedham in History*, pp. 108–9; BL Lansd. MS 61, fo. 73.

59. Collinson, *Religion of Protestants*, p. 249; J. Earle, *The Autograph Manuscript of Microcosmographie* (Leeds, 1966) p. 118.

60. Collinson, *Religion of Protestants*, pp. 243–4. Cf. the difficulty experienced by the Colchester incumbent Robert Lewis, a member of the Dedham 'classis', in holding his flock from straying to the counter-attraction of the popular town preacher George Northey (*The Presbyterian Movement*, 62).

61. C. H. and K. George, *The Protestant Mind of the English Reformation 1570–1640* (Princeton, NJ, 1961).

62. *A Century of Sermons*, p. xii.

63. G. Foxe, *Journal*, rev. edn by J. L. Nickalls (1952) p. 11; G. F. Nuttall, *The Holy Spirit in Puritan Faith and Experience* (Oxford, 1946) pp. 13, 164. With some of his reviewers I regard Professor John Bossy's classification of Quakerism outside the boundaries of Protestantism, in *The English Catholic Community 1570–1850* (1975) pp. 392–4, as too ingenious by half.

8.   THE CHURCH OF ENGLAND, THE CATHOLICS AND THE
       PEOPLE   *Christopher Haigh*

Readers will note that economy measures have been taken to keep what would otherwise have been a huge number of references within bounds; in particular, some detail which obviously derives from specific works listed in the bibliography is not separately referenced here.

1. C. Haigh, 'The Recent Historiography of the English Reformation', *HJ*, xxv (1982) 995–1007; D. M. Palliser, 'Popular Reactions to the Reformation during the Years of Uncertainty 1530–70', in *Church and Society in England: Henry VIII to James I*, ed. F. Heal and R. O'Day (1977) pp. 35–56.

2. H. N. Birt, *The Elizabethan Religious Settlement* (1907) p. 311; University of Durham Department of Palaeography and Diplomatic, Durham Probate Records 1596, will of James Nelson (I am grateful to Dr K. Wrightson for mentioning this document to me and providing a copy); *The Seconde Parte of a Register*, ed. A. Peel, 2 vols (Cambridge, 1915) ii, 166; F. G. Emmison, *Elizabethan Life: Disorder* (Chelmsford, 1970) p. 58; W. B[urton], *The Rowsing of the Sluggard* (1595) p. 27.

3. References to churchwardens' accounts are based on a study of almost 100 sets of Elizabethan accounts, from most parts of England. *English Church Furniture*, ed. E. Peacock (1866), *passim* (Lincs); Birt, *Elizabethan Religious Settlement*, pp. 428–9; R. F. B. Hodgkinson, 'Extracts from the Act Books of the Archdeacons of Nottingham', *Transactions of the Thoroton Society*, xxx (1926) 26–7.

4. *The State of the Church in the Reigns of Elizabeth and James I*, ed. C. W. Foster, Lincoln Record Society xxiii (1926) 457; *A Parte of a Register* (Middelburg, 1593) p. 62; R. F. B. Hodgkinson, 'Extracts from the Act Books of the Archdeacons of Nottingham', *Transactions of the Thoroton Society*, xxix (1925) 40; H. Hajzyk, 'The Church in Lincolnshire, c. 1595–c. 1640' (University of Cambridge PhD thesis, 1980) p. 422.

5. For a few examples of 'counterfeiting', etc., see W. H. Hale, *A Series of Precedents and Proceedings* (1847) pp. 152, 153; F. G. Emmison, *Elizabethan Life: Morals and the Church Courts* (Chelmsford, 1973) p. 195. R. Clark, 'Anglicanism, Recusancy and Dissent in Derbyshire, 1603–1730' (University of Oxford DPhil thesis, 1979) pp. 108–9; Wilts CRO, Diocese of Salisbury, Bishops' Records, Detecta Book 5, fo. 9; *A Hampshire Miscellany: Metropolitical Visitation of the Archdeaconry of Winchester, 1607–1608*, ed. A. J. Willis (Folkestone, 1963) pp. 10, 34–5, 41; K. R. Wark, *Elizabethan Recusancy in Cheshire*, Chetham Society (1971) p. 16.

6. T. Gibson, *A Fruitfull Sermon* (1584) sig. D; W. Perkins, *The Workes*, I (Cambridge, 1612) sig. A2; Hodgkinson, in *Transactions of the Thoroton Society*, XXIX, 35; F. Trigge, *An Apologie or Defence of our Dayes* (1589) pp. 24, 32, 35; Emmison, *Disorder*, p. 48; R. Greenham, *The Workes*, 3rd edn (1601) pp. 425–6.

7. *Archbishop Grindal's Visitation, 1575*, ed. W. J. Sheils, Borthwick Texts and Calendars (1977) p. 56; C. Haigh, 'The Continuity of Catholicism in the English Reformation', *P & P*, XCIII (1981) 41–53.

8. *Letters and Memorials of Fr Robert Persons, SJ*, ed. L. Hicks, Catholic Record Society XXXIX (1942) 319–21. For a much less optimistic version of early Elizabethan Catholic history, see the formative article by A. G. Dickens, 'The First Stages of Romanist Recusancy in Yorkshire, 1560–1590', *Yorkshire Archaeological Journal*, XXXV (1941) esp. 157–8, 180–81; J. Bossy, *The English Catholic Community, 1570—1850* (1975) esp. pp. 4–5, 11–12, 106–7, 147. For a balanced assessment, see A. Dures, *English Catholicism 1558–1642* (1983) pp. 3–8, 18–19.

9. See, for example, F. X. Walker, 'The Implementation of the Elizabethan Statutes against Recusants, 1580–1603' (University of London PhD thesis, 1961) *passim*; C. Haigh, *Reformation and Resistance in Tudor Lancashire* (Cambridge, 1975) pp. 202–94; R. B. Manning, *Religion and Society in Elizabethan Sussex* (Leicester, 1969) pp. 14–33, 129–50.

10. I here follow the argument elaborated in C. Haigh, 'From Monopoly to Minority: Catholicism in Early Modern England', *TRHS*, 5th ser., XXXI (1981) 129–47, where full references and supporting detail can be found. Cf. Dures, *English Catholicism*, pp. 20–6.

11. *Unpublished Documents Relating to the English Martyrs*, ed. J. H. Pollen, Catholic Record Society V (1908) 309; Haigh, 'Continuity', 59–62; *CSPD*, 1598–1601, p. 362.

12. Haigh, 'Monopoly to Minority', 136–43.

13. R. Challoner, *Memoirs of Missionary Priests*, ed. J. H. Pollen (1924) p. 232; *Unpublished Documents*, pp. 347–8.

14. Challoner, *Memoirs*, pp. 595–6; M. C. E. Chambers, *The Life of Mary Ward*, II (1885) 28, 35; Haigh, 'Monopoly to Minority', 143.

15. Borthwick Institute, York, HC.AB 9, fo. 164v; W. Harrison, *A Brief Discourse of the Christian Life and Death of Mistris Katherine Brettargh* (1602) sig. N.

16. N. Breton, *A Merrie Dialogue betwixt the Taker and Mistaker* (1603) pp. 12–13.

17. W. Pemble, *The Workes*, 3rd edn (1635) p. 567; *Seconde Parte*, II, 88, 94; R. G. Usher, *The Reconstruction of the English Church*, 2 vols (New York, 1910) II, 241; A. Peel, 'A Puritan Survey of the Church in Staffordshire in 1604', *EHR*, XXVI (1911) 352.

18. West Sussex RO Ep.I/23/5, *passim*; *Archbishop Grindal's Visitation*, p. vi; *Seconde Parte*, II, 130–42; *A Parte of a Register*, pp. 216, 305; G. Gifforde, *A Briefe Discourse of Certaine Points of the Religion which is among the Common Sort of Christians which may bee Termed the Countrie Divinitie* (1598 edn) p. 70; J. More, *Three Godly and Fruitful Sermons* (Cambridge, 1594) p. 69.

19. W. J. Sheils, *The Puritans in the Diocese of Peterborough*, Northants Record

Society xxx (1979) 45; W. Hinde, *A Faithfull Remonstrance of the Holy Life and Happy Death of John Bruen* (1641) pp. 83–4; C. W. Field, *The State of the Church in Gloucestershire, 1563* (Robertsbridge, Sussex, 1971)·p. 15; Gifforde, *Briefe Discourse of Certaine Points*, p. 41; Emmison, *Morals*, p. 116; Hale, *Series of Precedents*, p. 208; *A Parte of a Register*, p. 362; Hajzyk, 'Church in Lincolnshire', p. 160.

20. Gifforde, *Briefe Discourse of Certaine Points*, pp. 38, 121; A. Dent, *The Plaine-Man's Path-way to Heaven*, 21st edn (1631) pp. 289–90.

21. C. Haigh, 'Puritan Evangelism in the reign of Elizabeth I', *EHR*, xcii (1977) 47–8; Hodgkinson, 'Extracts from the Act Books', *Transactions of the Thoroton Society*, xxix, 52; *A Parte of a Register*, p. 208; Pemble, *Workes*, pp. 558–9.

22. Haigh, 'Puritan Evangelism', 47; R. Cawdrey, *A Short and Fruitfull Treatise of the Profit and Necessitie of Catechising*, 2nd edn (1604) p. 36; West Sussex RO Ep.I/23/5, fo. 32 and *passim*; *Bishop Redman's Visitation, 1597*, ed. J. F. Williams, Norfolk Record Society xviii (1946) 17–18.

23. West Sussex RO Ep.I/23/7, fo. 13v, Ep.I/23/5, fo. 23v; 'State Civil and Ecclesiastical of the County of Lancaster', ed. F. R. Raines, *Chetham Miscellanies*, Chetham Society, old ser., xcvi (1875) 2; Hodgkinson, 'Extracts from the Act Books', *Transactions of the Thoroton Society*, xxix, 36; *Bishop Redman's Visitation*, p. 79.

24. Hodgkinson, 'Extracts from the Act Books', *Transactions of the Thoroton Society*, xxix, 35; *The Archdeacon's Court; Liber Actorum, 1584*, ed. E. R. Brinkworth, Oxfordshire Record Society (1942) p. 159; Emmison, *Morals*, pp. 101, 118; Wilts CRO, Diocese of Salisbury, Bishops' Records, Detecta Book 5, fo. 35; *The Presbyterian Movement in the Reign of Queen Elizabeth*, ed. R. G. Usher, Camden Society, 3rd ser., viii (1905) 71; *Seconde Parte*, ii, 31.

25. T. Ratcliffe, *A Short Summe of the Whole Catechisme* (1619 edn) Epistle dated 1592, sig. A3; [E. Pagit], *Short Questions and Answeares, Conteyning the Summe of Christian Religion* (1583 edn) sig. A3.

26. Cawdrey, *Short and Fruitfull Treatise*, pp. 23, 99; T. Sparke and J. Seddon, *A Catechisme, or Short Kind of Instruction* (Oxford, 1588) pp. 1, 28, 55.

27. S. Clarke, *A General Martyrology* (1677 edn) pp. 12–15; M. Spufford, *Contrasting Communities* (Cambridge, 1974) pp. 327–8.

28. J. Nichols, *The Plea of the Innocent* (n.p., 1602) pp. 212–13; Cawdrey, *Short and Fruitfull Treatise*, pp. 87–9, 94, 117–18; Dent, *Plaine-Man's Path-way*, pp. 17, 25, 28, 237–8, 252–3, 264, 265, 271, 273, 278, 284; Gifforde, *Briefe Discourse of Certaine Points*, pp. 9, 69–70, 95, 116–17; Perkins, *Workes*, i, sig. A2. The final quotation is from Dent, *Plaine-Man's Path-way*, p. 25.

29. *A Parte of a Register*, p. 362; *Seconde Parte*, i, 238; W. Hunt, *The Puritan Moment: The Coming of Revolution in an English County* (Cambridge, Mass., 1983) pp. 146–7, 153–4; Haigh, 'Puritan Evangelism', 57; J. J. Goring, 'The Reformation of the Ministry in Elizabethan Sussex', *Journal of Ecclesiastical History* xxxiv (1983) 359.

30. *Hertfordshire County Records: Notes and Extracts from the Sessions Rolls*, ed. W. J. Hardy (1905) i, 18; Bod. Lib., Oxford Diocesan Papers, d. 5, fo. 60v; Haigh, 'Puritan Evangelism', 53.

31. C. Hill, *Society and Puritanism in Pre-Revolutionary England*, paperback edn

(1969) pp. 178–9 and refs; A. Beesley, *The History of Banbury* (1841) pp. 242–4, 615–16; *CSPD* 1581–90, pp. 586, 601, 602, 605; *APC*, 1588–9, p. 202; P. Clark, *English Provincial Society from the Reformation to the Revolution* (Hassocks, Sussex, 1977), p. 157.

32. Gifforde, *Briefe Discourse of Certaine Points*, pp. 2–3, 4, 45, 74; Dent, *Plaine-Man's Path-way*, pp. 24, 273; Hale, *Series of Precedents*, pp. 168, 221–2; Emmison, *Morals*, p. 215.

33. Hale, *Series of Precedents*, pp. 196–7; Wilts CRO, Archdeaconry of Wiltshire, Visitation Detecta Book 1586–99, fo. 172; Hodgkinson, 'Extracts from the Act Books', *Transactions of the Thoroton Society*, xxix, 42: Emmison, *Morals*, p. 215; Manning, *Religion and Society*, p. 173.

34. P. Collinson, *Godly People: Essays on English Protestantism and Puritanism* (1983) p. 11; *Seconde Parte*, ii, 44; Beesley, *Banbury*, p. 615; *Banbury Corporation Records: Tudor and Stuart*, ed. J. S. W. Gibson and E. R. C. Brinkworth, Banbury Historical Society xv (1977) 59–60; P. D. A. Harvey, 'Where was Banbury Cross?', *Oxoniensia*, xxxi (1966) 87, 93–4, 101–5; Sheils, *Puritans*, pp. 37, 68–9, 131; *Seconde Parte*, ii, 291–6.

35. *The Commission for Ecclesiastical Causes within the Dioceses of Bristol and Gloucester*, ed. F. D. Price, Bristol and Glos. Archaeological Society, Records Section, x (1972) 65; Emmison, *Morals*, p. 77; M. Spufford, *Small Books and Pleasant Histories* (1981) p. 34; *Bishop Redman's Visitation*, p. 69; Cheshire CRO, EDV 1/12a fo. 96, 1/12b fo. 122, 1/13 fo. 198v, 1/14 fos 186–7.

36. Gifforde, *Briefe Discourse of Certaine Points*, pp. 1–3; Cawdrey, *Short and Fruitfull Treatise*, pp. 79–80; *Seconde Parte*, ii 165–9. For examples of parishioners following such 'pot companions' in preference to godly preachers, see *Seconde Parte* i, 160–1, 163; Emmison, *Disorder*, pp. 190–1. For a sympathetic presentation of the model, see the 'Pattern for Pastors' in L. Wright, *A Summons for Sleepers* (1589) esp. pp. 49–51.

9. POVERTY AND SOCIAL REGULATION IN ELIZABETHAN
    ENGLAND   *Paul Slack*

1. E. M. Leonard, *The Early History of English Poor Relief* (Cambridge, 1900) pp. 29, 43; P. Slack, 'Social Policy and the Constraints of Government, 1547–1558', in *The Mid-Tudor Polity c. 1540–1560*, ed. J. Loach and R. Tittler (1980) pp. 107–8, 109, 113; W. T. MacCaffrey, *Exeter 1540–1640* (Cambridge, Mass., 1958) pp. 112–13; E. M. Hampson, *The Treatment of Poverty in Cambridgeshire 1597–1834* (Cambridge, 1934) p. 6; R. H. Morris, *Chester in the Plantagenet and Tudor Reigns* (Chester, n.d.) p. 360.

2. *The Norwich Census of the Poor 1570*, ed. J. F. Pound, Norfolk Record Society xl (1971) 7–9, 20–1.

3. One reason for calling the 1572 Parliament, according to the Speaker, was 'for punishment of vagabonds': *Proceedings in the Parliaments of Elizabeth I*, i: *1558–1581*, ed. T. E. Hartley (Leicester, 1981) p. 339.

4. *Victoria County History: Oxfordshire*, iv, 344; A. L. Beier, 'The Social Problems of an Elizabethan Country Town: Warwick 1580–90', in *Country*

Towns in Pre-industrial England, ed. P. Clark (Leicester, 1981) p. 75; A. Rosen, 'Winchester in Transition, 1580–1700', ibid., p. 158.

5. Even the most positive proclamation, one in 1600 dealing with dubious points in the poor-law, concentrated on rogues: *Tudor Royal Proclamations*, ed. P. L. Hughes and J. F. Larkin (New Haven, Conn., 1964–9) iii, 204–9.

6. P. Slack, 'Books of Orders: The Making of English Social Policy, 1577–1631'. *TRHS*, 5th ser., xxx (1980) 3–4; F. A. Youngs, *The Proclamations of the Tudor Queens* (Cambridge, 1976) pp. 114–17.

7. S. T. Bindoff, 'The Making of the Statute of Artificers', in *Elizabethan Government and Society. Essays presented to Sir John Neale*, ed. S. T. Bindoff, J. Hurstfield and C. H. Williams (1961) pp. 58–9, 92–3; Youngs, *Proclamations*, pp. 161–70.

8. J. R. Kent, 'Attitudes of Members of the House of Commons to the Regulation of "Personal Conduct" in Late Elizabethan and Early Stuart England', *BIHR*, xlvi (1973) 41–71; Leonard, *Poor Relief*, p. 74.

9. See, for example, P. Clark, ' "The Ramoth-Gilead of the Good": Urban Change and Political Radicalism at Gloucester 1540–1640', in *The English Commonwealth 1547–1640. Essays in Politics and Society presented to Joel Hurstfield*, ed. P. Clark, A. G. R. Smith and N. Tyacke (Leicester, 1979) pp. 175–6; D. M. Palliser, *Tudor York* (Oxford, 1979) pp. 255, 259, 285–6; *Records of the Borough of Nottingham*, iv: *1547–1625* (1889) pp. 229–30, 249, 253–61; *The Southampton Mayor's Book of 1606—8*, ed. W. J. Connor, Southampton Record Series xxi (1978) *passim*; A. H. Smith, *County and Court. Government and Politics in Norfolk 1558–1603* (Oxford, 1974) pp. 102–8; W. Hunt, *The Puritan Moment. The Coming of Revolution in an English County* (Cambridge, Mass., 1983) pp. 70–2, 76, 80.

10. See, for example, London Corporation RO, Repertories 17 fo. 388v, 18 fos 108v–110, 155v, 19 fo. 25v; Journals 19 fos 173v, 174, 20(ii) fos 483, 499v–503v; W. G. Hoskins, 'Harvest Fluctuations and English Economic History, 1480–1619', *Agricultural History Review*, xii (1964) 41; C. Creighton, *A History of Epidemics in Britain* (Cambridge, 1891) i, 341, 346–7.

11. P. Slack, 'Mortality Crises and Epidemic Disease in England 1485–1610', *Health, Medicine and Mortality in the Sixteenth Century*, ed. C. Webster (Cambridge, 1979) pp. 18, 33–43; J. S. Cockburn, 'The Nature and Incidence of Crime in England 1559–1625: A Preliminary Survey', in *Crime in England 1550–1800*, ed. Cockburn (1977) p. 67; *Bastardy and its Comparative History*, ed. P. Laslett, K. Oosterveen and R. M. Smith (1980) p. 14; P. Williams, *The Tudor Regime* (Oxford, 1979) pp. 327–30.

12. D. M. Palliser, 'Tawney's Century: Brave New World or Malthusian Trap?', *EcHR*, 2nd ser., xxxv (1982) 339–53; E. A. Wrigley and R. S. Schofield, *The Population History of England 1541–1871: A Reconstruction* (1981) pp. 416–30, 435, 451–3, 469–71.

13. For instance, in Robert Allen, *A Treatise of Christian Beneficence* (1600) sig. Aiii: 'poor labouring householders'.

14. Oxford City Archives N.4.2; P. A. Slack, 'Vagrants and Vagrancy in England, 1598–1664', *EcHR*, 2nd ser., xxvii (1974) 360–79; A. L. Beier, 'Social Problems in Elizabethan London', *Journal of Interdisciplinary History*, ix (1978) 204–5.

15. *Tudor Economic Documents*, ed. R. H. Tawney and E. Power (1924) III, 441; Beier, 'Social Problems in London', 204. I am grateful to Professor Mark Benbow for showing me an unpublished paper which discusses the wider activity of Bridewell.

16. *Tudor Economic Documents*, II, 335.

17. *The Book of John Fisher 1580–88*, ed. T. Kemp (Warwick, n.d.) p. 185; A. L. Beier, 'Vagrants and the Social Order in Elizabethan England', *P & P*, LXIV (1974) 11–14; Slack, 'Vagrants and Vagrancy', 362–5.

18. The following paragraphs are based on analysis of *Norwich Census; Book of John Fisher*, pp. 164–72 (Warwick); *Poor Relief in Elizabethan Ipswich*, ed. J. Webb, Suffolk Records Society IX (1966) 119–40; Staffs RO, Sutherland MSS, D 593/S/4/55/1, 4/14/12, 13 (Gillingham, Chatham and Grain, Kent, 1596–8); Lancs RO, UDCr 18 (Crompton, 1597). For other accounts of these records, see Beier, 'Social Problems of . . . Warwick', *passim*; P. Clark, *English Provincial Society from the Reformation to the Revolution* (Hassocks, Sussex, 1977) pp. 239–40.

19. Essex RO D/P 50/12/1 (Writtle), 1596–7 account and D/P 232/8/1 (Great Easton), 1581–2 account; F. G. Emmison, 'Poor-Relief Accounts of Two Rural Parishes in Bedfordshire 1563–98', *EcHR*, III (1931) 109–10, 112–13.

20. Bod. Lib., Jones MS 17, fo. 6v.

21. Beier, 'Social Problems of . . . Warwick', pp. 74–5; Chester City Records, QSF/27/86–93.

22. *HMC, Various*, VII, 128.

23. *Proceedings*, ed. Hartley, pp. 219, 311–13, 366–7, 384–5.

24. *West Riding Sessions Rolls 1597/8–1602*, ed. J. Lister, Yorks Archaelogical and Topographical Association Record Series III (1888) 84.

25. Allen, *Treatise*, pp. 41, 126–7. On other relevant literature, see F. Heal, 'The Idea of Hospitality in Early Modern England', *P & P*, CII (1984) 66–93.

26. K. Thomas, *Religion and the Decline of Magic* (1971) pp. 563–4.

27. *Book of John Fisher*, p. 29; Beier, 'Vagrants and the Social Order', 16–17.

28. W. K. Jordan, *Philanthropy in England 1480–1660* (1959). Although this work underestimates the number of rates (particularly after 1598) and their importance in some localities (particularly towns), its conclusion that in aggregate charitable giving was much more voluminous remains persuasive for Elizabeth's reign.

29. For instance, W. T., *A Casting Up of Accounts of Certain Errors* (1603) sigs B2v, B4, C3.

30. J. F. Hadwin, 'Deflating Philanthropy', *EcHR*, 2nd ser., XXXI (1978) 112–13, reworking Jordan's figures in *Philanthropy*.

31. For examples see *Archbishop Grindal's Visitation, 1575*, ed. W. J. Sheils, Borthwick Texts and Calendars (1977) 18, 19, 56, 75; *The Royal Visitation of 1559*, ed. C. J. Kitching, Surtees Society CLXXXVII (1975) 66, 69–71.

32. F. A. Youngs, 'Towards Petty Sessions: Tudor JPs and Divisions of Counties', in *Tudor Rule and Revolution. Essays for G. R. Elton*, ed. D. J. Guth and J. W. McKenna (Cambridge, 1982) pp. 210–12.

33. R. H. Tawney, *Religion and the Rise of Capitalism* (1926) ch. 4, pt IV; C. Hill, 'Puritans and the Poor', *P & P*, II (1952) 32–50.

34. *Proceedings*, ed. Hartley, p. 367. Cf. R. L. Greaves, *Society and Religion in Elizabethan England* (Minneapolis, 1981) pp. 572, 575.

35. Beier, 'Social Problems of . . . Warwick', p. 77.

36. *Norwich Census*, pp. 7, 19–20; *Tudor Economic Documents*, II, 322; P. Collinson, *The Religion of Protestants. The Church in English Society, 1559–1625* (Oxford, 1982), pp. 141–3; *H of C, 1558–1603*, I, 333, and III, 80–3, 658–63.

37. H. Ellis, 'Letter from Secretary Walsingham', *Norfolk Archaeology*, II (1849) 94. Cf. Smith, *County and Court*, pp. 104–5.

38. Collinson, *Religion of Protestants*, pp. 158–9; Kent, 'Attitudes of Members of the House of Commons', 41–2.

39. Norfolk and Norwich RO, Case 20, Shelf c, Mayor's Book of the Poore 1571–9 (boards), Proclamation 4 June 1571, Orders to overseers 1577, and loose paper 'Charge Given to the Overseers'; Collinson, *Religion of Protestants*, p. 182.

40. Ibid. p. 171; Essex RO D/P 232/8/1 [fo. 4] (Great Easton); Colchester Borough Records, Assembly Book 1576–99, 14 and 21 June, 33 Eliz.

41. Williams, *Tudor Regime*, pp. 152–4; P. G. Lawson, 'Crime and the Administration of Criminal Justice in Hertfordshire 1580–1625' (University of Oxford DPhil thesis, 1982) pp. 175–87; K. Wrightson, 'Two Concepts of Order: Justices, Constables and Jurymen in Seventeenth-Century England', in *an Ungovernable People*, ed. J. Brewer and J. Styles (1980) pp. 37–46.

42. Hadwin, 'Deflating Philanthropy', 117.

43. *Northamptonshire Lieutenancy Papers 1580–1614*, ed. J. Goring and J. Wake, Northants Record Society XXVII (1975) 24.

44. J. Walter and K. Wrightson, 'Dearth and the Social Order in Early Modern England', *P & P*, LXXI (1976) 40–2.

45. K. Wrightson, *English Society 1580–1680* (1982) ch. 6; K. Wrightson and D. Levine, *Poverty and Piety in an English Village: Terling 1525–1700* (1979) pp. 134–41, 156–8.

Notes on Contributors

SIMON ADAMS is Lecturer in History at the University of Strathclyde. He studied at Harvard and Oxford universities, and in 1973–5 held a Research Fellowship at the University College of North Wales. He has published a number of articles on aspects of Elizabethan and early Stuart politics, and edited *Queen Elizabeth I: Most Politick Princess*. He is now working on two studies of foreign policy 1558–1640 and a biography of the Earl of Leicester.

J. D. ALSOP is Assistant Professor of History at McMaster University, Hamilton, Ontario. He studied at the universities of Winnipeg, Western Ontario, and Cambridge, and completed MA and PhD theses under the directions of Professors J. R. Lander and G. R. Elton. He is author of a number of articles on Tudor finance and financial administration, and is working on a book in this area.

PATRICK COLLINSON is Professor of History at the University of Sheffield. He was formerly Professor of History at the University of Sydney and at the University of Kent at Canterbury, Ford's Lecturer at Oxford, 1979, and Birkbeck Lecturer at Cambridge, 1981, and is a Fellow of the British Academy. He is the author of *The Elizabethan Puritan Movement*, *Archbishop Grindal* and *The Religion of Protestants*.

G. R. ELTON is Regius Professor of Modern History at the University of Cambridge. He studied History at the University of London, and has been Fellow of Clare College, Cambridge, since 1954. He was Ford's Lecturer at Oxford and Wiles Lecturer at Belfast in 1972, and is a Fellow of the British Academy. He has published almost twenty books, including *The Tudor Revolution in Government*, *England under the Tudors*, *Policy and Police* and *Reform and Reformation*.

CHRISTOPHER HAIGH is Tutor in Modern History, Christ Church, Oxford. He studied History at Churchill College, Cambridge, and at the University of Manchester, and lectured at Manchester University between 1969 and 1979, before moving to Oxford. He has written two books on the Reformation in north-west England and a number of articles on the English Reformation and its aftermath, and edited *The Cambridge Historical Encyclopedia of Great Britain and Ireland*.

NORMAN L. JONES is Assistant Professor of History, Utah State University. He undertook his doctoral research at Cambridge, and has written many articles on early Elizabethan parliaments and religion, as well as *Faith by Statute*, which won the Archbishop Cranmer Prize in ecclesiastical history and the Whitfield Prize.

G. D. RAMSAY was Tutor in Modern History, St Edmund Hall, Oxford, 1937–74, and is now an Emeritus Fellow. His most recent publication was on the English woollen industry, 1500–1750, and he expects shortly to publish a work on the Merchants Adventures.

PAUL SLACK is Tutor in Modern History at Exeter College, Oxford. He studied at St John's and Balliol colleges, Oxford, and has taught at the University of York. He was co-editor of *Crisis and Order in English Towns*, editor of *Rebellion, Popular Protest and the Social Order*, and co-author of *English Towns in Transition*, and he has written several articles on social issues in the sixteenth and seventeenth centuries.

PENRY WILLIAMS is Tutor in Modern History, New College, Oxford. He studied at New College and at St Antony's College, Oxford, and lectured at Manchester University from 1951 to 1964. He is joint-editor of *English Historical Review*, and his books include *The Council in the Marches of Wales under Elizabeth I* and *The Tudor Regime*.

Index